UNFIT FOR MARRIAGE

THE BASQUE SERIES

Unfit for Marriage

Impotent Spouses on Trial in the Basque Region of Spain, 1650–1750

EDWARD BEHREND-MARTÍNEZ

University of Nevada Press Reno & Las Vegas

THE BASQUE SERIES
This book was funded in part by a grant from the Program for Cultural Cooperation between Spain's Ministry of Culture and United States Universities.

University of Nevada Press, Reno, Nevada 89557 USA
www.unpress.nevada.edu

Manufactured in the United States of America

Library of Congress Cataloging-in-Publication Data
Behrend-Martínez, Edward, 1970–
Unfit for marriage : impotent spouses on trial in the Basque region of Spain, 1650–1750 / Edward Behrend-Martínez.
p. cm. — (The Basque series)
Includes bibliographical references and index.
ISBN 978-0-87417-699-5 (hardcover : alk. paper)
1. Marriage—Annulment—Spain—History. 2. Marriage—Annulment (Canon law)—History—Sources.
3. Divorce—Law and legislation—Spain—History.
4. Impediments to marriage—Spain. 5. Impediments to marriage (Canon law) 6. Impotence (Canon law)
7. Ecclesiastical courts—Spain. I. Title
KKT555.B44 2007
262.9'2—dc22 2006034920

The paper used in this book meets the requirements of American National Standard for Information Sciences—Permanence of Paper for Printed Library Materials, ANSI/NISO Z39.48-1992 (R2002). Binding materials were selected for strength and durability.

University of Nevada Press Paperback Edition, 2014
ISBN 978-0-87417-957-6 (pbk. : alk. paper)

This book has been reproduced as a digital reprint.

Dedicated to Abril Martínez-Behrend,
without whose support and affection
this book would not have been possible.

CONTENTS

PREFACE

This book is about men—and women—accused by their spouses of being impotent in an era and place when such an indictment could dissolve unconsummated marriages. In itself, each impotence trial seems to be a trivial example of recognizable sexual and marital problems. There are the tales of a pathetic nobleman who could not "get it up," a wife wanting to escape a marriage she never agreed to, and a young man who accused *himself* of impotence in order to desert his pregnant wife and flee on a ship to Mexico. But impotence trials serve the historian as much more than lurid and tragic tales of everyday life. They were deliberate, well-documented events that enmeshed several important societal institutions (church courts, the law, marriage, and the practice of medicine) with fundamental aspects of daily life of early modern Europeans (sex, reproduction, gender, and property). Each trial involved issues that cut to the heart of the way early modern Europeans understood sex, religion, community, gender, and marriage. The authority of the church and its role as arbiter of the proper use of sex to order communities is revealed in the language of impotence cases. More importantly, the records of these trials allow us to see such practice at the level of commoners and in a parochial area of Europe: in this case, the Castilian/Basque borderlands of northern Spain.

My curiosity about impotence trials, and history in general, has always been guided by the conviction that the broadening of human knowledge should never be impeded by cultural taboos, especially nothing as petty as prudishness, bashfulness, or attempts to maintain gender stereotypes. Nevertheless, a challenging feature of this project from the start has been the taboo against speaking about impotence. Few men want to think of the condition. Recently, for instance, a colleague told me he would rather talk about incontinence than impotence. But the word itself has lost some of its frightfulness, perhaps because most impotence has been recently conquered by pills. And after I had pronounced the word dozens of times publicly, it seemed less and less daunting to me, too. Whatever the reason, it is my conviction that the bashfulness about impotence has caused impotence trials to be historically minimized. These cases were not uncommon and were about much more than a simple sexual malady.

Still, several intrepid historians—James Brundage, Natalie Z. Davis, Thomas Max Safley, Valeria Finucci, among others—have tackled the topic.

I first learned about the existence of early modern impotence trials from Jeffrey Merrick at the University of Wisconsin–Milwaukee. Speaking about early modern French sexuality, Merrick tangentially discussed impotence trials, drawing on Pierre Darmon's work as well as his own research. In the seventeenth and eighteenth centuries impotence trials reached "epidemic" proportions, according to Darmon, and they often included proofs of potency that could range from doctors' visits to a "trial by congress," an attempt by the accused husband to copulate with his wife in front of a judge and witnesses, thus proving his potency. These men invariably failed. Surely, I thought at the time, this was proof that early modern society, when compared to our own, was an alien place that had little respect for private sexual life or the individual.

A few years later, in 1997, I met with Renato Barahona to discuss his work on early modern Spain and Vizcaya and my own research plans. While explaining his work on sexuality in early modern Spain (later published as *Sex Crimes, Honour, and the Law in Early Modern Spain: Vizcaya, 1528–1735*), he mentioned that he had come across some impotence court cases in church archives in northern Spain and the Basque country. When I learned this I immediately knew that I wanted to tackle this research topic.

In the summer of 1999 I traveled to Calahorra (La Rioja), Spain, to visit its diocesan archive, which holds most of the church court business of that vast diocese for much of the past nine centuries. I expected to find the twelve or so cases briefly noted by Renato Barahona. In fact I found many times that number; there were eighty-three impotence cases between 1650 and 1750 alone. Most ranged between twenty to forty folios (paper leaves) in length. Many others, however, contained more than one hundred folios, and one in particular went on for four hundred folios. Supported by a Fulbright scholarship, I spent a year during 2000–2001 reading these and other cases in Spain.

These rich sources give modern historians the means to better understand early modern marital sexuality. More than anything, impotence cases demonstrate the early modern respect for sex as a public utility. Sex could create as well as destroy the idealized commune of towns in early modern Spain. According to the reasoning of early modern Spaniards, through legitimate reproduction and the licit gratification of lust, marital sex maintained society; conversely, sex outside marriage could bring social chaos. Male and female sexual potency, therefore, was a cornerstone of maintaining or reaching an idealized status quo. Impotence litigation reveals the important role that community and family members had in every couple's sex life.

The institutional church, however, treated spouses and their sexual behaviors as individuals. Technically, impotence was a discrete subject that involved only two people and the church court. According to canon law, it is true, matrimony was a spiritual and legal tie that connected husband and wife. Perhaps more importantly, as a sacrament it connected the couple to God. Regardless of the theological and technical characteristics of the church court—characteristics that would seem to separate spouses' private sex lives from the larger context of their communities—the church court actually became a venue for community members to involve themselves in the sex lives of couples. These impotence trials remind us that though sex most often occurs in private, sexual behavior unavoidably becomes a public issue. I believe this is truer in modern society than many would expect in an age when we think of sex as a private act. One's sexual behavior, as it is or is perceived to be, shapes family relationships, working relationships, and—need it be said?—political careers. If so-called private sex is still so important publicly today, then it was much more so in the past. "Private" sex was clearly a public act in early modern Spain.

This study is an appropriate addition to the University of Nevada Press's Basque Series because the diocese of the study spanned ethnic borders (see map). It allows a comparison of Castilian and Basque responses to the authority of the church. Today the diocesan borders respect political borders. In the seventeenth century, however, the Calahorran bishop, generally from Castile or Aragon, had authority over nearly all of the modern País Vasco, including most of Álava, Vizcaya, and part of Guipúzcoa. Naturally, there was a perpetual conflict between local parishes and the bishop's authority. Jurisdictional friction was more pronounced in the Basque areas of the diocese. In fact, several Basque communities maintained their parishes quite independently. The question of Basque independence is not the focus of this study, but the issue is important and unavoidable. When we compare the relative litigiousness of peoples north and south of the Ebro River, we find that Castilians made much more use of the diocesan court than Basques. There were, per capita, more impotence trials brought to court by people south of the Ebro. Although some Basque nationalists today would be pleased by the suggestion that Basque husbands were more virile than Castilians in the past and so did not end up as subjects in impotence trials, it is, of course, truer that Basques were simply more likely to resolve their marital disputes by means other than going to the bishop's court. Despite their lower participation compared to Castilians, many Basque couples did become involved in impotence trials. We know this not only by their surnames, and where they live, but also because many testimonies had to be translated and transcribed from the Basque language.

This study, then, is about sexuality, authority, and power. In the domestic sphere, it illuminates battles between spouses over the importance of sex in their marriages. Male authority, even male honor, was contingent on male sexual potency. Impotent wives, likewise, could not have sex and were therefore excluded from matrimony. This study also explores the ways that communities idealized the place of sexuality in the maintenance of social order. As we will see, communities did not simply see sexuality as a sin that had to be confined to the marital bed. Rather, communities expected sex to support matrimony; it promoted fidelity, peace, and reproduction, the social order and renewal that would ultimately guarantee the community's future. Finally, this study questions the Catholic Church's ability to assert its theological authority over sexuality, Basque or otherwise. The post-Tridentine Spanish church had a much weaker hold over the lives of the laity than has often been asserted. Rather than impose Catholic ideals of matrimony on Spanish communities, Spanish couples *used* the bishop's court to enforce their own ideals of marital sexuality. If impotent men were deemed "cold by nature" and the legal proceedings against them were naturally emotionally cold, it was only because the marriages that early modern Spaniards idealized were to be affectionate and sexual.

ACKNOWLEDGMENTS

This study owes its existence to two individuals: Renato Barahona and Angel Ortega López. Renato Barahona first noted a number of cases for marital separation and impotence trials on a visit to the Diocesan and Cathedral Archives of Calahorra more than a decade ago. Renato's intellectual generosity and practical knowledge of northern Spain have been the bedrock of this investigation. Perhaps more fundamentally important to this work have been the labors of archivist Angel Ortega López in his ongoing work cataloging the documents of the Calahorra archive. Father Ortega originally moved to Calahorra to serve as the cathedral's musical director. Seeing that the diocese needed to organize its extensive documentation, Angel sought further university training and refashioned himself as the cathedral's archivist. He has succeeded in creating a modern scholarly archive from what was an enormous amount of disordered material. I have been able to find and read the documents of this study only because they were first noted and cataloged by Father Ortega.

A research scholar generally requires either independent wealth, some type of position, or patronage to keep working. My main patron has been Abril Martínez-Behrend, my wife. Without her financial support I would never have been able to travel, photocopy, and otherwise purchase the equipment essential to this historical research. Abril has continued to support this project, though she may have long ago tired of listening to my stories of seventeenth-century spousal abuse and impotence trials. The Spanish portion of my research was made possible by a grant from the J. William Fulbright Foreign Scholarship Board and the Commission for Cultural, Educational, and Scientific Exchange between the Kingdom of Spain and the United States of America. The Fulbright grant allowed my family and me to live in La Rioja, Spain, in 2000–2001, where I was able to spend ten months reading materials from the Diocesan and Cathedral Archives of Calahorra. The study received further support from the History Department at the University of Illinois at Chicago in the form of a Bentley Brinkerhoff Gilbert Fellowship for 2001–2002, and a grant from Appalachian State University's University Research Council in 2004.

Several people have contributed to this study. Renato Barahona, Anne J. Cruz, and Abril Martínez-Behrend have all been helpful resolving translation problems. I thank Annette Chapman-Adisho and Chalice Wilkersen at the

University of Illinois at Chicago for reading versions of sections of the text. My colleagues in the Department of History at Appalachian State University, Jari Eloranta, Michael Krenn, Mary Quigley, Karen Greene, and David Reid provided me with further advice and criticism on portions of the manuscript. One of my students, Jessica Fowler, helped me with some particularly tedious editing. The encouragement, advice, and comments of Jeffrey Merrick and especially Merry Wiesner-Hanks from the Department of History at the University of Wisconsin–Milwaukee have been invaluable. I have learned much from the comments and examples of George Huppert and David Jordan, two superb historians and writers, from the Department of History at the University of Illinois at Chicago. Hispanists Anne J. Cruz and Susan Tax Freeman, both formerly at the University of Illinois at Chicago and experts in literature and anthropology respectively, have done much to shape my views of Spanish women and society. I also want to thank many of my colleagues in the Society for Spanish and Portuguese Historical Studies for their fruitful conversations over the years: Michael Crawford, Stephanie Fink DeBacker, Elizabeth Lehfelt, Allyson Poska, and Scott Taylor. Above all, I must again thank Renato Barahona, who has been a wonderful guide to the culture and history of northern Spain. His breadth and depth of knowledge are impressive and have served as an inspiration to me. Renato has been consistently unselfish with his time. He faithfully read the multiple drafts of this study, and has always given me his honest criticism and direction.

* * *

Portions of chapter 5 appeared in Edward Behrend-Martínez, "Manhood and the Neutered Body in Early Modern Spain," *Journal of Social History* 38, no. 4 (Summer 2005): 1073–93.ac

UNFIT FOR MARRIAGE

Towns mentioned in book

Introduction

> Es más facil atar que desatar.
> (It is easier to bind than unbind.)
> —Spanish saying[1]

In early modern northern Spain the church made marriages; and despite its own claim that matrimony was permanent, the church allowed divorces too. When church courts issued annulments, they bent and fitted Catholic laws in such a way as to appease the stubborn interests of beleaguered wives and husbands wanting to end their time in the purgatory of marriage. The Catholic Church still does this today, bureaucratically permitting huge numbers of annulments to couples divorcing in secular courts.[2] This book explores the most notorious type of trial in ecclesiastical courts: those in which an annulment, the equivalent of a divorce, was granted on grounds of impotence. Impotence was a very successful pretense for winning an annulment. Probably as a result, it was by far the most common basis for annulment in the busy church court of Calahorra and La Calzada.[3] By contrast, the small number of couples that asked the court for annulments on grounds of incest/consanguinity, lack of consent, or unequal status nearly all lost their pleas.

Aside from the sexual notoriety and the curiosity that impotence cases elicit, there are several reasons to study them. Most importantly, they demonstrate instances when women were able to litigate against their husbands. In fact, nearly all the demands for annulment were brought to the court by women against their male spouses. The church court was one of the few venues, and perhaps the only legal one, in which women could act independently to prosecute their husbands. Contrast this with secular courts and legal procedures in which, unless she were a widow, a woman had to be represented by a man who would speak in her name: a father, husband, or brother. Another significant aspect of impotence trials is that litigants clearly used these annulments as forms of de facto divorce. In some cases, in fact, litigants freely switched their pleas from separation to annulment and vice versa. A smaller number of plaintiffs were so uncertain whether to ask the court for a separation or an annulment that they allowed the judge to decide which plea seemed most plausible. Annulments based on impotence, like separations resulting from battery, were clearly early modern Catholic precedents to modern divorce.

At least three facts permitted a discussion of divorce in a Catholic legal system that did not recognize it. First among these, if we limit ourselves to the language of the day, both separations and annulments were commonly and legally called *divorcio:* divorce. Clearly, in the parlance and mentality of the day divorce existed, with remarriage permitted in the case of annulments. Second, the physical, social, and financial conditions that were part of Catholic annulments were just like modern divorces: the wife's titular property (dowry) was returned to her, the property accumulated during marriage was split between the couple, and even restraining orders could be promulgated to prevent menacing husbands from harming their wives. Finally, customary divorce was plainly present in the Basque and Spanish mentality. Plays, proverbs, and the records of public notaries reveal that, whether legally permitted or not, divorce was an option in the minds of early modern women and men.[4] What else could explain the wife in Cervantes' one-act play *The Divorce Judge* who demands "Divorce, divorce, divorce. A thousand times divorce!"[5] For all these reasons, throughout this investigation I will use the word *divorce* when referring to separations and annulments.[6] It was, after all, the word the litigants used.

The church's position, however, was that it never allowed the breaking of a legitimate marriage. This statement is true because the church could decide whether a "legitimate matrimony" existed or not by making use of complex and equivocal arguments.[7] Though ratified by consummation and consent, for instance, Henry VIII's marriage to Catherine of Aragon was eventually annulled using a sophistry alleging consanguinity because Catherine had married Henry's brother Arthur decades earlier.[8] That the church never allowed the dissolution of a legitimate marriage is also true because, no matter how permanent the physical and economic separation of a husband and wife, they were still married in the eyes of God.

Roderick Phillips, one of the foremost historians of European divorce, also rejects the idea that the Catholic Church allowed divorce.[9] He argues, first, that early modern Catholic divorcio was far removed from modern divorce because it did not allow for remarriage.[10] To accept this, however, one must assume that the ultimate purpose of all divorce is remarriage. This stems from the assumption that the desire to divorce is preceded by an adulterous affair. The view is that what leads to divorce is romance outside marriage rather than disaffection, and perhaps violence, within marriage.[11] The primary goal of divorce, however, is to get away from a spouse permanently, not find a new one. Especially for women, remarriage may be a secondary concern. On the question of annulment, Phillips disregards that they were often used as divorces. Perhaps giving the church the benefit of the doubt, he argues that church court judges were never so corrupt as to allow frequent breaches of Tridentine doctrine. Certainly, some clerical judges were, at times, bribable, and this did provide opportunities for church-sponsored divorce. But clerics hardly needed to be corrupt for annulments to be used as divorces. They could also be hoodwinked by litigants and attorneys who manipulated rhetoric to win annulment cases. They understood the legal grounds for annulments under canon law and fit their circumstances to those requirements. What seems most important to Phillips's purpose, though, is downplaying Catholic precedents to modern divorce so as to emphasize the roles of the Reformation and French Revolution in the history of divorce. Semantics aside, then, the annulments granted by the church that will be discussed hereafter were important forms of early modern divorce.

The history of modern divorce is part of a teleological history of progress, and it is unsurprising that Spain and Catholic Europe in general have been written about as the spoilers in this history. Divorce has frequently been used to measure both social progress and decline. Jeffrey Watt, for instance, used the frequency of divorces in Neuchâtel as a measure of the changing cultural perception of marriage in the eighteenth century.[12] Historians like Phillips and Watt have used changes in European laws allowing divorce, and the application of such laws, as measures of progress. Clearly any law that allowed women the legal option to litigate in their own right has been regarded as a promotion of individual liberty. Phillips sees the Reformation changes in divorce law as the significant break that allowed greater individual freedom.[13] Watt argues, instead, that the important social breakthrough making divorce a plausible option for married couples occurred later. In Neuchâtel he found that progressive change resulted from Enlightenment ideas that placed an emphasis on the role of sentiment in marriage. Both of these authors generally disregard Catholic societies in which divorce was officially considered anathema by Catholic theologians. Consequently, in many histories of divorce, Catholic Europe, and Spain especially, remains the antithesis of "progress." This study aims to temper such arguments by demonstrating that Spanish church courts actually provided several flexible legal devices for women to leave their husbands. Moreover, church courts were often used to protect women's property against their husbands. By looking at early modern Catholic divorces, we discover that Spaniards did have methods to cope with marital disaffection and breakdown in this period.

To show how Spanish women were able to challenge men at home, one must first dispel the myth that there was no way for women to escape marriage in early modern Spain. Divorce is one of the most useful tools that a woman can have to challenge the power of her husband over her person. After all, a key aspect of any society based on male governance, as defined by anthropologists, historians, and feminists alike, is the male-dominated household. The control of women by men was most fragile within the personally interdependent and microcosmic realm of marriage. Who actually governed a household, a husband or a wife, was a frequent source of tension in seventeenth- and eighteenth-century Spain, as it is today. This was even more the case in the Basque country, where women were occasionally named to head households *over* their brothers and other kin, in a society that has often been described as matriarchal.[14] What other situation explains why so many husbands turned to litigation to force wives to obey them?[15] Patriarchy was affirmed by the courts, but disputed within households. Though by our time period Spain had fully incorporated into law the concept that the husband was the head of the family, Spanish adages contained contradictory opinions on the traditional paterfamilias. Many sayings, to be sure, extolled the control of wife by husband: "Hell is a woman without guidance"; "Bring me, O God, to that house where the husband commands, and the wife does not." But other popular sayings, though not without irony, hinted at or even encouraged women's domestic authority over their husbands: "If you want to be well married, do what your wife commands"; "He who has a wife has someone to obey."[16]

Historian Allyson Poska as well as ethnographers working in Spain have found, in fact, that in Galicia, that distant and unique corner of Spain, marriages could be defined as matriarchal.[17] This contradictory evidence suggests that in Spanish custom competing ideals existed about sexual dominance and equality in the household. A patriarchal household was the model preferred by church and state and was clearly a dominant conception, but it was one that individuals, especially wives, disputed. The notion that a husband was to rule a wife, and not vice versa, required constant cultural reinforcement. Within marriage many women struggled and succeeded at undermining the paterfamilias ideal.

Impotence trials illuminate many of these private struggles between men and women over control of the early modern household. As such, these were not merely ugly domestic disputes. Matrimony was a fundamental economic institution. Usually, much money and property were at stake; even poor litigants fought jealously for possession of their few goods and lands. Using the rhetoric and principles of the male-dominated household, husbands asserted their rights over their marriages and wives. Women counterattacked by questioning the legitimacy of their husbands, arguing that they were sexually unfit and not true men. But whether they argued for or against an annulment, husbands and wives focused their arguments on their own bodies and those of their spouses.

Clearly, by customary definitions, marriage was made by physical coupling of a man and woman. Not all sex was marriage, of course, but there was no perfect marriage without sex.[18] Sex meant unification of male and female, but more importantly, it was a form of physical control. We will find in these trials that a husband's physical control of his wife's body, using violence, sustenance, and sex, constituted communally accepted daily foundations of wedlock. The wife's body was the proof, or disproof, of the husband's power over her. This observation is nothing new, of course; anthropologists who study Mediterranean honor have repeatedly demonstrated the important role women's virginity and chastity had in serving as the retainers of a husband's honor.[19] Evidence of such male control over a female body ranges from traditions of female sequestration to the symbolism of the chastity belt. What is often ignored, however, is that the proof of a husband's authority and legitimacy was documented in *his* body as well. A woman could challenge her husband's authority by asserting that his body was not a *man's* body after all.

Even though sexual consummation was the binding act of customary European marriages, church theology viewed sex as too crude a basis for marriage; matrimony was, after all, a sacrament.[20] Theologians from Hincmar of Rheims (845–882) to Gratian (twelfth century) never allowed sex, the uniting of flesh, which was evil by definition, to be central to a holy rite. Instead, canon law decreed that consent between man and woman officially created matrimony, and sex between them was a mere ratification of that union.[21] As we shall discover, however, there could be no legitimate marriage without consummation; even the church ultimately recognized that sex made marriage. What one finds in trials for annulment, then, is how Spanish church courts melded canon law and Catholic ideology with Spanish customs. This unique application of canon law did not involve altered or novel interpretations of church principles. Canon law, though one of the earliest and most highly developed law codes in early modern Europe, was sufficiently ambiguous and contained enough loopholes to accommodate the demands of Spanish customs. The church also had a stake in regulating and promoting matrimony for many reasons. Though there was money involved in licensing marriages and granting dispensations, for our purposes what was most crucial was the church's concern to create social order through marriage. Theologians had long conceived of matrimony, among other things, as a practical way to contain lust. For misogynistic clerical thinkers, suppressing lust meant controlling women's bodies; from their male perspective, preventing the social chaos that female beauty and sex threatened to bring about was the husband's duty. The social-sexual order would unravel if the husband were impotent.

This study focuses by necessity on the bodies of litigants because the majority of their arguments converged on physical facts. In annulment cases based on impotence, all actors of the church court worked to ascertain one slippery physical fact: was an accused spouse's genitalia apt or inept for intercourse? In the case of a woman accused of impotence: could her vagina be penetrated and receive her husband's seed? In the more common case of an allegedly impotent man: could the husband's penis become erect, penetrate the vagina, and sow the "true semen" that church theologians demanded? In all these divorces, therefore, the legitimacy of marriages depended on bodies and the interpretation of bodies by doctors, lawyers, spouses, and family members.

The particular court cases that are the focus of this book are recorded in documents in the Diocesan and Cathedral Archives of Calahorra, in Calahorra, Spain. This archive is the main depository for documents of the Diocese of Calahorra and La Calzada (see map). The diocesan ecclesiastical court records from the early modern period have only recently been fully cataloged, while materials from later centuries are still being organized. Though the archive is superbly staffed and cataloged, several factors affecting the bulk of the documentation make statistical data for social and legal trends precarious. First, it is unclear whether the archive has the entire run of the court's litigation. In modern times the existence of not one but two other seats for the diocese has resulted in the possibility that clerics in those cathedral chapters have jealously withheld from the main archive some documentation pertaining to the diocese as a whole.

Second, until recent decades the diocese stored the unorganized documents in a corner of Calahorra's cathedral, and humidity, water, and insects have certainly destroyed some cases. Yet, rot could have resulted in only a small number of paper victims; the occasional case that shows signs of worm and water damage indicates that these were minimal threats to the documentation. A third factor is that through the centuries the diocesan archive was usually housed where the bishop resided, either Logroño, Santo Domingo de La Calzada, or Calahorra. Therefore, some documents were possibly lost in their travels overland, when they did not fall behind shelves and bookcases. Finally, there is the likelihood that over the centuries some sensitive materials were purposely bought, removed, or destroyed by individuals hoping to prevent embarrassment to themselves, their families, or to certain institutions.

Keeping these factors in mind, however, the Diocesan and Cathedral Archives of Calahorra seems to be still relatively complete. Today it houses thousands of bundles of documentation, manuscripts, and books dating from the twelfth century to the present on all aspects of the church for a large expanse of northern Spain. Of these, our current study will focus on roughly eighty-three cases of marital annulment on grounds of impotence between 1650 and 1750 tried in the diocese's ecclesiastical court.

The records of these trials have helped to improve our dismal knowledge of Spanish ordinary church courts, for which very few studies exist.[22] Several logical reasons explain why historians have ignored the ordinary church courts. First has been a public fascination with that extraordinary ecclesiastical system of tribunals: the Spanish Inquisition. The historical imagination has clearly placed the common ecclesiastical courts in the shadow of the Inquisition. Unfortunately, the image of the Spanish Inquisition is so vivid that often even well-informed readers conflate it with the jurisdiction and role of ordinary church courts in early modern Spain. After the Spanish Inquisition monopolized many decades of historical study, a new generation of scholars turned to uncovering other aspects of Spanish life.[23] These historians generally preferred to examine secular Spanish history: its royal courts and municipal institutions. This focus on secular institutions, though a much needed corrective, again left church courts unstudied.

Not only have church courts been of less interest to historians than other institutions, but their archives have been far less accessible. Both secular archives and those of the Spanish Inquisition were earlier and much better organized and cataloged than ecclesiastical archives housed in the dozens of diocesan seats throughout Spain. Also, the bishops and clerical archivists in charge of church archives have traditionally been suspicious of secular historians' motivations. It is unsurprising, then, that many clerics in Spain have often worked to limit, or prevent entirely, entry into and use of ecclesiastical archives. Happily, in recent decades greater trust and cooperation between state, church, and academic authorities in Spain have made a few of these archives more accessible.

A study of the Diocese of Calahorra and La Calzada also breaks new ground geographically. Though a small number of Spanish ecclesiastical and local historians have produced studies using materials from the Diocesan and Cathedral Archives of Calahorra and La Calzada, many archival documents have not often been used to uncover aspects of social history, especially for our time period.[24] In contrast, materials from the Diocese of Pamplona, which lies just to the northeast of our bishopric, have yielded many studies owing to its better funded archive. Among these studies is María del Juncal Campo Guinea's investigation of matrimonial church court disputes in the Kingdom of Navarra.[25]

Aside from the fact that it has been very little studied, many characteristics make the Diocese of Calahorra and La Calzada a particularly interesting object for investigation. It was a vast, ethnically diverse bishopric whose institutional authority issued from Old Castile south of the Ebro River. Because it was in the heart of Old Castile and was a formally Castilian institution ruling over an area that was highly parochial, mountainous, and locally diverse, the Diocese of Calahorra and La Calzada was, strangely enough, a typical Spanish diocese. The fact that it covers nearly all of the Basque country makes this diocese even more important for studying the impact of a Castilian institution, the church court of Calahorra and La Calzada, on a population that was largely Basque.

In the seventeenth and eighteenth centuries the Diocese of Calahorra and La Calzada included most of what are today the Spanish provinces of La Rioja, Álava, and Vizcaya (see map). It also held jurisdiction over parts of western Burgos, eastern Guipúzcoa and Navarra, and northern Soria. Half of this widespread diocese therefore fell into what was culturally Castilian Old Castile, while the rest of it consisted of Álava and the Basque Provinces. The three administrative centers, however, were located in Old Castile. Appeals from the diocese of Calahorra and La Calzada proceeded to the metropolitan see of Burgos.[26] The diocese maintained two cathedrals in the eighteenth century, though it now has three. The cathedral and town of Santo Domingo de la Calzada began as an important stop for medieval pilgrims traveling the Camino Francés that stretches from the French Pyrenees to Santiago de Compostela on Spain's western Atlantic seacoast. A second cathedral originated in the ancient Roman seat of the Diocese in Calahorra. As the documents of these trials show, however, the majority of litigation actually took place in Logroño, the larger and centrally located city situated on the Ebro River.

There were no truly large cities in the diocese. Important urban centers included the port of Bilbao, the inland provincial capital of Logroño, and Vitoria and Nájera. The bishop usually resided in Calahorra, Santo Domingo de La Calzada, or Logroño. One historian has estimated Logroño's population to have been no more than 7,000 at the end of the seventeenth century. The number of residents in Calahorra hovered around 3,600, and Santo Domingo de La Calzada boasted no more than 3,000.[27] However, the majority of the diocese's population lived in the hundreds of small towns, villages, and hamlets scattered throughout mountain valleys. Most were tiny by any standard.[28] Very small urban populations and single homesteads characterized the mountainous Basque-speaking areas of the north of the diocese. Two hundred thousand, or 80 percent of the bishopric's citizens, lived in the more largely Basque area north of the Ebro. In sum, those residing north of the Ebro constituted the majority of the diocese's inhabitants.

Only fifty thousand, or a fifth of the people in this study, lived south of the Ebro in Old Castile. Yet these Castilian subjects of the diocese appeared before its court much more frequently than those living in Álava or the Basque Provinces to the north. The majority of litigants in this study came from towns south of the Ebro. There are three possible explanations for this difference in litigiousness between the north and south of the diocese: urbanity, cultural difference, and language.

Living close to the diocesan court, whether it was in Logroño, Calahorra, or Santo Domingo de La Calzada, naturally made the church court's justice more accessible. Owing to proximity, then, residents of La Rioja had easier access to the court. The three principal cities of the diocese were all south of the Ebro River. Towns south of the Ebro in this region were more Mediterranean in character than those in Vizcaya and Álava to the north; that is, the cities of Old Castile tended to be more centralized, with greater numbers of their populations concentrated into urban areas. Several historians have shown that in early modern Europe urbanity made litigation more likely.[29] Attempting to determine how frequently rural residents litigated in early modern Spain, for instance, Richard Kagan studied the Fiel del Juzgado, a special judge assigned to oversee cases from Toledo's mountainous rural jurisdiction. He concluded that landholding peasants, but especially artisans and urban professionals, were more likely to bring personal disputes before a court.[30] We can only guess at the impact that an institutionally Castilian court manned by Castilian-speaking notaries and lawyers had on extending the church's jurisdiction in the Basque-speaking provinces. Aside from the differences in the number of cases from north and south of the Ebro, however, there is little qualitative evidence that ethnic differences directly inhibited couples from approaching the ecclesiastical court. It is probable nonetheless that, though the diocesan court employed translators to serve Basque-speaking litigants, the different languages might have created an obstacle to litigation for some. A good comparison is the French diocese of Cabrai. This officially French diocese included a large Flemish-speaking population. J. R. Machuelle found that Flemish-speakers were far less likely to litigate in the ecclesiastical court than French speakers.[31]

The period 1650 to 1750 is well suited to a study of Spanish legal institutions, but even more so to an investigation into the Spanish church courts. Traditionally, historians have split Spanish history at the dynastic political change from Hapsburg to Bourbon that occurred at the turn of the eighteenth century. Several factors make the mid-seventeenth century an equally useful division in Spanish institutional and social history. First, the decades following Spain's 1654 treaty with France that ended an international conflict beginning with the Thirty Years War mark the nadir both of Spain's political power during the early modern period and its demographic and economic decline. Traditionally, historians had described Spain's recovery as a result of Bourbon reforms after the turn of the eighteenth century. More recent studies, however, have actually found signs of recovery during the reign of Spain's last Hapsburg, the personally pitiful Charles II.[32]

The century of this study, which straddles the seventeenth and eighteenth centuries, also precedes the influences of the Enlightenment in Spain. Ending at 1750, this investigation stops just before the reign of the enlightened Bourbon monarch Charles III (king of Spain 1759–1788). He would eventually institute the Real Pragmática of 1776, a legal reform that severely curtailed the jurisdiction of the church in marital disputes. As such, this study remains squarely within Spain's *antiguo régimen.* There is continuity in the mentality, procedure, and decisions of the ecclesiastical court over the many decades that make up these impotence trials.

Though there was little change in the mode of thought of diocesan officials in the church court, institutionally there was change in the Diocese of Calahorra and La Calzada between 1650 and 1750. The diocese experienced a great growth in activity in the last decades of the seventeenth century and then declined after the turn of the century. This tendency confirms the surges and dips in legal activity noted by Richard Kagan in his general history of litigation in Spain 1500 to 1700. Though not the primary focus of this investigation, over the century we will follow the growth in litigation in the ecclesiastical court, an apex in its activity, and then a leveling off and decline in the institution's power. But before entering into how the church court functioned and a description of its regulation of marriage and divorce, I will focus on the twists and turns of a single impotence trial, wife Gerónima Martínez de Texada versus husband Diego Belasco, which reveal how many of these cases proceeded.[33]

1: Gerónima Martínez de Texada *v.* Diego Belasco, Logroño, 1681

> He was not to be taken for a man . . .
> —Gerónima Martínez de Texada

Anyone attempting to explain the rudiments of an impotence trial to an interested audience will be met with a flood of questions. How did judges test a litigant for impotence? How long did a husband have to be impotent for an annulment to be possible? How could a woman litigate independently in such a male-biased society? How could a woman be judged impotent? How common were these trials? Answering these fundamental questions can be complicated by the fact that marital annulments on grounds of impotence varied considerably; each case followed unique and twisted courses shaped by the assorted political, economic, and sexual situations of particular husbands and wives. And yet, impotence cases that came before the court shared numerous features. The present case serves as a superb example because it incorporates several characteristics found in many different impotence cases. The case of Gerónima Martínez de Texada *v.* Diego Belasco included a variety of rhetorics and legal procedures not seen together in other cases. For example, out of eighty-three cases, roughly a dozen were litigated against castrated men; three husbands used witchcraft as an explanation for their impotence; descriptions of impotence cures, apothecaries, and drugs occurred rarely; and only a minority of cases involved the medical examination of the wife by midwives. Furthermore, lawyers only occasionally resorted to calling witnesses. Yet these phenomena could and did occur in many impotence cases. The trial considered here had it all. All these issues can be introduced by dissecting this one case.

But Gerónima Martínez's case against her husband, Diego Belasco, despite its twists and turns, did return to the primary questions of every impotence trial: Was the husband perpetually impotent? Could the wife demonstrate his impotence by proving herself a virgin? Had the couple ever consummated the marriage? Their case also reveals how ecclesiastical judges often applied canon law with practicality, and not necessarily sacramentality, as their foremost concern.

One of the few facts that Gerónima and Diego agreed on during a year's litigation in the ecclesiastical court of Calahorra and La Calzada was that they legally wed before the church in accordance with the ritual and manner decided by the Council of Trent nearly a century earlier. That celebration took place on April 1, 1662. Philip IV (1621–65) was still on the Spanish throne, and the nation was recovering from four decades of wars at home and abroad. Diego had been twenty-three years old and Gerónima had been seventeen. The case meant to dissolve their marriage came before the court an amazing nineteen years later, making Diego forty-two and Gerónima thirty-six. Now the year was 1681, and the feeble and sterile Charles II (1665–1700) ruled Spain. Just as with his predecessor two centuries earlier, Henry IV (1454–74), known as "the Impotent," Charles II's impotence and inability to produce offspring would ultimately plunge Spain into civil war. Henry IV's supposed impotence had resulted in a war when his alleged daughter Juana and his sister Isabella fought over the succession to the throne. Charles II's sterility during his reign would lead, upon his death, to another war of succession: the War of the Spanish Succession (1701–1714).

Though Diego inhabited a much humbler social world and economic level than the king of Spain, like Charles II he too was in a desperate fight to prove his virility at the end of the seventeenth century. The validity of Diego's marriage was being questioned in the local bishop's court in his home town of Logroño. Gerónima had publicly denounced Diego as impotent and had begun a suit for annulment. Diego also fought, therefore, to defend his reputation and manhood to a community completely aware of his wife's accusations and the couple's sexual problems. Furthermore, the dangers that sterility and impotence posed to public order could not have been lost on a citizenry concerned about the impending consequences of Charles II's childlessness. The succession crisis was likely a common topic of public conversation and jokes.

Gerónima had filed her suit for annulment on February 5, 1681. She had much to gain from the dissolution of her marriage to Diego. In reality, she was fighting for her complete independence. If she could prove that she was a virgin and that her husband, for nearly two decades, had never consummated their marriage, she would reclaim full power over her dowry and take half of all that she and Diego had earned in their profession as tailors. Gerónima would avoid ever living again with a man whom she disliked and may have hated. She might live where she pleased; perhaps she would even remarry. Her marriage to Diego had proved to be a sterile union. With remarriage at age thirty-six, Gerónima might have looked forward to a last opportunity to have children.

Though her plans for life after Diego can only be guessed at, we do know that Gerónima was trying to wrest goods and money from the control of her husband, giving her much more actual autonomy. As we shall discover below, she had already easily avoided living with Diego. To be physically separated, Gerónima had not needed to turn to the courts. But for further liberty, she needed the return of her dowry and property, and only the courts could force Diego to give those to her. Gerónima would, of course, have been better off as a widow because she would have inherited all of the couple's wealth. And given the mortality rates for men in the seventeenth century, her chances were not too bad. Instead, Diego was still alive after nineteen long years and Gerónima was still legally bound to him, as the majority of women in the seventeenth century were attached to a father, husband, brother, son, or confessor.[1] With an annulment, however, Gerónima could become a marriageable single woman and could hope to direct her own life more completely.

Much was also at stake for Diego. First there was the substantial question of his rights over Gerónima's dowry. Even though it was not permitted for him to squander or otherwise alienate the dowry, Diego could still use and make money from it. Their home and all the goods that he held in common with Gerónima were also at risk. Because she had worked with him for many years in his tailor's shop, Gerónima could also take half of all they earned and owned. However, Diego's main concern may not have been economic at all. He may have been more worried about his public reputation as a man. If he could prove that he controlled his wife's sexuality, and that he had, in his words, "deflowered her and deprived her of her virginity with his natural member without force or violence whatsoever," he would maintain his legal power over Gerónima and all that was hers.[2] He would also protect his status as a man and a *vecino,* a full citizen, in the city of Logroño. If he lost the case, however, his customers, neighbors, and friends would consider him a eunuch, *un capón.* If he lost his case and was proved to be impotent, the court would prohibit him from ever marrying again. And, as was true for so many men in early modern Spain, without the financial cushion of a woman's dowry, he would be forced to live the remainder of his life in poverty.

The ecclesiastical court had its own agenda in this case and others like it. If the court were to allow individuals to annul their marriages on the basis of spurious claims of consanguinity or impotence, it would weaken the importance of marrying in the church. The bishop had to enforce the church's control over marriage formation and authority over legitimating who was and was not married. Because it was a sacrament, matrimony was to be treated, as much as possible, as a single momentous step. The Catholic Church throughout Europe had spent centuries wresting the legitimization of matrimony from the grasp of long-held customs and the aristocracy, and brought it into the doors of the church and cathedral. By the mid-sixteenth century it registered marriages in its books, and the church's notaries kept track of profits from the sale of marital dispensations. Not long after 1681, the year of Gerónima and Diego's trial, the defense of the church's jurisdiction over marriage would become more intense. The Enlightenment, and the resulting anticlerical reforms, soon recommended that the state rather than the church have jurisdiction over many matrimonial issues.[3]

A great deal rested, then, on the determination of a single fact: had Diego and Gerónima ever had sex? Money, property, status, legal rights, and even salvation of both husband and wife depended on whether they were legitimately united by the holy sacrament of matrimony. Canon law clearly defined sexual consummation. A marriage was only consummated via erection, penetration, and insemination *intra vas.* Diego and Gerónima had conflicting stories as to whether this had happened or not. Diego claimed that he had been "in the act" with his wife on several occasions in the days after they married: "on the first, second, or third night that I began sleeping with [Gerónima] I deflowered her and deprived her of her virginity with the natural member without force or violence whatsoever."[4] Later in their marriage, however, Diego admitted to having used "two fingers . . . so that the virile member could enter with ease."[5]

Gerónima adamantly maintained that her husband was lying. She asserted that Diego never had been able to penetrate her and deprive her of her virginal seal, her *claustro virginal,* and furthermore, that she had suffered and persevered in her chastity for the nineteen years since their marriage. Though she had lived apart from Diego for many years, Gerónima claimed that she had also never lost her virginity to any other man. Thus, she defended her public reputation as a virgin, a status that was always crucial for any woman planning to marry in early modern Spain.[6] Gerónima's virginity, after all, was worth a great deal of money.[7] In claiming her virginity she asserted that Diego had no legitimate rights to her dowry and goods and that they were hers. As a virgin, Gerónima could claim control over her physical person; she had rights, therefore, to the property that was attached to that person. If Diego had not taken her virginity, he had no legal claim over her and her property. Juan de Gámiz Hidalgo, her lawyer, argued that "on no occasion during the entire [marriage] was [Diego] able to copulate with [Gerónima]."[8] But what proof was there? All claims would eventually need to be proved to the court by physical examination. To trump any conclusion by a midwife that her claustro virginal was no longer intact, Gerónima made an excuse for the state of her vagina in a deposition to the court.[9] If her genitalia were at all lax or otherwise corrupted, she argued, it was because her husband, driven mad by his inability to consummate the marriage, "had done [the penetration] with his fingers and fingernails seizing her as on different occasions he would seize her by her parts and insert his fingers."[10] Gerónima's accusation was not common enough to be considered a rhetorical formula, but neither was it unique in defloration and impotence cases. It was also one of her lawyer's favorite allegations. Juan de Gámiz used it in the 1692 case when wife Josepha de Echabarría accused her husband, Antonio Ruiz, of "planning to break the virginal seal with his hands."[11] And it appeared in two other of Gámiz's impotence prosecutions, one in 1697 and one in 1704.[12] The charge that a husband illegitimately used his fingers, rather than his penis, to effect consummation was not peculiar to Gámiz and Spain. We find it used in a 1736 French impotence trial between Marie-Catherine Chardon and her husband, Nicolas Séné.[13] Not only did such indictments explain the loss of the hymen, according to the prosecution's rhetorical approach, they helped expose the trickery of these alleged imposters who claimed to be real men. In Gerónima's testimony about her husband's inabilities, she told the court "that the said Diego de Velasco would cry recognizing that [he] was not a man."[14]

Juan de Gámiz Hidalgo had written Gerónima's initial petition for an annulment on grounds of impotence. In it he claimed that Gerónima married her husband seventeen years earlier. Gerónima and her counsel may have been already attempting to downplay the long duration of their marriage. Gerónima would later admit in a declaration that she actually married Diego nineteen years earlier. Still, they had only lived together for a fraction of the time that they were legally wed. Three years after the wedding, Juan de Gámiz explained, Gerónima recognized that her husband was incapable of consummating the marriage because he was impotent. On advice of her confessor and other learned persons, the couple voluntarily separated *quoad torum et mutuam cohabitationem,* from hearth and cohabitation.

Note the ease with which Diego and Gerónima separated. The couple did not need to litigate for a formal separation. They parted mutually on the simple advice of local clerics. Gámiz argued that they parted for the protection of their souls; the marriage not having been consummated, Gerónima and Diego were technically man and woman living alone under one roof. They were living in sin. No doubt, however, there could have been problems for the couple had their makeshift separation come to the attention of an ecclesiastical visitor. Gámiz ended Gerónima's petition by asking that Diego make a declaration to the court concerning his alleged impotence, that medical experts visit the husband to confirm his affliction, that the tribunal annul the marriage and give Gerónima license to marry whomever she pleased.

Diego and his lawyer had many arguments to counter the suit begun by Gerónima. The most suspicious aspect of this lawsuit, his lawyer Juan de Soldevilla argued, was the nineteen-year lapse between the day Gerónima married Diego and when she finally decided to sue for an annulment. Why had she waited so long if her husband's impotence was so obvious? "For if it were as certain as [Gerónima] holds that the impotence of [Diego] from the first was visible and natural, she would not have remained quiet such a long time [before] now issuing her plea."[15] A second issue was the condition of Gerónima's vagina, which Diego hoped would show that she was no longer a virgin. Juan de Soldevilla persistently demanded that medical experts examine her, in addition to the traditional examination of the allegedly impotent husband. The true motivation for the suit, Juan de Soldevilla claimed, stemmed from the couple's separation that brought to an end three years of domestic discord. He argued that Gerónima wanted to transform the separation into the marriage's complete dissolution: an annulment. Finally, he had several explanations for Diego's inability to perform his conjugal duties consistently. Though the husband did admit to having suffered from a lack of sexual vigor later in his marriage, he blamed this on *maleficio,* evil potions or witchcraft.[16] Diego also claimed that a botched impotence cure had resulted in his persistent sexual weakness. He blamed the malpractice on an apothecary whom he and Gerónima had consulted in Estella. In any case, Diego asserted that because his bouts of impotence had occurred long after they had had sex, the marriage was therefore consummated and legitimate.

Such were the competing and contradictory claims of husband and wife. Whom were the judges to believe? Following the regular procedure in annulment trials based on impotence, the court looked to medical experts to substantiate or refute the assertions of litigants. The ecclesiastical tribunal depended heavily on the diagnoses of doctors and surgeons as the most reliable evidence to substantiate charges of impotence. The man's potency, rather than the woman's viginity, was the court's primary concern. Unless there were extenuating circumstances, the husband had to demonstrate his capacity for "the use of matrimony" before a wife would be examined to confirm her virginity. Little more than a month after Gerónima initiated the suit, Dr. Don Mathias Femat Lobera and surgeon Matheo de Urrondo visited with and inspected Diego.

The ecclesiastical tribunal generally relied on a familiar list of medical professionals to provide their learned opinions. Between 1679 and 1683 Dr. Femat appeared before the tribunal and gave medical testimony in three other cases. In 1681 he declared a man from Castillo potent; two years earlier he found a husband from San Román impotent. And, in a curious case from Alegria, in 1683, he absolved a young husband of having intolerable bad breath.[17] Surgeon Matheo de Urrondo was more of a regular in the court than Dr. Femat. He appeared as an expert witness in more than fifteen cases between 1673 and 1686. Urrondo's job as a surgeon was to examine the subject with his hands while following the instructions of the doctor, whose privilege it was not to have to actually touch the patient at all. During the examination Dr. Femat was not an uninformed and blind arbiter of Diego's sexual potency. Before meeting Diego, the doctor had been fully appraised of the marriage and the circumstances of the case. The court had apparently provided him with the statements made by the litigants and their lawyers. In Dr. Femat's declaration he demonstrated that he was conversant with the details of the case and the marriage in question. Before physically examining his patient, Dr. Femat had a lengthy interview with Diego. The husband revealed the details of his bout with impotence and efforts to find a cure. After nine years of marriage Diego believed that he had been bewitched. Diego told Dr. Femat that he and his wife had made a trip north of Logroño to the Basque town of Arbeyza in search of a cure. There they were exorcised by a cleric famous for ridding couples of impotence. Such exorcisms, according to this and other trials, involved acts of penance and a clerical exorcist who physically exorcised the husband of the evil spirits causing the impotence; however, few of the cases provide specific descriptions of what these exorcists actually did. Some testimonies describe that in the process of exorcism the afflicted men trembled or sweated heavily. The exorcists themselves cited the *Fustis dæmonum* of Hieronymous Mengus as their guide to exorcism of impotence. Many of these exorcists insisted that both husband and wife needed to be exorcised.[18]

By the beginning of the eighteenth century few educated professionals believed in witchcraft. As Keith Thomas has demonstrated, European intellectuals had clearly defined the belief in the supernatural powers of the devil in the temporal as superstitious.[19] Dr. Femat was such an educated man. He did not believe that witchcraft could have caused Diego's impotence. He testified before an ecclesiastical tribunal, however, and acknowledged the fact that the Catholic Church made provisions for exorcism. Canon law allowed for the possibility that impotence could be caused by diabolic spells, defined as *maleficium.* Still, Dr. Femat made it clear that he disavowed witchcraft as a cause and placed little faith in the spiritual cures of clerics. For example, referring to the couple's visit to a Basque priest in Arbeyza known for curing individuals of impotence, Dr. Femat stated that "the abbot who exorcised them for the span of nine days deceived them."[20] Diego went on to tell Dr. Femat that after exorcism had failed to restore his potency, the couple traveled across the Ebro River and through the mountains northeast of Logroño to Estella, a small Basque town tucked between the jagged green mountains that begin the Pyrenees. There they visited a special doctor and apothecary in further hopes of a remedy. In Estella, Diego told the doctor, the apothecary Francisco Zete gave them some tablets: "those same tablets irritated him so much that they caused such an inflamation to the virile member and fistulous nerve that he was in danger of mortification."[21] Diego told Dr. Femat that he had not had an erection since undergoing this treatment in Estella.

Continuing his exploration of Diego's medical history, Dr. Femat discovered that he had also been partially castrated as a young boy. As was the common practice of hernia surgeons in seventeenth-century Spain, one of Diego's testicles had been removed while the other was "cleaned" and put back inside the groin.[22] It is unclear whether such a hernia operation was actually a medical treatment or instead a method of castration in which curing a "hernia" was simply a pretext. In any case, such a procedure was not uncommon; we find more than a dozen such "castrates" and monorchids in these impotence trial cases. Diego, however, insisted that this operation had not affected his ability to have sex. In a number of cases the ecclesiastical court substantiated the fact that such "castrated" men could indeed marry and have children. But Dr. Femat was skeptical on this point: "even though Diego Belasco says that he has nocturnal emissions, they are acrid and caustic."[23] Citing Thomas Sánchez and other authorities, including the "angelic" doctor Saint Thomas, Dr. Femat believed that he could conclude by Diego's polluted and caustic complexion that the humors that descended from the head and other upper regions of the body to form semen must also be corrupted and weak. It was a widely accepted medical belief in medieval and early modern Europe that the substance of a man's semen descended from his head and other parts of his body through ducts to the testicles where it was then expelled from the penis. This belief originated with Aristotle and explains why Dr. Femat felt he could judge the quality of Diego's sperm by studying his overall complexion.[24] Before examining Diego, therefore, the doctor had already settled on a conclusion.

Dr. Femat's actual physical examination of Diego was brief, or at least unimportant, in his final determination: "I have done the research on classic and modern [experts] that speak to my science, and also [the penis] does not erect to the touch."[25] Unlike most other impotence examinations in which medical experts placed their faith in a physical test involving cold and hot water baths of the genitalia, Dr. Femat made his decision based mainly on his knowledge of classical authorities and Diego's medical history. Also unlike other doctors solicited by the court, Dr. Femat reverted to Latin in his description of sexual information. While he may have used Latin for its exact medical terminology, more likely he wrote sexual terms in Latin to lessen the scandalous impact of certain terms. He preferred to write that Diego "insomnis habet pollutionem" rather than state in Castilian that he had ejaculated during the night.[26] Dr. Femat's final conclusion was that Diego had always been impotent, before and after the wedding. He could not have consummated the marriage. Furthermore, in Dr. Femat's opinion, Diego was impotent with virgins as well as with corrupted women. This final conclusion was an important verdict. It meant that Diego would never be able to consummate a marriage with any woman, virgin or otherwise. If the court trusted the doctor's judgment, Diego would never be allowed to remarry.

Surgeon Matheo de Urrondo added little to the doctor's learned declaration. Dr. Femat's conclusions were founded, after all, on the knowledge of centuries of sexual and medical study. Matheo de Urrondo gave a short affirmation of his colleague's opinion. With little reference to texts or authorities, he testified that he had administered hot and cold water baths, a common test used to reveal penile expansion and contraction. Urrondo described Diego's member as "impaired."[27] He therefore concurred with his medical superior, Dr. Femat.

The categorical medical diagnosis against Diego could have ended the case. But Diego's lawyer successfully convinced the court to order a medical examination of Gerónima. In most other Spanish impotence cases an examination of the wife occurred only after the husband had proved his virility. But the fact that Gerónima had waited for nineteen years before claiming nonconsummation to a court made her claims of being a virgin suspicious. If she wanted to claim virginity now, Gerónima had to prove it to the court. In order to determine whether she was a virgin or not, the tribunal again looked to medical experts. The court added midwife Cathalina de Oronz to the medical team to assist in the physical examination and add her experience regarding female sexual subjects. Cathalina de Oronz was a fifty-year-old midwife practicing in Logroño. Though clearly an expert in her vocation, she had had little or no formal education, as suggested by the fact that, unlike the male medical experts, Oronz did not sign the declaration that she presented to the court. Judge Juan Joseph de Texada y la Guardia trusted her enough to solicit her opinion in at least one other virginity test, in October of 1681.[28]

Little more than a week after Diego had presented himself for medical inspection, Gerónima did the same. Her visit must have been just as humiliating as her husband's was for him. Dr. Femat began his declaration to the court with a review of the medical literature concerning the determination of virginity. The doctor found the Book of Almansor by medieval Persian physician Rhazes (860–932) most useful to define virginity: "[Almansor] states that [virginity is] the path that has not been tread, neither penetrated nor sown with man's seed within the birth canal."[29] Dr. Femat also quoted the same author's acknowledgment that "the determination of virginity is very difficult."[30] When he diagnosed Diego, Dr. Femat had mainly resorted to medical authorities. Now, however, Dr. Femat relied heavily on the midwife's examination to determine whether Gerónima was a virgin or not. He gave no evidence of having systematically questioned Gerónima. As part of the crude virginity test, Oronz inserted a candle into Gerónima's vagina. After this humiliating examination, the experts agreed that Gerónima was a virgin.[31] Judging from lacerations that they found on Gerónima's genitalia, the medical experts also concluded that Diego had, indeed, violently torn the entrance of her vagina with his hands. The medical expert's conclusions, therefore, neatly echoed and corroborated Gerónima's own declaration. In all likelihood, their diagnoses had been influenced by the prosecution's arguments. The stories that a spouse told before an examination could greatly influence the opinions of medical experts who were attempting to practice a science as uncertain as the determination of virginity and impotence. One must remember, of course, that Dr. Femat had full knowledge of the testimonies of both Diego and Gerónima. Cathalina de Oronz included her declaration to the court just below that of Dr. Femat. Surgeon Mateo de Urrondo apparently acquiesced, adding his signature to the declaration.

Expert medical testimony decidedly favored Gerónima against her husband. According to them, Diego was clearly impotent now and probably was when he married Gerónima two decades before the trial. The ecclesiastical tribunal, then, relied on these informed opinions when it attempted to pry into the hidden sexual lives of litigants. Against such assessments how could Diego's lawyer hope to win the case for his client?

Soldevilla escalated the legal battle with a weapon rarely used in impotence trials: witness testimonies. Soldevilla composed a list of questions and began seeking witnesses to testify in defense of his client. In August of 1681 he submitted his client's proof to the ecclesiastical tribunal. The questions were leading and biased, which was exactly what a church court expected. The questions were, after all, written by one of the litigants. Soldevilla focused on the most important points of Diego's defense. He wanted to confirm that any alleged impotence occurred long after Diego consummated the marriage, and that any lasting impotence was related to the unfortunate events involved in trying to find a cure in Estella. Soldevilla asked witnesses to corroborate the story of Diego's search for an impotence cure. He asked witnesses to acknowledge the assumption that Gerónima would have sued for an annulment soon after their wedding if Diego had not actually consummated the marriage.

By appealing to witness testimony, Soldevilla pitted Diego's popularity and public standing in the community against Gerónima's reputation. At this stage, the tribunal was subjected to long lists of informants who gave lengthy testimonies. Many of these stories were based on hearsay evidence and influenced by personal opinion. The defense submitted a relatively long list of the couple's neighbors. The selection of witnesses showed no gender bias: five of the witnesses solicited by Diego were women, four of them men. Two were widows, and five of them were relatively close in age to Gerónima and Diego, in their late thirties, early forties. In fact, witnesses Joseph de González and his wife María de Artigue seem to have been close to Diego and Gerónima.[32] Even though these witnesses were selected by Diego's defense, only two of them gave evidence that supported the husband. Seven of the witnesses actually supported Gerónima, claiming that Diego had not consummated the marriage. Overall, then, the witness testimonies did not refute his wife's claims.

Most witnesses focused on Diego's journey for an impotence cure to the cities of Pamplona and Estella. This shed little light on whether or not Diego had actually ever consummated the marriage. If witnesses were in doubt they could, and often did, skip a question and simply go on to the next one. Most of the individuals questioned could not, and did not, attempt to explain why Gerónima had waited nineteen years to seek an annulment. Few seemed at pains to defend their neighbor's sexual reputation. Dr. Phelipe Baptista Martínez Garijo, however, recalled that when he first learned of Diego's impotence, he suggested to Gerónima that she ask for an annulment.[33]

From the testimonies Soldevilla and Diego did find some hope for victory. Two witnesses unquestionably affirmed that Diego and his wife had had sex, and that he was therefore her legitimate husband. Christobal Pérez began his testimony by admitting that he was related to Gerónima. He was married to Gerónoma's sister. But Christobal reassured notary Miguel de Irazu that his relationship to the litigating wife would not prevent him from telling the truth. After making the sign of the cross, thirty-year-old Christobal gave a detailed account about how he once overheard the couple having sex. Early in their marriage Christobal had spent a week in Diego and Gerónima's house to learn something of Diego's trade as a tailor. According to Christobal, he slept for several nights in the same room with Diego and Gerónima. On one occasion the young couple called to Chistobal to see if he was awake. Christobal slyly feigned that he was asleep and did not respond. While lying awake, he claimed, he heard the couple having sex. "The witness slept in the same room and on more than four or five nights heard noises from the bed of the said Diego and Gerónima Martínez, giving one another their said kisses, and that, wanting the said Diego Belasco to sleep with the aforementioned his wife . . . [she] called to this witness to see if he was awake or not. And this witness, maliciously, didn't want to respond, and [then] heard different acts and noises made of the kind that seemed to this witness to indicate that they were having *copula carnal,* and after they finished he heard Gerónima Martínez say 'I beg God that this boy didn't hear us and tell the officials in the morning.'"[34] Exactly what "officials" Christobal might have informed, we do not know. Yet, from these incidents Christobal concluded for himself that Gerónima could not be a virgin, and therefore was Diego's wife. With Christobal's testimony Soldevilla had gained an eyewitness to the consummation of Diego's marriage to Gerónima. This was the first corroboration of Diego's claims to be legitimately married to Gerónima.

María Maesto, a twenty-seven-year-old widow, also came forward in full support of Diego. When asked about Gerónima's virginity, María Maesto claimed to have spoken with surgeon Matheo de Urrondo who had been present at Gerónima's physical examination. In her deposition María Maesto claimed that, after asking Matheo de Urrondo if Gerónima was a virgin, the surgeon responded "swearing to Christ that she was more open than a funnel."[35] She claimed that she was certain that Diego and Gerónima had consummated their marriage. With the favorable depositions of two witnesses, Soldevilla and his client now had some grounds to defend the validity of Diego's marriage.

Still, overall, Diego's case was weak; ecclesiastical tribunals did not often give men accused of impotence the benefit of the doubt.[36] Diego's case would have been in much better shape had all of his witnesses supported his claims. Christobal Pérez and María Maesto's testimonies, because they were singular and effusive, could not have been very convincing in the face of the other witnesses and the doctor's reports that attested to Diego's impotence. After all, if the young couple had made love as loudly as Christobal claimed, why was there so much doubt as to Diego's potency? Had Diego been fighting to prevent a separation based on a charge of spousal abuse, one favorable testimony generally would have won him the case. In pleas of wife battery before the court, the burden of proof rested with the wife. She had to demonstrate that she was abused and feared for her life. A charge of impotence, on the other hand, began with the assumption that the man was impotent. Potency, like masculinity, was always in doubt and had to be proved when it was impugned publicly. The court began by forcing the man to prove otherwise. When Diego's own witnesses failed to fully support his assertions in the case, there was little hope he could sustain the onslaught of the proofs made by the opposing attorney. Diego's arguments were weak, and Gerónima had yet to reply.

The wife's attorney offered his own questions to prove Gerónima's assertions. Gámiz made several points to substantiate the three bases of Gerónima's case for annulment. First, he asked the witnesses to verify that Gerónima had left Diego because he could not consummate the marriage, rather than because he beat her. Second, Gámiz asked witnesses to confirm that Gerónima was, indeed, a virgin; he also asked them to confirm that if her hymen was broken it had been from Diego's violent hands rather than legitimately breached by his "male member."[37] Lastly, Gámiz hoped that his witnesses could attest to Diego's impotence. Gerónima's lawyer asked the impossible of his witnesses, and he knew it. The attorney understood that witnesses would rely on public gossip because they had no direct knowledge of Diego's penis or Gerónima's vagina. Gámiz could reasonably hope that neighborhood gossip would put Diego's potency into question. Again, Juan de Gámiz made use of the assumption of male impotence.

Gerónima's support among her neighbors must have been weak. Because even though her lawyer provided an impressive list of questions to the court, he could not submit a long list of witnesses. Gámiz questioned only two individuals. Even worse than the small number of testimonies was that fact that one witness spoke decidedly against Gerónima. Perhaps Diego was more popular in the community or better connected politically. Licentiate Phelipe de Atavie, a middle-aged cleric and royal lawyer, provided testimony in Gerónima's favor. Atavie told the court about a day when he met Gerónima just after she had left confession. Gerónima was in tears. When he asked why she was crying, she told him that her confessor had just ordered her to stop living with Diego "because the marriage is not legitimate."[38] Atavie's evidence was clearly hearsay.

Worse still was the testimony of Gerónima's confessor, licentiate Phelipe Francisco de Olibán. As Gerónima's confessor, Olibán would have had knowledge of her sins as well as the couple's marital problems. His testimony, therefore, must have been more influential in the court than much of the hearsay evidence that formed the majority of witness declarations. Olibán's opinions, as a cleric, would also have been especially important in an ecclesiastical court. Contradicting Gerónima's assertions, Olibán stated in his declaration that the couple's separation had been caused by domestic abuse and the inability to live together. He also claimed that Gerónima and Diego had confessed to him that they had consummated the marriage. He apparently had attempted to bring about peace between the couple, and blamed Gerónima's charges of impotence with causing the domestic troubles between her and Diego.[39]

In the fall of 1681 Diego's case against his wife looked better than when the doctor and surgeon declared him impotent earlier in the spring. Though the medical testimony and a number of witnesses asserted that he was impotent, a handful of testimonies had fully substantiated his claims. Juan de Soldevilla, perhaps hopeful for a determination in his client's favor, petitioned the court repeatedly in September to make its decision. Gerónima's representative gave no response to his efforts. The court, however, must not have had a clear opinion in the case. Instead of announcing its decision, now that the litigants had presented all the medical and witness testimonies, the court transferred the papers and details of the litigation to the tribunal's prosecuting attorney, the *fiscal general,* for another opinion.

The prosecuting attorney defended the interests of the court rather than those of the litigants. He was to protect the jurisdiction, laws, and sanctity of the court. Generally, cases were transferred to the prosecuting attorney when there were suspicions that litigants were manipulating the court for their own purposes or when one of the parties failed to appear before the tribunal to defend themselves. The court's prosecuting attorney usually argued against the demands of a petition, preferring to uphold the status quo rather than allow a questionable annulment. For example, in a case in which a husband's impotence seemed certain and the husband did not defend himself against the accusations, the prosecuting attorney would commonly argue against an annulment. In such a case the prosecuting attorney would demand that the tribunal force the couple to live together, at least for a trial period. In Diego and Gerónima's case, however, the prosecuting attorney seemed to have been brought into the case because its determination was problematic, filled as it was with contradictory evidence. The case was further complicated by the fact that even if Diego had consummated the marriage according to canon law, it was also clear that he had done so many years ago. He was clearly no longer able to have sex, a situation proved by numerous testimonies. The tribunal may not have wanted to send Gerónima back to a sexually moribund union, even if the marriage was valid according to canon law. It was often assumed that a sexually unsatisfied wife would turn to an extramarital affair, disrupting social peace and order. In essence, the court had to find a way to reconcile a canon law that regarded the marriage as legitimate and indissoluble with the cultural expectation that a husband and wife be able to fulfill the conjugal debt. The prosecuting attorney's decision, tellingly, made no mention as to whether Diego had ever consummated the marriage in the first place, only that he was now impotent. The prosecuting attorney asked that the court annul the marriage.

Inexplicably, the ecclesiastical court waited for some time before announcing its decision. On April 18, 1682, Juan Joseph de Texada y la Guardia, vicar and provisor general of the diocese, issued the court's conclusion. He handed down a harsh decision against Diego. First and foremost the tribunal declared Diego impotent with virgins as well as nonvirgin women, *impotente ad virgines et ad corruptas.* The fact that the tribunal began its decision with its condemnation of the husband reveals that this particular determination was unique and problematic. Generally, proclamations by the court in impotence cases first annulled the marriage, gave license to the wife to dispose of her person as she saw fit, and, almost as an endnote, ordered the husband not to contract marriage again without the court's approval. In this case not only was Diego condemned to a life of solitude and shame, but the court also held him responsible for the costs of the year-long litigation.

Texada y la Guardia went on to annul the litigants' marriage and awarded Gerónima power over her own person. She also received license to marry whomever she pleased. Alternatively, she could enter religious life, or simply live as she desired. Furthermore, the court's conclusion that her marriage had never been consummated meant that Gerónima was still considered a virgin, despite the fact that she was thirty-six years old. Her status as a virgin and the restitution of her dowry along with half of the nineteen years' worth of money and goods accrued during her marriage to Diego meant that Gerónima could plan on finding a satisfactory husband.

The court had defended its interests, even though it may have had to disregard a strict interpretation of canon law. It had avoided prolonging a marriage that, whether initially consummated or not, would have been a further source of headaches for the court, the community, and the wife. Confronted with a woman who was not being sexually fulfilled and thus controlled by her husband, the church court, following early modern reasoning that a woman's sexuality had to be guarded and contained, feared that Gerónima posed a threat for scandal in her community. If Diego was not satisfying Gerónima, the reasoning went, she might seek sex in an adulterous relationship; a married woman who engaged in a public affair, in *amancebamiento,* would cause public shame and sin, and engender further social disorder.

Perhaps the most important aspect of Gerónima and Diego's case that gave the ecclesiastical court the ability to make an arbitrary and subjective decision was the tribunal's use of medical testimony. Medical experts brought the weight of experience, authority, and education to resolve a question that was truly as unanswerable as it was fiercely debated. Both the determination of virginity and impotence were often little more than educated guesses. While educated church officials like Judge Texada y la Guardia may have abandoned "superstitious" beliefs that blamed witchcraft for impotence a century before, they were now inclined to trust in a science that was not very reliable. Judges of the tribunal had to rely on the opinions of doctors who, in their diagnoses of impotence, cited a strange variety of sources that ranged from Pliny the Elder to local surgeons. Decisions in impotence cases were uncertain and subjective because the medical science they were based on was questionable and capricious.

Nonmedical evidence could counter unfavorable medical opinions and give the judge a wider range of opinions to choose from. Occasionally, witness testimonies refuted medical evidence in impotence cases. If a lawyer could demonstrate, for instance, that a wife had had a miscarriage, he might then substantiate his client's claims of potency. Witness testimonies could also be a way for a couple's community to influence the court's decision. This community included family and friends, local professionals, neighbor women and men. Even if ecclesiastical functionaries might not be able to decide whether a couple should continue living together or not, a consensus of neighbors' opinions might decide the question in court. Aside from the couple, after all, it was the community that would have to live with the court's decision. Witness testimonies also gave litigants another way to use their political connections. In the case of Diego and Gerónima, the husband was able to find three witnesses to support him, while his wife was ultimately backed by eight community members. Witness testimonies, therefore, could often be just as ambiguous and inconclusive as the medical evidence and the competing claims of the litigants themselves. And again the court would have great latitude in making its final decision.

This case also reveals the connections and similarities between potency and virginity. The difficulties that Diego had to surmount to defend his status as a husband and man demonstrate the power that charges of impotence had over men in the seventeenth century. A man could not hope for a viable and legitimate marriage, life, and family if he was not esteemed as virile by the community. But in Gerónima and Diego's case, both litigants had to defend their sexual reputations. In a struggle similar to that of her husband, Gerónima had to undergo the same humiliating medical examination to defend her public sexual status that was just as uncertain as her husband's potency: her virginity. Women in Spain had traditionally resorted to litigation to refute gossip and insinuations that besmirched their honor, rumors that questioned their virginity.[40] Potency was to Diego what virginity was to

Gerónima; he could not lay claim to a marriage and to a "normal" life without it. Both Gerónima and her husband needed to assert these statuses in order to fit into the normative roles prescribed for them by their communities as well as by the church and the state.

The ecclesiastical court of Calahorra and La Calzada faced considerable problems when making decisions in cases like Gerónima and Diego's. Most difficult was how it should come to a decision based on the laws of the church. Nonconsummation and impotence were unlike any other impediment to matrimony. The impediment of consanguinity could easily be proved or refuted with the aid of meticulously kept parish baptismal, marriage, and death records. It could also be resolved with a dispensation. When the marital impediment was servitude—that a slave could not give himself or herself in marriage without the consent of his or her owner—the court only had to find the accused spouse's alleged master. But the impediment of nonconsummation and impotence placed the judge in the absurd position of determining what was often impossible to know. Yet the ecclesiastical court had to make decisions in annulment cases that rationalized and justified its adjudication of marriage altogether. In addition, church courts were already regularly forced in the seventeenth century to fight secular jurisdictions that attempted to grant de facto separations.[41] Plainly, it was important for the ecclesiastical court to make practical decisions that legitimated its powers and pleased weary litigants and their retinues. In the case of Gerónima and Diego the court did just that when it annulled a marriage that all involved knew was dead, regardless of whether it had ever truly existed.

2: The Reforms of Bishop Pedro de Lepe Dorantes (1686–1700)

> Because many in this our bishopric, especially in the mountains, betroth one another, and later from some displeasure that occurs between them, they litigate in our court to part with and leave one another . . . and the judges are [then] in much doubt, not knowing what, with good conscience, they should determine.
>
> —*Synodal Constitutions of the Bishopric of Calahorra,* 1555[1]

As the earliest synods took up questions of matrimony, canon law on marriage became increasingly elaborated, with glosses and enumerations of edicts on laws. Occasionally, movements of legal reform prompted church canonists to make canon law clearer and more concise. The church's decisions regarding questions on the sacrament of matrimony became absolute after the Council of Trent. But how such laws were received, understood, and used by communities and couples in towns and parishes is far murkier. Historians of marriage often suggest that the church foisted an alien concept of marriage on Christians and then molded their behavior into the form that the church chose. This chapter suggests a model of mutual adjustment and reciprocity between church law on marriage and the people who married. Individuals manipulated canon law as much as its statutes shaped their behavior. When they needed to use the courts Spaniards accommodated their own diverse marriage customs to the legal requirements and opportunities presented to them by their local vicars and priests. Using the services of the ecclesiastical court, for instance, a wife who already lived separated from her husband might also be able to force him to return her dowry and half the goods of her marriage.

Even if the church affected social behavior with Christian ideology, instilled through confessional literature for instance, church dogmas like marital indissolubility and sexual chastity had to overcome long-held, stubborn customs that clashed with these ideas. Bishop Pedro de Lepe Dorantes' attempt at reform during the late seventeenth century strongly suggests that diocesan mechanisms of social control were completely inept at policing people's sexual behavior.

The seventeenth-century synodal legislation on matrimony in the Diocese of Calahorra and La Calzada was a discrete and distinctive body of local canon law. Yet, though the diocesan laws maintained distinct local characteristics, such as special provisions for translators for trials in the Basque-speaking provinces, the laws were fundamentally based on wider European matrimonial canon law. The theological and legal conflicts that resulted in one European-wide ecclesiastical law on marriage, as valid in Cologne as it was in Calahorra, occurred in universities and cathedrals far removed from the cities of northern Spain. One of the most comprehensive trends in European history since the late Middle Ages and into the seventeenth century was the ever increasing ability of larger governments, secular and religious, to affect the lives and harness the resources of common people.[2] This tendency is clearly demonstrated by the development of marriage law in the late medieval period. When a man and woman legitimately married in seventeenth-century Spain, they did so in obedience to many higher powers. Not only was their relationship sanctioned by each other, but it was also made legitimate by their families, neighbors, local clergy, and ultimately by the larger institution of the Roman Catholic Church. The changes that brought the various methods of medieval marriage to the strictly defined and state-endorsed matrimony of the seventeenth century began with the elaboration of ecclesiastical law on marriage in the twelfth century. Between the twelfth and sixteenth centuries church leaders developed comprehensive answers to the prickly questions raised by European matrimonial dilemmas.

The Roman Catholic Church's greatest asset was a universalized ideology that it then used to claim dominion over every aspect of the temporal and spiritual world. The church utilized its authoritative Christian doctrine, extensively elaborated over the centuries by theologians from Saint Augustine to Thomas Aquinas, in persistent attempts to affect the behaviors of medieval Europeans. Marriage and human sexual comportment were clearly within the purview of ecclesiastical theologians and functionaries. Church elites in medieval Europe, for instance, influenced by biblical teachings, promoted celibacy and sexual continence among the clergy and throughout society. Yet the degree to which the church could have actually changed sexual behavior remains open to vigorous debate.

Early church convictions regarding matrimony often conflicted with local marital traditions and laws. Some of these local traditions may have originated, for example, from Germanic or Celtic rites, or were part of Roman or Jewish traditions.[3] Generally, canonists looked to the Bible, especially the New Testament, for their rationalization of marriage and sexuality. Their interpretations of scripture greatly affected the marital legislation that they made.[4] Canonists contradicted many local matrimonial laws regarding the importance of the marrying couple's mutual consent, the indissolubility of marriage, and the nature of sex during marriage.

At the heart of the church's conception of marriage was the belief that an individual could enter the sacrament of matrimony only by his or her freely given consent. Church canonists placed enormous emphasis on the principle of mutual consent for the formation of legitimate marriages. Not surprisingly, there was a clear political motivation behind the church's defense of individual consent in the making of marriage. By defending sons and daughters with claims to inheritances against their parents and relatives, the church undermined the power of aristocratic families.[5] Such families commonly used the marriages of their offspring to consolidate land and power. Over the centuries canonists rarely questioned the importance of consent between man and woman. Lack of consent would persist as an effective cause for annulments of betrothals and marriages throughout the medieval and early modern eras in ecclesiastical courts. Such trials generally pitted individuals and clerics against coercive families as well as against jilted spouses and fiancés. Rather than question the importance of consent in the formation of matrimony, later theologians would instead debate the merit of sexual intercourse over consent as the key to marriage.

Canonists saw marriage as an unbreakable bond between husband and wife. By insisting on marital indissolubility, church laws again repudiated customs more familiar to local populations. Biblical scripture both asserted the permanence of matrimony and defined marriage as a sacrament, and in so doing the Bible provided the basis for the marital canon law. Could any canonist avoid Mark 10:11–12, a scripture that bluntly stated, "Whoever divorces his wife and marries another commits adultery against her. And if a woman divorces her husband and marries another, she commits adultery"? Church authors used the disciple Paul's analogy that defended matrimony as a sacrament; they likened the relationship between man and wife to the spiritual bond that existed between Christ and the church. Yet, despite church law and the efforts of Catholic canonists, the principles and customs of a landholding nobility most often prevailed in the early Middle Ages. During the medieval period Christianity was not yet dominant enough to allow church institutions to enforce many of its social prescriptions. Marriages in early medieval Europe could often be dissolved. Couples separated and remarried for reasons ranging from adultery to illness, long absence, and separation.[6]

Unlike most medieval secular law that, if anything, regarded marital sex as a husband's prerogative, medieval clerical authors viewed sex as a generalized evil; and this opinion included sex between a husband and wife.[7] Early church fathers and later canonists were led by New Testament scripture that generally depicted sex as immoral and praised chastity. Paul, for instance, wrote in his instructions to the Thessalonians, "It is God's will that you should be sanctified: that you should avoid sexual immorality."[8] For early canonists marriage existed as a means to contain this sexual immorality. Still, matrimony was an imperfect solution because the best Christian abstained from sex entirely. An early-fifteenth-century Spanish synod in Salamanca reiterated this attitude toward sex: "in the church the virgins have the first place, the continent the second, the married the third.[9] Because Christians could be spiritually contaminated by their sexual actions, canonists placed conjugal restrictions on married couples. According to early medieval penitentials, some of these prohibitions included sexual abstinence during Lent, on holy days, on the fast days of Wednesday and Friday, on Sunday, during menstruation, during pregnancy, and during a period following childbearing.[10] The creation of such austere sexual regulations greatly expanded opportunities for Europeans to sin. Sexual legislation also provided for equally new adventures in litigation. Canonists could not accept the customary markers of European marriages—sex, cohabitation, and an exchange of money—as the basis for a holy sacrament.

They became divided over the crucial question of whether coitus was needed to validate a marriage. Judgments by early canonists such as Hincmar of Rheims (845–82) suggested that marriage could truly be validated only by coitus between husband and wife. Hincmar's opinions, however, seriously differed from later reformers, represented by canonists like Peter Damien (1007–72) and Ivo of Chartres (1040–1115), who harbored extremely chaste attitudes toward sex. They rejected coitus as an integral element of marriage and held up the biblical example of Mary and Joseph as the ideal example of continent matrimony. The *Concordia discordantium canonum*, written by Gratian around 1140, issued solutions to these conflicting views.[11]

Gratian settled many issues. Like his predecessors he considered sex a social disease; fornication was a moral crime. On the important question of whether or not a legally binding marriage required coitus, Gratian attempted to find a middle course. He ruled that consent made a valid marriage if it were at some point followed by the sexual act of consummation. This was not, of course, a true compromise. The simple fact that Gratian recognized coitus as a marriage requirement meant that he rejected the concept of a chaste marriage. Gratian actually placed great importance on sex in marriage. He ruled that a consummated marriage could not be broken to enter religious orders. He felt that coitus validated clandestine marriages. Gratian even embraced the concept that husbands and wives had a conjugal debt owed to one another; they were responsible for submitting to sex on the request of their partner. Gratian provided a framework from which a rational, pan-

European canon law could develop.[12] The fact that twelfth- and thirteenth-century Spanish canonists like Pedro Hispanus, Johannes Garsias Hispanus, and Martinus Zamorensis all wrote glosses on the *Concordia discordantium canonum* demonstrates that Gratian was known by clerics in Spain.[13] Crucial for the purposes of this study, Gratian's recognition that sex was inseparable from marriage became a permanent characteristic of Catholic doctrine. Freely and mutually given consent between a bride and groom, however, would remain the act that technically formed a marriage. This formula, consent contingent on sex, would be repeated and reaffirmed at the Council of Trent (1545–63).

Development of Spanish Canon Law Regarding Matrimony

Ecclesiastical legislation in Castile benefited from an unusually well educated king, Alfonso the Wise (reigned 1252–84). Regarding marriage, Alfonso x of Castile's thirteenth-century law code drew directly from canon legislation.[14] The *Siete Partidas* explained the specifics of the sacrament of matrimony and was to be applied throughout the Kingdom of Castile. Castilians were to wed according to clearly stated phrases provided in the *Partidas.* Following Pope Alexander's 1179 reconciliation between the opinions of Peter Lombard, who favored consent as the essence of matrimony, and Gratian on marriage, the exchange of words in the future tense, *palabras del futuro,* constituted a betrothal.[15] If the couple then had sex, they were legitimately married. Words said in the present tense, *palabras del presente,* immediately created a marriage. These two tenses created an important distinction because they made betrothal a crucial step toward matrimony.[16]

In the medieval Iberian kingdoms of Aragon and Portugal, canon law was incorporated earlier and became more firmly established than in other parts of the Iberian Peninsula. Medieval Aragonese synods were influenced by Parisian didactic works such as those of Eudes of Sully, bishop of Paris (1196–1208).[17] Despite the *Siete Partidas,* in Castile aristocratic marriage traditions prevailed among the laity, a fact that is not surprising considering that the interests of the nobility naturally took precedence in a society that depended on martial talents to defend and advance against the Muslims. The Castilian secular model of marriage tended toward endogamy among the nobility, often allowed for the feasibility of divorce and remarriage, and usually required the consent and participation of the uniting families. However, Castilian synods continued to expound on canon law in spite of the prevalence of local marriage customs.

As in other parts of Europe, Spanish synods interpreted and expounded on the canon law they received from higher church authorities. Medieval synods used the canon law developed in the twelfth and thirteenth centuries as their foundation for ruling on problems unique or troublesome to their dioceses. The first and most important step toward marriage in medieval Spain was betrothal. Spanish medieval synods suggested that the couple say their palabras del futuro before a clergyman, that they have the betrothal notarized, and that they post banns to inform the community.[18] Betrothals lasted for at least months; some early modern examples continued for years.[19] The bride and her family could use this time to amass a dowry and the groom to find a stable vocation. Sex between the betrothed created a de facto marriage before the couple properly established a household. Canon law bound the betrothed by the sexual act of consummation. Canonists intended such legislation to make it more difficult for spouses to escape commitments made by palabras del futuro.

Despite the growth of canon law in the thirteenth and fourteenth centuries, Spanish ecclesiastical matrimonial legislation still left much room for ambiguity. According to the *Libro sinodal* of Gonzalo de Alba (1410), there were five methods of betrothal in medieval Salamanca. The first manner was for the man to declare "I will take you as wife," to which the woman would respond "I will take you as my husband." This method, of course, coincided with the French model that depended on specific words in the future tense. Gonzalo de Alba's second and third ways to betroth were expressions of sincere commitment: giving "oneself to another in faith" and "confirming [the betrothal] by swearing." The fourth and fifth ways to enter into betrothal were by older secular rituals that depended on the exchange of money or symbols of betrothal. "Giving coins, such as money or other things" resembled marriage traditions throughout Europe that placed an importance on a material transaction to bind the couple and the families together. Finally, "placing a ring on the hand," a tradition that has flourished in the modern West, was in medieval Spain one of the most important symbols of engagement.[20]

However, Spaniards often did not follow many of these legally defined steps regardless of the amount of legislation Spanish synods dedicated to how betrothals ought to be made. Most of the problems decried by synods concerned the private and uncertain nature of many betrothals. As we have already seen from the epigraph for this chapter, clerics of the Diocese of Calahorra and La Calzada celebrating a 1553 synod lamented the haphazard way some couples betrothed in their bishopric: "Because many in this our bishopric, especially in the mountains, betroth one another, and later from some displeasure that occurs between them, they litigate in our court to part with and leave one another . . . and the judges are [then] in much doubt, not knowing what, with good conscience, they should determine."[21] The main purpose of synod legislation regarding betrothal was to ensure that the entire community knew who was betrothed and to whom. If the betrothal and wedding were generally known, then church authorities could expect that anyone aware of marital impediments or previous marital commitments made by either of the betrothed individuals would come forth and prevent the marriage. In order to guarantee that the public would recognize who was and was not married, a synod held in Mondoñedo in the mid-sixteenth century ordered "that, from here forward, no woman, after living a married life with her husband, will dare to go about without the headdress of a married woman."[22] This prescription alluded to the common practice, after betrothal, for Spaniards to "join together and live a married life as if they were [married]."[23] Because betrothal often led directly to living as a married couple, it was treated as the most serious step in the marriage process.

The usual method to announce a betrothal and upcoming wedding was through the publication of banns. Most synods required that a couple announce their wedding at mass on three Sundays before the wedding. The public betrothal announcement was of utmost importance if the parish was to avoid subsequent problems; therefore the presentation of banns was one of the most consistent concerns of medieval Spanish synods. Thus a thirteenth-century synod held in Santiago de Compostela stated: "for when matrimony is contracted, it is first to be announced in church at mass by a priest, for three Sundays or for three holidays before the community.[24] Yet customs naturally varied from bishopric to bishopric. Many synods allowed for the banns to be announced at "festivals before the townspeople" as well as at church.[25] According to the *Constituciones antiguas del obispado de Orense* (Galicia), banns had to be announced on only two Sundays before the wedding, instead of the typical three.[26] The church had little concern so long as couples followed the general principles that promulgated their wedding intentions so that the participation of parishioners might prevent crimes of bigamy, consanguinity, and desertion.

Spanish synods recognized as valid several types of legitimate and illegitimate marriages. Most weddings were simply final confirmations of what were already serious betrothals. The most preferred course was to conclude a marriage between a betrothed couple by benediction. The pair exchanged vows in the present tense in front of a priest either in the church or on the church steps. By directing that the ceremony be done in the day and in the presence of witnesses, the church attempted to ensure public awareness of the marriage.

The second means by which parties often married was by common public knowledge. Termed *pública fama,* or common knowledge, the general recognition by a community that a couple lived as man and wife undoubtedly formed the basis for many rural peasant marriages as well as for poorer urban couples. In her study of separation and annulment in Navarre, Campo Guinea believes that the numerous ecclesiastical trials for public fornication in the sixteenth and seventeenth centuries were actually prosecutions against couples whose marriages were not considered legitimate by the church.[27] While the church had not originally created or sanctioned these marriages, it did recognize their validity and tried the spouses accordingly in ecclesiastical courts. Men and women could also marry by reciting oaths to one another, either alone and in private, or more often before family and friends in a public venue. The celebratory atmosphere of holy day festivals and fairs provided an opportune occasion for known couples to solidify their relationships in public. As with marriage by pública fama, the church grudgingly acknowledged that these spontaneous marriages by *juras,* or oaths, were valid. The church punished couples who married illegitimately with fines and/or excommunication.

By taking measures to prevent clandestine unions, the church promoted public order, increased its authority, and augmented its wealth. Illegitimate and clandestine marriages, recognized as licit by the church in Spain, easily became sources of public discord. The church, along with secular authorities, increasingly punished couples who made marriages secretly. For example, a couple in Tuy (Galicia) who married without receiving the benediction would incur a "sentence of excommunication and six hundred maravedis for our treasury." The man and wife would remain ostracized from the parish and any children they had would be considered illegitimate, until whenever the church was satisfied to pardon them.[28] Without a public wedding a couple could not ensure that their children would be treated as legitimate before the church or secular authorities.

Spanish synods seemed even more concerned with controlling the behavior of their clergymen than that of the laity and therefore held them culpable for performing unauthorized marriage practices. The Diocese of Calahorra and La Calzada still spent much of its efforts on chastising and attempting to discipline its clergy a century after the Council of Trent and two centuries after the sweeping reforms of Spain's Cardinal Ximénez de Cisneros. Clerics could be subjected to heavy fines and punishments that threatened their livelihood, such as excommunication. A cleric in Tuy who performed a clandestine wedding ceremony could be fined three ducats, and if he did so outside his own parish he could be fined ten.[29] Illegitimate weddings often caused misunderstandings between husbands, wives, and their families concerning the nature, legality, and terms of the marriages that they had made. The vague nature of illegitimate marriages also facilitated offenses like desertion, the breaking of a betrothal, adultery, or bigamy. Marital ambiguities led to a profusion of litigation in both ecclesiastical and secular courts. Women who brought men to trial for desertion, bigamy, or for the support of children had difficulty proving the validity of marriages that may have been made in secret. Ambiguous marriages also made for puzzling cases for annulment.

Annulments could be procured by husbands and wives for a variety of reasons. They could chose from the many obstacles that existed to prevent couples from marrying in the early modern Spanish church. Iberian synods recognized all the impediments acknowledged by decretists throughout Europe. The main concerns ranged from lack of consent and consanguinity, to age, to promises of marriage made to other individuals. Physical afflictions such as insanity and impotence were also impediments to marriage. Finally, Spanish synods also declared that Christians must marry within their religion and according to their law; that is, they could not marry "a nun or woman who has taken orders or jewess or mooress or any other woman who is not of his law."[30]

The proximity of Castile and Aragon to Muslim kingdoms, and the large presence of Jews in Spain, produced some problematic cases of mixed marriages. In the Diocese of Calahorra and La Calzada, before the expulsion of Jews in 1492, the city of Calahorra had a considerable Jewish community, making up nearly a quarter of its population.[31] Ecclesiastical court records also reveal the presence of gypsies in the diocese.[32] Early Catholic decretists considered many of the questions regarding marriages between Christians and "infidels." However, they usually deliberated on cases where one of the spouses converted to Christianity while the other remained outside the faith and also considered whether a convert should then be compelled to remain married to a pagan. Gratian regarded marriage as a part of natural law and therefore viewed marriages made by heathens as binding.[33] Marriages directly between Christians and Jews or Muslims, however, were not recognized as valid by the church. The ancient customs of Orense (Galicia) denounced all Christians "that accompany Jews or Moors and attend their weddings or festivals and are their lackeys."[34] Curiously, few synods in Spain commented on the problem of mixed marriages until the mass conversions to Christianity by Jews and Muslims in the later medieval period brought new rituals and customs into Catholic weddings and Spanish churches.[35] The Synod of Guadix in 1554 is one of the few that does mention Muslim wedding traditions. There clergymen complained about the prevalence of

Muslim wedding customs among Muslims recently converted to Christianity, called *moriscos*. They specifically expressed dissatisfaction that moriscos made wedding contracts "in the moorish fashion."[36]

By encouraging couples to marry legitimately, the church augmented its importance in communities and widened its control over an important sacrament. Much synodal legislation allowed Spanish clergymen to use their essential role in legitimate weddings to ensure that couples understood many of the rituals and doctrines of the Christian faith. By the sixteenth century clergymen could oblige couples to memorize the Nicene Creed, the Pater Noster, Ave Maria, Salve Regina, the Ten Commandments, and the seven deadly sins. The church was also better able to impose its views on sexuality on married couples.

The Salamancan *Libro sinodal* of 1410 listed four reasons for sex during marriage: for reproduction, to fulfill the conjugal debt, to prevent one's wife from seeking sexual gratification elsewhere, and to "carry out evil," meaning sex for pleasure. Sex done for pleasure flatly constituted a sin. In effect, the *Libro sinodal* mentioned five criteria that could further determine whether sex was sinful or not. The time a Spanish couple had sex could make it a sinful act; sex was immoral if, for example, they copulated during Advent or on a Sunday before mass. Place was important, because sex in a church or graveyard was sinful. Consent on behalf of both partners was necessary as well. The physical condition of a wife was important to avoid sinful sex; she could not be menstruating or be pregnant. Finally, the manner in which a married couple had sex could be sinful. Having sex with a wife "as if she were a prostitute" was altogether wicked in the eyes of the church.[37]

Churches in Spain were also in accord with other parts of Europe regarding the concept of conjugal debt. A husband and wife owed one another sex if requested. The conjugal debt attempted to prevent married individuals from seeking sexual satisfaction outside their marriage. Adultery affected everyone because it disturbed public order and in a broader sense spiritually contaminated the community. In the *Libro sinodal*, Gonzalo de Alba describes conjugal debt in terms of marital property: "Item, after the consummation and they know one another carnally, the husband does not have power over his body, nor the wife over her body . . . moreover the one to the other pays his debt, being careful of the time and place, the condition and manner."[38]

Both secular and ecclesiastical courts fought over the regulation of marriage and jurisdictions over marital questions. Questions regarding property and the dowry were ordinarily left to the secular authorities. Issues involving the state or dissolution of marriage, sexual offenses such as adultery and sodomy, and petitions for annulment were most often handled by ecclesiastical courts. European canonists had disputed the legitimate grounds for annulment throughout the Middle Ages. The Bolognese school of canon law allowed for more occasions for annulment than did the Parisian canonists. The Italian decretists defended dissolution early in marriage for cases involving impotence, the entry into religion of one of the spouses, long absence, chronic illness, serious crime, rape, adultery, and bigamy. However, in Spain only impotence, entrance into holy orders, and long absence were accepted as legitimate grounds for annulment. There, a spouse could leave a consummated marriage only with great difficulty. A synod held in Astorga (Castile), for example, required proof of a spouse's death before it would annul a marriage on the grounds of long absence.[39]

To allow for an annulment on grounds of impotence, the condition ordinarily had to have existed before sexual intercourse between the husband and wife had consummated the marriage. Once consummated, marriages could not be dissolved on such grounds. European canonists often distinguished between two types of impotence: that which was permanent due to a physical disorder and that which was temporary or conditional. Conditional impotence included cases where a husband was impotent only in the presence of his wife yet virile with another woman. Such cases could also involve impotence thought to have been caused by magic spells. In cases of conditional impotence, ecclesiastical courts often suggested solutions other than annulment. Because of the differences in impotence, courts in England and France considering annulments for such reasons often required that an examination of the sexual organs be performed on the impotent spouse, usually the husband. Some medieval English courts employed women knowledgeable in matters of sex, called "wise women," to perform these examinations.[40] French courts added male surgeons to the examining panel of female experts. In cases where permanent physical impotence could be proven, ecclesiastical courts allowed the sexually able spouse to remarry while they ordered the impotent spouse to remain single.[41] While little has been written on impotence trials in the Iberian Peninsula, synod pronouncements hint that annulments for such reasons did occur in Spain. For example, a synod of 1303 held in León, summarizing its ecclesiastical jurisdiction, declared that "they can part, after three years, those that are married and are bewitched in such a way that they cannot know one another carnally."[42]

Spanish churches also annulled marriages to allow one or both of the spouses to enter holy orders. In these cases an individual could not leave a marriage if it had been sexually consummated because they could not abandon the conjugal debt owed to their spouse. If, however, both spouses consented, a marriage could be annulled for one or the other to enter the service of the church.[43] Spanish ecclesiastical courts also sanctioned annulments and remarriage in cases of the long absence of a spouse. Husbands not returning from battle after several years without word as to their fate were ordinarily presumed dead, and the wife was permitted to remarry.

In its assertion that the sacrament of marriage was indissoluble, the church naturally did not consider divorce an option for Christians. However, there is evidence in the proclamations of Spanish synods themselves that Spaniards did divorce, or at least attempted to. Some married couples simply left one another to remarry other people. This practice is bewailed by a synod held in Mondoñedo in 1447: "it has occurred and occurs many times that those who are legitimately married leave one another, in fact and not legitimately, to the great danger of their souls."[44] Some couples formalized their divorces through official documents. Bishop Diego de Deza, at a synod held in Salamanca in 1497, ordered public notaries to cease issuing "letters of freedom" to married couples.[45] Throughout the Spanish synods, clergymen had to assert the church's authority and reiterate that married couples could not separate "without license of a judge."[46]

The medieval history of Spanish marital canon law, and Spanish marriage customs in general, was consistent with that of the rest of Europe. The church was involved in an increasingly successful campaign to replace secular and aristocratic marriage custom, law, and celebration, which stressed familial consent and allowed divorce, with its own conception of matrimony, ecclesiastical legislation, and wedding ritual, which emphasized individual consent and indissolubility. Spanish synods persistently implemented the wider European Catholic resolutions pertaining to marriage and sex: the posting of banns, Christian sexual mores, the indissolubility of marriage, mutual consent, and so on. However, as in many other parts of Europe, the church in Spain had difficulty enforcing its doctrine in the face of stubborn local customs. As can be seen in studies of early modern Galicia, León, the Basque Provinces, and Navarra, people from rural villages continued marrying informally and clandestinely even a century after the Catholic Reformation.[47] The marital practices and problems that existed in Spain were similar to those in other parts of medieval Europe. Paralleling Spanish custom, for example, communities in England and Burgundy often condoned couples' sexual exploration after betrothal.[48] And as in the rest of Europe, secret betrothals and illegitimate marriages in Spain caused the greater part of litigation. The ambiguities caused by broken betrothals, sexual affairs, and cohabitation encouraged further European synod legislation that addressed specific problems. Spanish synods replied to marital equivocation by insisting that banns of marriages be posted and by stiffening punishments for couples who married illegitimately.

During the High Middle Ages the church in Spain, as in the whole of Europe, established and broadened its control over the marriages and sexual mores of the laity. By making itself the arbiter of legitimate matrimony and therefore of legitimate offspring, and using the threat of fines and excommunication to enforce its laws, the church enlarged its authority during the four centuries leading up to the Protestant Reformation. Communities, in turn, grew more dependent on the church to validate their unions. The church also increased its revenues by bringing more couples into the parish and making them aware of their financial obligations as Christians. The importance and power that religion would have during the early modern period was the result of the church's success in increasing its domination over private life in the previous era. The Protestant Reformation and the religious wars of the sixteenth and seventeenth centuries were, perhaps, reactions to a church that had become too catholic, too universal.

Pedro de Lepe Dorantes and the Application of Canon Law in a Spanish Diocese

The Council of Trent is often presented not only as the legislative event that resulted in the crystallization of canon law but also as the beginning of vigorous ecclesiastical reforms that affected dioceses and Catholics throughout Europe.[49] The sweeping and vigorous edicts of the Council of Trent, however, were less impressive when seen from the level of the local Spanish church parish, even by the end of the seventeenth century. In their studies of dioceses in Galicia and Catalonia, respectively, Allyson Poska and Henry Kamen are only two historians of many who have questioned the ultimate effects on the general population of Tridentine pronouncements.[50] José Manuel Cifuentes Pazos emphasizes that Tridentine reforms were deeply felt in Vizcaya only after 1700.[51] My study of ecclesiastical litigation in parishes in La Rioja, Navarra, Álava, and Vizcaya supports their conclusions. Judging from the documents left to us from the seventeenth-century activities of the Diocese of Calahorra and La Calzada, by any measure it appears that Tridentine reforms were very late in coming, especially to the laity. Even by the end of the seventeenth century, the ecclesiastical tribunal was more preoccupied with convincing its clergy to adopt behavior in accordance with that prescribed by Trent than it was with indoctrinating the laity. However, this study is not primarily concerned with measuring the effects of Tridentine legislation in northern Spain. Instead, the aim of this investigation is to describe and interpret divorce litigation in the ecclesiastical tribunal of Calahorra and La Calzada. To that end it is necessary to adopt a perspective that acknowledges that the court served as a legal arbiter in sexual and marital disputes between spouses, individuals, and communities. I therefore hope to partially dispel the notion of Counter-Reformation church courts as oppressive, centralized institutions that enforced a strict sexual and matrimonial code. During the seventeenth century the ecclesiastical tribunal was used by Spaniards more often as an institution that they could turn to in order to resolve matrimonial conflicts. If there was a concerted attempt to enforce ecclesiastical laws in the diocese of Calahorra and La Calzada, it came only at the end of the seventeenth century motivated by the energy of an individual bishop.

The stunted reforms of impassioned bishop Pedro de Lepe Dorantes serve as a good example of the difficulties that prevented the church from using canon law as a domineering tool to control the laity. The end of the seventeenth century was the beginning of an era of reforms in Spain. Several historians have argued that the reform of Spanish institutions, attempts to revitalize government from the lethargy and parochialism experienced during the reigns of the later Hapsburgs, began at the end of the seventeenth century. Bishop Lepe's reforms are one more example that institutional reforms antedated the much touted "Bourbon reforms" of Spain's new eighteenth-century dynasty. Modern Caliguritanos, as the residents of Calahorra call themselves, compliment one another's intelligence by saying that one is "sharper than Lepe," in homage to the work of Bishop Pedro de Lepe Dorantes (1641–1700).[52] The saying that honors the intellect of the scholar-bishop became so widespread in Spain that Castilian dictionaries of the nineteenth century included it.[53]

Clearly one accomplishment that brought Bishop Lepe fame as a scholar-bishop was the synod he organized in 1698. That year the Diocese of Calahorra and La Calzada celebrated in Logroño its first synod since 1620. Such synods were not easily convened in a diocese as extensive as that of Calahorra and La Calzada, which was also one of the most ethnically diverse dioceses in seventeenth-century peninsular Spain. To attend the synod, priests, vicars, and other clerics made the trek from disparate corners of the diocese. They came from northern, mountainous Basque towns and from the northern coast, one hundred miles north of Logroño. They also traveled from towns as far south as Yanguas, a village nestled in the also mountainous Cidacos River valley, another sixty miles to the southwest of Logroño. The Diocese of Calahorra and La Calzada was a quintessential example of how distance, rough geography, and differences in language were obstacles to the imposition of political centralization in early modern Spain. As a partial remedy to its expansive jurisdiction, the diocese happily maintained administrative posts in the two cathedral towns as well as one in Logroño. The synod of 1698 and its subsequent pronouncements and publications were clear evidence of a renewed effort by the bishop to reform his diocese and increase the presence of the church in the region.

Bishop Lepe obviously hoped that the diocese's new constitution would lead to sweeping reform. Each parish was supposed to buy and maintain a copy of the new constitution in their parish church. In the constitution, Bishop Lepe admonished all clerics to read and familiarize themselves with its decrees, which included declarations of the Council of Trent in Castilian. For instance, he ordered them to read Tridentine doctrine on matrimony aloud to the laity in Castilian on Christmas, the Sunday of Quasimodo, the day of the Virgin Mary in August, and All Saints' Day.[54] In fact, the constitution was filled with such remonstrances and with long lists of concomitant fines to be imposed when they were ignored.

The learned bishop's master work, a new constitution for his diocese, was published in 1700 in Logroño. The *Constitutiones,* not surprisingly, contained several reiterations of Tridentine doctrine. Most of its chapters also cited and restated pronouncements from earlier diocesan synods and texts, the earliest being those from Diego de Zuñiga's synod in Logroño of 1410, followed by synods in 1480, 1502, 1533, 1539, 1600, and 1620.[55] The diocese built on its own long history of local legal and doctrinal production that dated from the reestablishment of the bishopric after the reconquest of Calahorra from the Muslims in 1045.[56] To these centuries-old doctrinal foundations Bishop Lepe added many extensive new decrees that tackled problems discussed at the synod of 1698. This massive legislative effort, when published, resulted in a tome of nearly eight hundred pages.

The number of *amancebamiento* trials heard by the ecclesiastical tribunal during Bishop Lepe's reign as bishop is compelling evidence that he attempted to leave his mark on his diocese, especially its clergy. Amancebamiento was the crime committed by two generally unmarried individuals who carried on a long-term public sexual relationship, in effect cohabiting. The zeal, or lack thereof, with which the court accepted and prosecuted amancebamiento cases was a measure of the tribunal's desire to impress the church's conception of sexual behavior on society. Though such crimes could involve a variety of wrongdoers, from womanizing priests and adulterous husbands to betrothed couples fornicating before marriage, amancebamiento was a charge solely concerned with sexual behavior and the public scandal that it caused. Such cases could be initiated by a variety of ecclesiastical people. The local priest could begin a trial against a person in his parish. The tribunal's prosecuting attorney was commonly responsible for prosecuting any instance of amancebamiento that he discovered or of which he was informed. A visiting ecclesiastical magistrate could also initiate a prosecution of a sexual offender. Finally, the bishop himself, often in his role as *visitador general,* could begin inquiries into such sex scandals.

The ecclesiastical tribunal maintained a steady docket of amancebamiento trials when it was under the leadership of Bishop Lepe, bishop from 1686 to 1700. This regular prosecution of sexual misconduct was in sharp contrast to the decades before and after his tenure, 1630 to 1685 and 1701 to 1720, respectively. The twenty years following Bishop Lepe's reign saw a drastic decline in the prosecution of amancebamiento trials, as can be seen in graph 1 (appendix B). When amancebamiento crimes were tried prior to Bishop Lepe, such prosecutions occurred in spates. For instance, in 1641 there were ten indictments for amancebamiento. Yet there was not another such prosecution for an entire decade thereafter. Over the twenty years preceding Bishop Lepe's reign the diocese had not heard one case for sexual misconduct. Yet beginning in 1686, the year Pedro de Lepe became bishop, the ecclesiastical tribunal tried, on average, slightly more than one amancebamiento case every year, for a total of eighteen cases during Lepe's reign. In fact, all types of litigation before the court reached their seventeenth-century peaks under Bishop Lepe, and began to dwindle soon after his death. The tribunal would not see as much business until well into the eighteenth century. Another example of Bishop Lepe's personal hand in increasing the stature of the ecclesiastical tribunal was his prosecution of a large number of parishes for corruption in the collection of the tithe.[57]

The simple personal presence of an authority figure is often an important aspect of the law's imposition, especially in the early modern period. Consider, for instance, the importance of the ubiquitous presence of Isabella and Ferdinand in their effort to mete out justice and establish control over Spain after a devastating war of succession. Much unlike his predecessors, Bishop Lepe took the charge of pastoral visitation seriously. An important factor in Bishop Lepe's program of diocesan reform was his effort to visit the multitude of tiny towns scattered across his far-reaching diocese. Though he may have concentrated his activity on visiting the distant Basque-speaking towns scattered across the northern half of the diocese, Bishop Lepe also traveled to the populations in the mountainous southern half. Many bishops prior to him had perturbed the dual cathedrals of the diocese by instead residing and directing ecclesiastical business from Logroño. This perpetual absence from the episcopal seats had been the cause for unending litigation by the cathedral towns against their bishops. Though the ecclesiastical tribunal remained in Logroño, Bishop Lepe wisely placated Santo Domingo de La Calzada and Calahorra with his frequent presence and adulation.

The result of a bishop who personally carried out the administration of his diocese was a direct increase of the church's power and presence. However, the clergy rather than the laity was the group most affected by the new bishop and his reforms. Bishop Lepe himself prosecuted several sexually incontinent priests during his visit to Elorrio, for example. One such cleric was Antonio de Garaiçabal who, over several years and three trials, had left five young unmarried women pregnant.[58] Had it not been for Bishop Lepe's visit to the town of Elorrio, another priest, Diego de Gamarra, would never have had to explain to the ecclesiastical tribunal why his two illegitimate children lived in his house and off the fruits of his benefice (indeed, in time his son probably could have expected to inherit his father's benefice). Once he discovered Diego de Gamarra's embarrassing example, Bishop Lepe ordered that the section of diocesan legislation prohibiting priests from having their illegitimate children in their residence be read aloud to the priest's parish. The laity heard the pronouncement against their priest on April 8, 1691. Arguing against the bishop in an appeal to the tribunal, Diego de Gamarra maintained that his situation was not uncommon, nor did it surprise or offend anyone in his parish. After all, he pleaded, several other priests in towns of the Basque-speaking region also raised their own children. Furthermore, to remove his fifteen-year-old daughter from his care would threaten her "honesty." According to the priest, every person in his flock was aware of his children's presence and that they lived with their father. The tribunal's prosecuting attorney, however, used this very fact, that clerics with children abounded in Vizcaya, to argue that an example needed to be made of Diego de Gamarra. And so they did.[59]

The ecclesiastical tribunal often oversaw the sexual disciplining of the clergy, but rarely punished the laity. Diego de Gamarra's case was not only indicative of Bishop Lepe's efforts to reform his diocese, it also demonstrated how far the church in northern Spain still had to go in order to compel Catholics to behave according to the church's sexual and spiritual norms 130 years after the Council of Trent. Far from regulating the laity, Bishop Lepe needed to focus the majority of his reforming efforts on controlling the conduct of the clergy. Only four years after the bishop's tenure, in 1705, the ecclesiastical tribunal had no fewer than eight clerics in the diocese's prison, and may have had many more. All eight testified in the case of one of their cell mates: Alonso de Mena Yborya. The accused was a young man who before and after ordination had had sex with a fellow cleric's sister.[60] The ecclesiastical administration was far too occupied with the supervision of its own clerics to be able to punish the sex crimes of the laity. Furthermore, the jurisdiction of secular courts overlapped that of the church court regarding sexual misbehavior. Though the diocese had jurisdiction over lay as well as clerical amancebamiento, it only occasionally used its tribunal to punish the sex crimes of the laity. Rather than being pursued by the court, more often Spaniards invited the intervention of the ecclesiastical court into their personal lives, approaching the court themselves and entering charges against one another.

Instead of the church using canon law to regulate the people, Spaniards made use of canon law to their own ends. Husbands and wives, for example, brought the vast majority of matrimonial cases to the court themselves. The aggregate volume of the court's business shows that the majority of its time was devoted to administering its vast properties, calculating its profits, and conferring benefices. Only a small fraction of its business was criminal trials.[61] Yet there was still the *fiscal general,* the court attorney charged with defending the laws of the church; surely his prosecutions in defense of church law, forcing individuals to comply with its sexual and marital ideals, was an example of church regulation of society. The prosecuting attorney could initiate prosecutions ex officio against couples who lived separated without permission, who lived together without being married, or who lived in a state of public scandal. Yet few if any of these crimes came to the distant prosecuting attorney's attention through his own aggressive investigations. Fellow citizens zealous to correct the sexually immoral misbehaviors of their neighbors undoubtedly denounced such criminals to the ecclesiastical tribunal. Such individuals then submitted their testimonies against their neighbors to the court with the satisfaction that they were correcting the sinful behavior of members of their community. In the accusations of the prosecuting attorney, then, we should not see the actions of an oppressive institution being used "against the people" but instead the tribunal being used by communities to enforce sexual conformity on the individuals of a village or town.

One example of such communal denunciation and sexual correction is the case of Beti de Venitt (Betty Gros). Beti's plight shows how ecclesiastical laws, even criminal prosecutions, were sometimes used by townspeople to limit members of a parish to a prescribed normative behavior. What may have seemed to the community to be arrogant individualistic behavior came under attack by neighbors in the name of the church. Beti was an English woman who had moved to a small coastal community near the port of Bilbao with her Irish lover in 1695. Though she professed to be Catholic and joined the local church parish claiming to be married to an Irishman, Pedro de la Cruz (Peter O'Crosbi), she was hopelessly an outsider. So when the pregnant Beti and Pedro could not produce proof of their marriage, and he fled Bilbao, and Beti began living publicly with a fellow Englishman, she became a target for the entire community. The trial against her was filled with denunciations by Spanish neighbors. They complained that Beti scandalized the community by her sexual behavior, that she had stopped attending church and had flouted the Lenten prohibitions on eating meat; after all, they argued, she had professed to be Catholic. After a lengthy trial, the publicizing of her name and crimes, and the seizing of all her belongings, the local vicar finally decided that she should not be too harshly punished. After being warned not to relapse, she was freed. The judge wanted to prevent her from fleeing Spain with her infant daughter. What could have been worse than losing an infant soul, baptized Catholic, to that island of "heretics," England?[62]

The laws of the church, then, were not necessarily imposed on and resisted by Spaniards. Instead, communities and people at all levels of early modern society could accept, use, and manipulate canon laws. When historians interpret canon law designed by the church to correct sexual behavior, they must consider that these regulations were far from actually affecting the comportment of individuals. As in the case of Beti above, community members, using law as their tool to chastise and reform, were a more powerful force in shaping an individual's behavior than the church itself. Though canon law on marriage had been developed over centuries and was, in fact, quite refined and sophisticated in the manner in which it was applied, the church simply did not have the power to enforce these codes of Christian marital and sexual behavior.

The church was perhaps most successful, on the other hand, in its education of Catholics regarding the canon laws that regulated marriage. Knowledge of canon law was an important prerequisite for its manipulation. Once aware of the outlines of canon law, individuals and communities could then use and abuse such matrimonial laws as they chose. Because a woman knew, for instance, that she could escape her marriage if she avoided its consummation, for example, she could use canon law to seek an annulment. Bishop Lepe aided this general public education on church law by printing thousands of new copies of the diocese's constitution and asking that sections of it be read regularly to the laity. Bishop Lepe also furthered the goal of an educated and quality clergy by founding the diocese's first two seminaries.

Of course, today we have little way of gauging the ultimate impact of the Bishop Lepe's attempts to reinvigorate the church in the Diocese of Calahorra and La Calzada. We have no way of knowing, for instance, whether parish priests read Lepe's work regularly to ensure that they were in compliance with the rules governing the diocese, or whether they bypassed consulting it altogether and instead enjoyed a game of pelota with the local children in the village plaza. What the existence of the synod and its constitution give us, however, is a demonstration of the resources and effort that Lepe and the diocese put into late-seventeenth-century reform.

But whether the diocese could coax its clergy into service and revitalize its institutions, the effects of reform on the laity must have remained distant. Inevitably, a warped image of Spanish society emerges from these glimpses of cases tried by the ecclesiastical tribunal; sex scandals appear to be everywhere, as do incontinent priests and troubled marriages. These cases were extraordinary, and only for that reason were they tried in a court at all. Trying to understand everyday life from litigation documents also makes it seem that the ecclesiastical court was omnipresent, when it clearly was not. Still, the ecclesiastical tribunal was important for many Spanish families, men and women; it served them as a means to expose and eliminate public sexual scandals and to enforce or dissolve marriage betrothals and contracts. In essence, the court's most valuable services in the realm of sex and marriage, as far as the laity was concerned, were to protect and promote the creation of their legitimate progeny.

The Administration of the Diocesan Court and Pleas for Annulment

Church courts remain a murky institution in Spanish history. There are few studies that describe their role in society and how church courts functioned. Richard Kagan repeatedly laments in his survey of litigation in early modern Castile that "little is known about these tribunals."[63] He was writing two decades ago, but our overall knowledge of Spanish church courts has not improved appreciably. Though there have been a number of works that explore how the Council of Trent's legislation was received at the diocesan level in Spain, few have dealt directly with ecclesiastical courts.[64] Several factors have caused this gap in our knowledge. We have already noted how the flood of work on and interest in the Inquisition, for one, has eclipsed attention to the ordinary ecclesiastical courts.

The purpose of this section, then, is to outline the institutional characteristics and functions of an ecclesiastical court in Spain. Two salient attributes emerge from this cursory overview of the court. First, because of professional nepotism, salaried positions, and the immutable characteristics of canon law, the ecclesiastical court experienced little fundamental change in its approach to matrimonial disputes over the century of this study. Second, the change that we do find, the increases and decreases in the court's activity between 1650 and 1750, was primarily attributable to the efforts of individual bishops.

By the end of the seventeenth century the reforms of the Council of Trent had come and gone. The council's sweeping reforms had already been institutionalized in the diocese but were far from realized at the parish level. Its decrees were already published and a part of synod legislation, but in remote local churches one might still find a number of practices running contrary to the spirit of Tridentine legislation. What remained of the diocesan court during the depression of Spain's mid-seventeenth century must have been a fiefdom of an institution. The court's activity had clearly dwindled while its offices had probably become venal, if not hereditary.[65] For the court to exert any centralizing force over such an expansive diocese, it needed life breathed into it through the energies of a committed reform-minded bishop.

The Bishops

As witnessed in the case of Bishop Pedro de Lepe Dorantes, bishops were crucial figures that determined how effective and powerful the ecclesiastical court would be. For the greater part of the seventeenth century, the bishops of Calahorra and La Calzada neglected enforcing the Tridentine reforms of their immediate predecessors. Instead the bishops became better known for patronizing devotional art in the episcopal palace and church chapels scattered throughout the diocese. Henry Kamen has noted a similar increase in expenditure on church buildings in seventeenth-century Catalonia.[66] Many of the exquisite baroque chapels, ornately covered in gold leaf, found in the cathedrals of La Rioja date from the seventeenth century when wealthy nobles and prelates spent impressive amounts of money in their foundation. Not until the end of the century did a new wave of reform come to the diocese with Pedro de Lepe (1686–1700) and, to a lesser degree, with his predecessor Gabriel de Esparza (1670–86).[67]

Bishops were appointed by the Spanish king, a right conceded to the monarchs of Spain in 1523 by Pope Adrian VI.[68] As such, the seat of Calahorra and La Calzada was a political appointment by the Crown, though in the seventeenth century no bishops from the diocese served directly on any of the royal councils. For the men who became bishops, the Calagurritan seat was seen as a significant stepping stone.[69] The personal residence of the bishop in the diocese, however, was required for only a quarter of the year. Even when many of the early bishops did reside in the diocese, they stayed in the episcopal palace in Logroño, usually insulting by their absence the municipalities and cathedral chapters of Calahorra and Santo Domingo de La Calzada, the official seats of the bishopric. Bishops were required to visit the length and breadth of their diocese, but only the most devoted took this requirement seriously. As we have seen in the case of Bishop Lepe, however, bishops who visited many towns, thereby making their presence felt throughout the diocese, more often perturbed than pleased local vicars and clerics. To begin with, local towns had to house and feed the bishop and his entourage upon such visits.[70]

The ecclesiastical tribunal was adjacent to the bishop's palace in Logroño. Logroño, during the period of this study, was the de facto seat of the diocese because it served as the main residence of the bishop and his court. Logroño's importance, however, would make it the official seat only in the nineteenth century.

The Vicar General (Vicario y Provisor General)

Without a doubt the vicar general of the diocese was the most important individual in the ecclesiastical tribunal; the bishop himself rarely participated directly in cases. The vicar general was the lone judge of the court and acted individually in promulgating its decisions. Most of the vicars general in the court of Calahorra and La Calzada seem to have been lifetime servants of the court but were, of course, ultimately chosen by the bishop when they advanced to the vicarage. Documents show that certain clerics, for instance, served several temporary stints judging single cases in the absence or illness of the vicar general. Only years later were they elevated to the seat of vicar general themselves. The vicar general was often chosen from one of the cathedral chapters by the bishop.[71] Eighteen different judges served in the cases under scrutiny in the current study. By far the most important judge in this investigation was Bernardo de La Mata, vicar general from 1684 to 1701. Vicar General La Mata served during the court's most fervent period of activity, encompassing the reign of reformer Bishop Lepe (1686–1700). As an example of La Mata's personal role in the study, he adjudicated 43 percent of the annulment trials during the period under consideration, 1650 to 1750.

The church court of Calahorra and La Calzada shared in wider general trends within the Spanish ecclesiastical judiciary. A basis of this shared legal culture was the exchange of personnel between dioceses. High officials from other ecclesiastical institutions and dioceses often temporarily filled the seat of vicar general in Logroño. We find canonists from the neighboring diocese of Palencia and Burgos serving as Calahorra and La Calzada's vicar general for single years. Antonio Manuel de Lodeña, for instance, from the distant University of Alcalá, was also a vicar general. Further cooperation within the

Spanish church occurred at the institutional level; as can be seen in table 1 (appendix A), two vicars general of the ecclesiastical court were also consultants to the Inquisition.

Unfortunately, the opinions and legal reasoning that were crucial to forming the final case decisions of any of these judges never formed part of case documentation. The judgments they wrote were brief, leaving scant evidence of their motivations for ruling one way or another. This leaves us with many unanswered questions: Did judges make their decisions because they were influenced by factional ties, family affiliations, or local politics, for instance? Did litigants improve their chances with bribes?[72] In another study of divorce in Europe, Jeffrey Watt argues that judicial decisions were influenced by new notions that made sentiment the foundation of marriage.[73] Were ecclesiastical judges in Spain affected by ideas similar to those Watt found in early modern Neuchâtel?

We might hope to see the trees for the forest by comparing the overall rulings of one vicar with those of another. If some individual judges were more corrupt, surely the results would be reflected in the percentage of annulments they permitted. Similarly, by comparing the percentages of annulments that the ecclesiastical judges allowed over time we should be able to see any appreciable change in judicial attitudes toward annulment; either it became more abhorred and discouraged or the judges became more lenient. Surprisingly, at least in regard to matrimonial disputes, judgments were quite consistent from one vicar to the next. For instance, instead of showing that one judge was a stubborn opponent of marital dissolution while another was quite liberal, the percentages of spouses allowed to annul their marriages show that no judicial regime was appreciably harsher or more lenient than another.[74]

The decisions of the church court demonstrate the negligible effect that new modes of thought regarding marriage and divorce had on traditional Spanish legal institutions. Such judicial consistency over time may have resulted from the institutional stability of the court itself. Individuals serving together over several decades, mentoring and consulting with one another, would bring about a great deal of consensus within the court, even over a century. As will be seen in the discussion below about the court's attorneys, most of the positions in the ecclesiastical tribunal were filled by long-term appointees. In the case of the vicarage general, officials were more likely to be from a prominent nobility than from a competitive corps of judicial officials. Unlike the Enlightenment texts that Watt claims influenced his secular court officials administering marital disputes in Neuchâtel, the Counter-Reformation education in canon law that typical canonists received in Spain changed very little from 1650 to 1750.[75] Furthermore, as Antonio Domínguez

Ortiz has argued, rather than being influenced by new Enlightenment ideals, Spain before the mid-eighteenth century actually experienced a retrenchment in and resurgence of scholasticism. As such, we should not be surprised by the consistency with which the church court adjudicated its cases over time. And as an institution that employed personnel relatively entrenched in their positions and mindset, the ecclesiastical court was an apt example of what Domínguez Ortiz described as the devolution of the powers of the Spanish state and a increasing insularity of its institutions in the seventeenth century.

The Prosecuting Attorney

The court's prosecuting attorney served to defend the interests of the church. According to the 1698 synod, the court's prosecuting attorney had to have a degree in canon law. The prosecuting attorneys in this study were usually licentiates. Unlike some of the vicars general, they never carried the mainly honorific title of doctorate. The prosecuting attorney was empowered to prosecute and investigate individuals who transgressed canon and/or diocesan law within the diocese. In theory the topical jurisdiction of the court's prosecuting attorney was nearly limitless. The church court's jurisdiction included any issue involving one of the sacraments, sins, a transgression of diocesan law, church property, or the clergy. The *Constituciones,* for instance, urged the prosecuting attorney to supervise local markets "on Holy days in order to see if [people are] working in any of them on those days, and [the fiscal] is to proceed against the lawbreakers among them."[76] In reality, however, the powers of the church court's prosecuting attorney were severely limited economically, logistically, and by competing jurisdictions. To begin with, there was only one prosecuting attorney for the entire diocese. The court itself did not possess the money and presence to prosecute all the possible infractions of its code.

Other crimes clearly fell into the bailiwicks of either the Inquisition or royal courts. Bigamy, for instance, was a criminal offense that defiled the seventh sacrament. The *Constituciones* specifically compelled the attorney general to investigate cases of bigamy. Yet there were no bigamy cases tried in the ecclesiastical court during the century of this study, or before or after. The Inquisition had successfully taken bigamy for itself.[77] Data from the sixteenth century shows that the tribunal of the Inquisition in Logroño prosecuted many bigamists. In the year 1576 alone, Logroño's tribunal of the Holy Office reconciled twenty-five bigamists to the church.[78] The Inquisition won the right to try bigamists from ecclesiastical courts by defining bigamy as a form of heresy. Though there were clearly jurisdictional disputes between the Inquisition and the church court, there might well have also been a great deal of cooperation in which an official such as the prosecuting attorney or visiting magistrate directed criminals for prosecution in the proper court. Physically, diocesan and inquisition officials were quite close to one another. Between 1521 and 1562 the Spanish Inquisition was located in Calahorra and had jurisdiction over the Diocese of Calahorra and La Calzada as well as the Kingdom of Navarra. After 1562 it moved to Logroño, where it would stay for the period of this study.[79]

As was true with the Inquisition, denunciation was a common manner by which the court's prosecuting attorney learned of a crime against the church. According to the laws of the diocese, a denouncer was liable for trial costs if the prosecution that he or she initiated came to naught. Furthermore, a denouncer could not testify in the trial. There is no evidence from these trials or the synodal legislation that denouncers were paid when their information resulted in a successful prosecution. Such regulations for denunciation mainly pertained to criminal cases. There is no evidence that any person who informed the prosecuting attorney about an individual being impotent, for instance, ever participated in the actual marital litigation against that man. One suspects that the recourses that the *Constituciones* provided for holding denouncers liable was a punitive measure to prevent false accusations; it did not necessarily pit denouncers against denouncees in a court battle.

In a separation or annulment trial the prosecuting attorney often defended the interests of an absent or uncooperative party. In the separation of Antonia Feliz from her husband, Antonio de Herze, residents of Calahorra in 1701, the husband refused to litigate in his own defense. The court was reluctant to allow a case to proceed uncontested. Therefore, in order to defend the husband's position, prosecuting attorney Diego de Moreda argued a blanket refutation of Antonia's petition for a separation.[80] Because matrimonial trials were a form of civil case, the prosecuting attorney's role was sporadic. In these types of trials he usually did not litigate ex officio in defense of the church's laws. Instead, he defended the interests of one of the litigants. The judge ideally acted as the objective agent, fairly applying the laws of the church in the dispute at hand. In this capacity the prosecuting attorney of an ecclesiastical court was unlike his counterpart in the Inquisition. In an Inquisition trial the prosecuting attorney and the judge colluded, planning a secretive investigation and prosecution. In the church court the prosecuting attorney was truly on equal footing with the opposing parties.[81] This was especially true in matrimonial disputes, which were neither secret nor criminal cases. The demands and accusations of the prosecuting attorney were regularly ignored and contradicted by the vicar general's final decisions.

The participation of the prosecuting attorney in trials for annulment was rare and limited. However, several circumstances could result in the participation of the tribunal's prosecuting officer in a marital dispute. First, he could act ex officio and initiate litigation either to begin annulment proceedings against an illegally married couple or to end the de facto separation of a husband and wife living apart from one another. Second, the vicar general could call on the prosecuting attorney to participate in a case if one of the litigants refused to cooperate. Third, the judge could also bring him in to examine a case if he suspected deception, such as a case in which a husband and a wife conspired together to receive an annulment.

As will be described in more detail below, the prosecuting attorney could act against marital circumstances that caused public scandal. Of these, amancebamiento may be the most studied by historians, but any circumstance between a husband and wife that produced concern in the community could draw the attention of the church court's prosecuting attorney. According to Bishop Lepe's *Constituciones,* the prosecuting attorney was to prosecute "those separated from Matrimony."[82] Husbands and wives were expected to live together; those spouses who did not occasionally became notorious in a town, and their situation could draw the attention of local ecclesiastical authorities. The prosecuting attorney brought several cases before the court against estranged spouses. Generally, this initial ex officio censure by the prosecuting attorney acted as a catalyst. His order to the couple to return to "married life" would initiate a civil dispute in the church court between the wife and husband. The result would be a church-approved separation replacing the earlier de facto divorce. The court's prosecuting attorney could also move against marriages that community members suspected to be unconsummated. In a few cases the church court forcibly segregated allegedly impotent men from their wives. The couple would then have to defend their marriage against the prosecuting attorney and, ultimately, the community's charges of nonconsummation.

Separation trials only rarely involved the prosecuting attorney. In annulment trials based on impotence, however, his participation was far more common. The court's prosecuting attorney entered cases of annulment in two ordinary circumstances. Either the court was suspicious of the evidence or the litigants' motivations, or one of the litigants, usually the husband, refused to defend himself in the lawsuit.

The prospect of an annulment, which would provide a clean and official end to a marriage, occasionally tempted litigants to deceive the church. If the court suspected deception, at the end of the litigation the judge usually called on its prosecuting attorney to investigate. Often the vicar general may have felt that litigation was proceeding too easily in an annulment trial based on impotence. Perhaps a husband freely admitted his impotence to the court, a strange and rare act. When the ordinarily hostile husband failed to defend his interests, this prejudiced the outcome of the annulment. A quick and accusatory reevaluation by the prosecuting attorney was a last attempt by the court to prevent false annulments. In even the most indisputable impotence cases, the prosecuting attorney frequently urged discretion, a period of trial cohabitation, or rejection of the annulment. In the end, however, the vicar general usually granted annulments despite the final efforts of the prosecuting attorney.

Often in trials in which a wife accused her husband of impotence, the man would refuse to defend himself in court. Without evidence to the contrary, the vicar general was compelled to take the husband's silence as proof of his impotence. But the tribunal was not comfortable holding hearings without a full cast of litigants. When a party refused to participate, the prosecuting attorney often entered litigation to defend the absentee's interests. In this role the prosecuting attorney ordinarily contradicted all claims that the accusatory party made out of hand. Still, lacking the aid of the man whose marriage he aimed to preserve, the prosecuting attorney generally lost these types of cases. Therefore, whenever the court brought the prosecuting attorney into an annulment trial, he was usually in a strategically weak position.

The Attorneys (*Los Procuradores*)

Several ecclesiastical lawyers were attached to the bishop's court, and throughout these cases many of their names will become familiar. Other lawyers appear intermittently, perhaps participating in only one marital dispute before the ecclesiastical court. Therefore, even though a small number of attorneys handled the majority of business in the diocese's docket, any lawyer licensed to practice canon law could represent a client before the court. Still, when moving a case from court to court in early modern Spain, litigants would have hired a local lawyer familiar with a particular court rather than present an attorney foreign to the tribunal in question. Though rarely clerics themselves, attorneys were well versed in canon law and were closely associated with the business of the church and the bishop's palace.

There is evidence that practicing law in the ecclesiastical court was a family business. Kagan has found that, in secular courts at least, legal positions were often passed from father to son.[83] This seems to have been the case in church courts as well. Over the century of this study we find three instances in which attorney positions were most likely bequeathed from father to son (see graph 2, appendix B). Francisco López Aguado tried his last case in 1688, ending twenty-three years before the court; in 1696 a Lorenzo López Aguado began his thirteen-year career in the court. Thomás Pérez de Baños practiced before the court from 1691 to 1702, Gabriel Pérez de Baños from 1706 to 1729. Finally, Juan Bauptista de Zuazu's long practice lasted from 1655 to 1683. From 1687 to 1699 Manuel Bauptista de Zuazu argued cases before the court. All six men were long-term lawyers in the bishop's court, and none of their careers, from elder to younger, overlapped. Though one cannot be certain that these positions were father-son patrimonies without spending days sifting through parish baptismal records, the appearance of the same surnames from one decade to the next clearly suggests the presence of nepotism in court positions. Because these court offices were part of a family tradition and occupation, the court's activities were probably quite closed and resistant to change over time.

Early modern attorneys were not lawyers in the strict sense; they performed the rhetorical and strategic aspects of practicing law but did not necessarily have a degree in canon or secular law.[84] Many had not reached the degree of licentiate. Offices as attorneys attached to a court were normally purchased. The attorneys of the ecclesiastical court also likely purchased their positions and therefore needed to make a return on their investment over their time in office.

At least in marital disputes, attorneys did not seem to have been wedded either to defending or prosecuting cases. We find Juan de Gámiz Hidalgo, for instance, in one case arguing on behalf of an abused wife and in another defending an allegedly abusive man. The assignments of who would defend and who would prosecute a case happened quickly and were likely a simple bureaucratic matter. Litigants nearly always accepted the attorneys assigned to them by the court. Often the signatures of both the adversarial lawyers of the husband and wife are found on the initial aggrieved spouse's power of attorney.

The Provisional Judge (*Juez de Comisión*) and Lower Courts

A great deal of the diocesan tribunal's activity occurred via correspondence and in venues far removed from the episcopal seats in Logroño, Calahorra, or Santo Domingo de La Calzada. In distant towns the ecclesiastical court was represented by clerics designated as provisional judges by the vicar general for specific cases. The duty of these individuals, who could be parish priests, abbots, or local vicars, was to fulfill the court's orders and act on its behalf in any particular case. These actions included censuring and excommunicating recalcitrant spouses; sequestering, inventorying, and liquidating a litigant's property; hiring medical experts, accountants, and notaries; placing abused wives in safe houses; and publicizing the names of those excommunicated or sentenced by the court. The most common activity of the provisional judge was arranging for and overseeing the taking of testimony.

The role of the provisional judge as a liaison between the bishop's court and the local vicarage and parish must have been a point of contention within the diocesan hierarchy. The *Constituciones* of 1700 contained many provisions that limited the autonomy of local vicars and priests. Some clerics clearly acted independently of the bishop's court in a variety of efforts to control the laity. Evidence of such ecclesiastical control at the local level extended from an instance in which itinerant Jesuit missionaries ordered a man and wife to live separately to a local vicar who formally investigated and prosecuted an English woman who was cohabiting with an English sailor.[85]

The efforts at the 1698 synod to reform the diocese clearly aimed to bring distant judicial activities under the supervision of the diocesan court: "We decree and order that no provisional judges will be [deputized] to ascertain offenses unless in grave and serious cases."[86] But the church's juridical activity at the local level was wildly variable. In one parish we find the despotic behavior of a priest who refused to provide a blessing to a woman without a chicken as payment.[87] In other towns we discover lax clerics who regularly drank, gambled, and danced when they were not fathering illegitimate children.

Parish priests had no authority to intervene and rule in cases of annulment; instead, litigants had to appeal to the ecclesiastical court directly.[88] Matrimonial disputes before the diocesan court were first-instance cases. First-instance cases were those cases that were not heard on appeal and had never been tried before in a lower church court, such as a local vicar's court. The vicars were to inform the court once every two months about any "public sins" so the prosecuting attorney could act appropriately.[89] That only the diocesan court was supposed to prosecute wrongdoers does not mean that clerics and the church had not intervened earlier in these cases. Litigants occasionally complained in their pleas to the tribunal about the orders of an individual confessor, priest, or diocesan visiting magistrate. Yet the orders of priests and confessors were not judicial decisions and, at most, amounted to insistent, coercive spiritual advice. More frequently, a couple would approach the court after being forced by the bishopric's visiting magistrate to separate or cohabit. Even the visiting magistrate's orders did not amount to a trial, however, and, most importantly, records of his deliberations never formed part of the subsequent marital trials.

There is, however, scattered evidence that the diocese contained lower church courts. The abbot of Nájera, for instance, tried one case of annulment based on impotence independently of the diocesan court, though the abbacy still fell within the jurisdiction of Calahorra and La Calzada.[90] In another instance, a vicar on the diocese's Atlantic coast, far removed from the diocesan court in Logroño, independently prosecuted a case of publicly scandalous adultery.[91] But the fact that none of the cases considered in this study directly proceeded from a lower court demonstrates that local church tribunals, when they existed, operated very intermittently.

Notaries and Scribes

Bishop Lepe extensively revised sections of the diocese's *Constituciones* describing exactly how the ecclesiastical court should function. The heart of these additional sections was his instructions pertaining to the tribunal's permanent notaries and ecclesiastical notaries in general. Writing during and immediately after his extensive visits to many of the towns of the diocese, Lepe wrote these mandates on notaries to standardize church business. Certainly the vitality of the ecclesiastical court depended on these secretaries. Notaries in the tribunal itself organized documents and dispatched all court papers and copies thereof to the various parties involved in the separate cases. Certified ecclesiastical notaries in the far-flung towns of the diocese were hired and paid per service. The court charged them with transcribing testimonies, serving court papers on accused individuals, and other matters.

In its main office the tribunal employed two notaries who divided court business between them. Cases were to be handed to the judge for a decision only after all formalities had been secured: signatures, affidavits, and so on. The notaries also maintained the court's open hours "at their desks in person, with their aides: in the mornings from six to ten in the summer, and in winter, from seven to eleven."[92] Evening hours were from two until nightfall. That Lepe specifically listed the court's hours tells us several things. It is strong evidence of his struggle to reform the diocese. Clearly, during his reign as bishop, he would have enforced these extensive court hours. Such hours suggest an approachable judicial institution openly seeking and practicing business. The church court, at least under Lepe, must have been quite active and revitalized.

Lepe's attention to licensed ecclesiastical notaries throughout the diocese was even more excessive. He had obviously witnessed several abuses of the title of "notario apostólico." Men licensed to practice as ecclesiastical notaries had to be reviewed and their licenses renewed upon the annul visitation of the diocese's visiting magistrate. Apparently, however, practicing notaries often eluded such inspections. By many indications they were poorly qualified. In Lepe's words "many are inducted into this profession with titles given by people, that, according to common law, do not have the authority to create notaries . . . many annulments of public [legal] institutions can come of this, causing grave harm to the commonweal."[93] In an effort to ensure the quality of notaries, the tribunal prosecuted those in charge of their certification. The court prosecuted licentiate Joseph Maldonado y Pardo, for example, for selling ecclesiastical notary licenses.[94] As an added effort to improve ecclesiastical notaries, Lepe urged that, when possible, the diocese should hire clerical rather than lay notaries.

The diocesan court often dealt with litigants and witnesses who spoke only Basque, termed in the documents *lengua vascongada*. The court hired translators to assist scribes and notaries to receive testimony from Basque witnesses. Translators were often hired and assigned by the court on an adjunct basis. Like medical experts who were associated with the court but not officially part of the institution, the tribunal consistently turned to a number of known interpreters when their services were needed. The *Constituciones* of the diocese provided for two interpreters when taking testimony: "in such cases when examined witnesses do not understand or know how to speak Romance, [the scribe is to] receive the information and witness depositions with the use of at least two interpreters, and that there not be just one: because from this there can result that the entire proof is based on the truthfulness of one person, something that is a great detriment."[95]

Clearly the participation of translators in the transcription process and production of documents removes us further from the actual sentiments of the deponents. Happily, for our purposes, many Basque litigants could also speak Castilian, what the documents refer to as "romance." Therefore, only a fraction of the cases in this study involved translated testimony.

Medical Experts

The opinions of doctors, surgeons, and midwives were critical in the trials for annulment based on impotence and occasionally separations based on abuse. Medical testimonies attempted to answer one or more of three questions that we will consider in detail: the sexual potency of a man or woman, a woman's virginity, and physical evidence of abuse. As such, the court asked medical experts to be able to show that there was physical proof of marriage or domestic tyranny within a marriage. The *physical* aspect of all medical testimony is central to this study. The concern that the ecclesiastical court showed for physical facts demonstrates that the bodily control and treatment of a wife by a husband, through sex and violence, was the central element of how early modern Spaniards understood matrimony.

During the period under study, doctors and surgeons invariably worked in pairs. At some level they dealt with their medical practice as a partnership. Doctors were clearly university trained, usually carrying the title of licentiate. They would direct the course of physical examinations verbally by instructing their medical associate. Doctors also researched and cited the appropriate opinions of esteemed medical authorities from Aristotle to Paolo Zacchia.

In an impotence examination, surgeons would perform the actual tactile examination of the subject. Though they had generally received less formal education than doctors, only rarely carrying the title of licentiate, surgeons often composed an additional declaration for the court, usually written in their own hand. Despite their independent voice in documents, however, they invariably concurred with the opinions of the doctor with whom they worked. As witnesses in wife-battery cases, surgeons did not form part of a doctor-surgeon team. Women with broken bones, contusions, and open wounds often needed the urgent help of surgeons, and the latter, along with other deponents, would later give the court their descriptions of abuse.

Midwives joined the doctor-surgeon teams in cases requiring the examination of female subjects. Midwives were not only employed to perform the physical examination of a woman in order to protect her modesty; the court also clearly valued their opinions, especially in the determination of virginity. Unsurprisingly, none of the professional midwives we find in these cases had received a formal education, though a few were able to sign the declarations that they submitted to the court. María Pérez, this study's most prominent midwife, having served in more than twelve cases, could not sign her name. Perhaps a midwife's most important quality was her experience; and experience was generally equated with age. To determine a case of virginity in the town of San Pedro Manrique in 1699, for instance, one of the litigating parties complained that "there is no experienced and satisfactory midwife because the one that [the town] has at present is of a very young age and not very proficient."[96] Like the attorneys we have seen, María Pérez may have practiced her occupation because it was a family profession; we find a Juana

Pérez eight years older than María working for the church court during the same year, 1699, and in the same city.

The church court always solicited—and seems to have trusted—midwives' diagnoses, chiefly regarding virginity. Still, because medical women lacked a doctor's knowledge of written medical opinion and a surgeon's experience of anatomy from having, among other things, dissected cadavers, midwives did not command the forensic respect that their male colleagues did. At least one doctor devoted part of his declaration to an invective against the abilities of midwives. Dr. Juan Muñoz of Vitoria disregarded the conclusion of midwife Catalina de Orenz, glibly claiming that "midwives are ignorant about this material."[97]

Doctors, surgeons, and midwives were not formally on the bishop's payroll. Yet the church court regularly hired the same medical experts, especially when determining impotence cases. The Logroño medical trio, Dr. Don Diez de Ysla, surgeon Juan Bauptista de Soraluçe, and midwife María Pérez, assisted in determining a large number of impotence cases. In his career before the court between 1690 and 1710, Dr. Diez de Ysla assisted as forensic expert in twenty-nine, or 35 percent, of the impotence trials. These individuals likely became professional court experts simply because of their proximity. Because the tribunal was based in one main city, Logroño, and only occasionally in Calahorra, medical experts in those cities received the court's business. When litigants went to physical examinations in other cities, the court enlisted the services of the closest reputable medical practitioner.

The vicar general usually chose the medical experts to perform physical examinations. However, attorneys had the opportunity to challenge the selection of medical experts, and on occasion doctors were rejected. Litigants would either object by citing the distance of the expert in question from where they lived or, more rarely, that the doctor was biased against them. The court had little hesitation accepting depositions from other forensic professionals when litigants refused the vicar general's first choice. Most impotence cases were resolved with the aid of one team of experts, but many contentious cases required more. Defense teams could initially attempt to rebut unfavorable findings of the first medical examination by asking for a second opinion by another doctor and surgeon. Third teams were then usually hired to settle the conflicting opinions; additional medical opinions rarely did anything but further muddle the potency question. Finally the court could send the various medical declarations for an opinion from a more learned medical expert at a university. Ultimately all the medical testimonies would ridiculously read as a gloss on a gloss on a text, the subject of which was the sleepy performance of a simple penis. Litigants' money, more than anything, permitted this impressive marshaling of doctors, surgeons, and their educated opinions.

Impotence Trial Procedure

The official start of a typical charge of impotence in the ecclesiastical tribunal was always clear according to the documents. A woman interested in fighting for an annulment of her marriage would enter the diocesan offices, solicit the court, and enter her charge. If the litigating individual lived near the ecclesiastical court, which held audience in one of the two recognized episcopal cities (Santo Domingo de La Calzada and Calahorra) or the de facto seat of the bishop in Logroño, he or she had ready access to the tribunal's services. If the *Constituciones* of the diocese are to be believed, the ecclesiastical lawyers were supposed to be open to the public every workday morning between eight o'clock and nine o'clock in the summer, and an hour later in the winter.[98] A notary and the attorney assigned to the accusing spouse's case would draft a power of attorney for the wife, ceding jurisdiction in the charge to the lawyer and the court. The power of attorney would ordinarily include a description of the charge and might also contain a narration of extenuating circumstances. Other lawyers attached to the court would certify the power of attorney with their signatures; occasionally one of these men might defend the opposition in the case. At this early stage the court often assigned a defense lawyer for the allegedly impotent individual, though the accused spouse was usually absent. In the same session that the power of attorney was composed, the prosecuting spouse's attorney would write the initial demand that would begin the case. Again, the spouse accused of impotence was rarely present to hear the first charge read against him or her.

In his formal acceptance of an impotence case, the vicar general would order the accused spouse to appear before the court within three days after receiving the court's subpoena (*carta de justicia*). He would also order the spouse to respond to the charges and submit to a physical examination. At this point the court might also acquiesce to other of the wife's demands: that she be removed from the company of her husband during the litigation, that she be defended gratis due to poverty, and others. In the first stages of the case the court acted rather quickly; the three initial documents (the power of attorney, initial petition, and official acceptance of the case by the court) were often completed on the same day.

If an accused husband cooperated with the court, he met with the attorney assigned to him and proceeded to the medical examination. The medical experts then submitted their reports to the court and both litigating parties.

The defense attorney then formally responded to the wife's initial charges and to the doctor and surgeon's diagnoses. Cases could take several different directions at this point, depending on evidence, counter-accusations by the defense, and other considerations.

After the interested parties had submitted all proofs and arguments to the vicar general, he would promulgate his decision. Judgments appear to have been read orally before the interested parties. Only later would the court compose an official written document of the verdict that would allow the victor in the case to claim his or her rights. Occasionally, wives complained that they were waiting for the final publication of the court's decision so they could demand the restitution of their dowry in a secular court or remarry. Attorneys for losing parties often automatically submitted an appeal. The vicar general was legally compelled to allow almost any appeal. Losing clients frequently gave up pursuing an appeal. Still, attorneys generally drafted an initial letter of appeal the same day that they lost a case. Lack of money probably prevented most litigants from taking their fight to the metropolitan court in Burgos.

Costs of Litigation

The price of any particular trial depended, of course, on its length. Appendix C provides an example of the costs for one of the parties in a case for separation based on abuse. The husband in this case had to pay these costs as well as his own legal expenses. Because the losing party was responsible for the final payment of legal costs, litigants may have been tempted to continue "upping the ante" of a legal battle with additional petitions, testimonies, and appeals. The first individual to run out of money, or creditors, would have to quit the suit, lose, and be responsible for the huge debt of the case. Wives, perhaps, had less to lose financially than husbands because if a woman lost her case she would simply forfeit her dowry. Her husband would remain responsible for her financial maintenance. A husband who lost, however, had to pay the costs of litigation after returning his wife's dowry intact, turning over half the goods of marriage, and paying alimony.

Court functionaries received regular salaries, but clearly earned a large part of their income directly from the court's itemized work. The tribunal obviously incurred many expenses itself, however. These ranged from paying for paper to the ample costs of bread and board for its notaries when they ventured to distant towns to take testimony.

Competing Jurisdictions

Clearly, the many types of legal polities in early modern Spain led to confusion and competition between the several jurisdictions. In cases of separation and annulment, however, the ecclesiastical court had little trouble policing its sovereignty. Royal courts seemed to be well aware that if a case they were considering brought into question the legitimate existence of a marriage, that particular issue could only be resolved in an ecclesiastical court. Likewise, though secular courts might fine, jail, and otherwise penalize abusive husbands, they never issued formal separations and left such issues to the church.

We have already seen that the Inquisition reserved certain types of crimes for itself, such as sodomy and bigamy. There may have been a certain amount of cooperation between the ecclesiastical court and the Inquisition, especially since higher members of the tribunal occasionally acted as consultants to the Inquisition. Two vicars general, for instance, aided the Inquisition with their legal knowledge in this capacity. However, we encounter little of the Inquisition's presence and jurisdiction in marital disputes. Only rarely do we find in court documents the personnel and familiars of the Inquisition, who usually proudly identified themselves as such.

In matrimonial cases the tribunal of Calahorra and La Calzada had to defend its geographic jurisdiction against other dioceses more often than against other types of courts. This mainly resulted from the fact that the spouses could come from different dioceses. One party might prefer his or her influence or chances in one church court over another. In one impotence trial, for instance, a wealthy and highly influential husband attempted to relocate the case against him to the diocesan court of Pamplona in his home Kingdom of Navarra rather than in Logroño. The Calahorran tribunal was forced to appeal to the archbishop's court in Burgos to gain jurisdiction over the case.[99]

Historians have been forced to make many assumptions about Spanish church courts because they lacked concrete information. Some have assumed that church courts were dying institutions whose jurisdiction and powers had been ebbing for centuries compared to the Inquisition and royal courts.[100] As this chapter has demonstrated, however, this particular ecclesiastical court witnessed a revitalization through the end of the seventeenth century. One historian has erroneously assumed that church courts proceeded by *inquisitio* in the same manner as the Inquisition, the accused not knowing who charged him and why.[101] Others, such as Abigail Dyer, have correctly supposed that church courts were more akin to municipal courts, settling disputes between aggrieved parties as much as they prosecuted crimes ex officio.

The institution of the church court, however, seemed less able to change itself or be changed than other courts. First of all, its laws were unchanging and legal training in canon law remained mired in scholasticism even into the eighteenth century in Spain. Second, it is clear that positions in the court itself functioned according to family and patronage if not venality. There is little evidence of corruption, especially since decisions in separation and annulment cases seem consistent over time. For the period of our study the church court's traditional methods for resolving marital disputes were still important in Spanish society. By determining the legitimacy of all marriages, church courts remained vital to people's everyday lives. Royal law, however, would soon encroach on the powers of the ecclesiastical courts; after the end of our period of study, Charles III's Enlightenment reforms of 1776 would remove several aspects of marriage law from the church.

3: Impotent Women, Discarded Wives

> Fría es y más que fría la que ni pare ni cría.
> (Cold and colder still is she who neither bears nor rears children.)
> —Spanish saying[1]

As with men, but more so, societies have defined women by their bodies and their sexuality (e.g., virgin, wife, prostitute). So the fact that women were prosecuted for sexual impotence may not be all that surprising, even though impotence has most often been described as a male curse. Indeed, descriptions of impotence in early modern Spanish dictionaries refer exclusively to men.[2] The debates about women's bodies in female impotence trials reveal three important ways women's sexuality fits into the early modern worldview. Foremost was the uterus's economic role in creating legitimate new generations. Without these new people, of course, there would be no one to continue the life of the community, care for the elderly, and pray for the souls of the dead.[3] Second, men's licit use of women sexually in marriage maintained the male socio-sexual order. Third, women's sexuality and genitalia were thought to be connected to greater supernatural and physiological forces, beyond the comprehension of men. The church court could define women as "impotent," and even "castrated," because such language clearly resulted from typical early modern concepts of the female sex.[4] Early modern women could be and were determined to be sexually *im*potent because their sexual organs were considered to be potent. Early modern concepts of female sexuality imbued women with considerable power in their sex.

Between 1650 and 1750 the bishop's court decided eight cases of wives charged with impotence. It also heard one case against an allegedly castrated woman. Seven of the eight women charged with impotence came from rural Spanish villages, and only two of the eight women came from the Basque area north of the Ebro River. Spanish doctors, surgeons, and midwives of the period generally referred to female biology using male terms. They regularly cited scholastic authorities on female sexual anatomy, including ancients like Galen and Aristotle, as well as moderns like canonist Thomas Sánchez or medical jurist Paolo Zacchia. Like men, "impotent" women could not participate in the penetrative sex act using the "natural" sexual members;[5] like men, in order to conceive a woman had to emit a white, foamy seed during coitus; and like men, women had "testicles" rather than ovaries. The clitoris, were it to be recognized at all, and it never was in these cases, might have been explained away as a diminutive penis.[6] The Spanish functionaries of the court and its medical experts employed what today is seen as a deficient male anatomical vocabulary to discuss women's genitalia and sex. These Spaniards, then, were steeped in the medical scholasticism that still dominated education in Salamanca and Valladolid (as well as Oxford and Cambridge, for that matter). Like Galen and Aristotle many centuries earlier, they understood women's sex as imperfectly formed male genitalia.[7]

Early modern Spaniards, then, did not comprehend female sexual behavior and biology using any single logic. Attorneys selected the most appropriate understanding of the nature of female sex for their particular purposes in arguing a court case. Medical experts did the same when they tried to diagnose or explain a woman's particular condition. When necessary, these legal and medical professionals described women as sexually unique and unlike men. As we will see, in some cases doctors portrayed women as having sexual powers men did not have. However, a medical expert would equate a wife's sex with that of her husband if a lawyer's case would better be supported by such an interpretation. Attorneys and the expert witnesses they employed used concepts of women that would make the best argument in court. They might just as easily argue that women were cold, moist males as that the female sex was unique and different from the male sex. The speaker or the writer of any particular statement about women often determined what lens they used to understand female sexuality. Husbands often focused on the reproductive mission of their wives' sexuality. Many of the court functionaries were more concerned with the role of marital sex in preventing scandal, adultery, and illegitimacy. More rarely, litigants and witnesses referred to female genitalia as magical or physiologically powerful.

It is impossible, then, to reconstruct a unified early modern Spanish discourse on women's bodies and female sexuality because there were competing and/or parallel sexual views of women. Nicolas Abercrombie and Bryan Turner have asserted that a single dominant paradigm through which the world was understood did not exist in early modern Europe. They have argued convincingly against Marx and Foucault's emphasis on the power of an ideological superstructure created by those who produce knowledge in society: "At the very least," they assert, "the [dominant ideology] theory must assume that there is a common culture in which all classes share and that the content and themes of that common culture are dictated by the dominant class. In fact it is typically the case that subordinate classes do *not* believe (share, accept) the dominant ideology."[8] Addressing the effect that the Council of Trent had on Catholics, supposedly making them more religious, Abercrombie and Turner maintain that subordinate orders of society instead escaped participating in the orthodoxy of their supposed social superiors.

Counter-Reformation ideology, they argue, primarily dominated the lives of elite members of society.[9] These impotence trials bear out Abercrombie and Turner's argument, not only in terms of the effect of the Council of Trent, but also by the fact that litigants, doctors, and attorneys used contradictory rhetorics to discuss early modern anatomy, sexuality, and marriage.

As we have already seen, impotent spouses could be sued because canon law dictated that marriages were only legitimate if they were sexually consummated. This law code enabled at least eight husbands to take their wives to court seeking annulments and freedom to remarry. Evidence exists from a few impotence trials that some spouses might have colluded with each other to gain an annulment. But because the losing spouse could not remarry, such cooperation was rare. All of the wives considered here vigorously denied accusations of impotence. Indeed, the allegedly impotent woman used desperate measures to convince the court and public that she was sexually potent. The prosecuting man, however, sought to expose his wife as sexually defective. Ultimately these accusations led to medical experts giving their opinions. Medical examinations that purported to prove whether an individual was impotent or not then became the focus of court rhetoric. Much was at stake.

For commoners, marriage was society's normative institution; women excluded from matrimony likely lost access to sustenance, status, family, and support in their old age. A woman threatened with an annulment that excluded any possibility for remarriage thus risked losing more than a man facing a similar accusation. She would lose the financial support of a husband and the possibility of having children and a family of her own. Less tangible, but perhaps more important in a small community, she would lose the status and respect that married women enjoyed. As a single woman, she would have to find a local niche to fill, perhaps as an auxiliary member of her parents' or a sibling's family. If she had enough money or property, she might join a convent. Without support, a single woman could do domestic work for a wealthy family or religious institution. Whatever the scenario, a deserted woman's future was very likely less secure than the married life she had been planning. It was, after all, the promise of predictability and familiarity that made even the most miserable early modern marriages difficult for women to escape, if they were given the rare opportunity to do so. In the Basque area of the diocese, a woman's standing, and thus marital status, could be even more crucial; it was not uncommon for Basque women to be promoted to the head of the ancestral house and its estate, the *baserri,* over brothers and male relatives.[10]

Canon law's definition of female impotence did not differ substantially from its explanation of male impotence. It consisted of any physical defect that prevented a person from participating in vaginally penetrative sex, which was the only understanding of "natural" sex during this era.[11] Female impotence corresponded to the three male criteria of impotence: erection, penetration of the vagina, and ejaculation therein. It was the inability to be penetrated, to accept the penis, and receive the semen. Raymond of Peñafort first codified female impotence under the papacy of Innocent III (1198–1216).[12] In Gratian's *Decretals*, "De Frigidis," women could be impotent because they had an extremely narrow vagina, flesh covered the vagina, or a tumor closed the uterus.[13] Even though this definition could be confused with sterility, barrenness could not prevent marriage and did not constitute grounds for annulment. According to the Catholic interpretation, after all, Joseph and Mary had never had any children of their own, yet their holy marriage was undoubtedly valid.[14] More practically, canonists had found it necessary to recognize that elderly women past menopause could marry even though they were assumed to be sterile.[15]

There is a good deal of evidence that female impotence cases were not at all unique to northern Spain. Rather, because canon law had explicitly discussed female impotence as a grounds for annulment since the High Middle Ages, it is likely that these trials are representative of greater Catholic Europe. Natalie Zemon Davis's version of the Martin Guerre case provides us with one of the most infamous examples of female impotence. In attempts to understand the reason the couple was not able to consummate their marriage, Bertrande de Rols, Martin Guerre's wife, was suspected of impotence.[16] Martin Guerre was, unsurprisingly, also accused of impotence. After all, it was much more common for husbands to be accused of impotence than women. Pierre Darmon estimates that during the epidemic of impotence trials that plagued early modern France, 5 percent of all cases were against women.[17] His estimation is confirmed in the Diocese of Calahorra and La Calzada, where more than 8 percent of all impotence accusations in the court were against women. Into the nineteenth century wives continued to be subject to such trials. Rather than disappear, the canonical debate on female impotence became more problematic in the modern age with the advent of new surgical techniques like hysterectomy and ovariectomy. With the introduction of modern surgery, allowing the relatively safe removal of ovaries and/or uterus, the Vatican had to reconsider definitions of female potency in the nineteenth century. Yet, the debate over whether a woman who had undergone a hysterectomy could marry or not continued well into the twentieth century.[18]

Of the many impotence trials that historians have documented throughout Europe, it is likely that a small percentage involved allegedly impotent women. Joanne Ferraro studied many impotence trials that came before Venice's ecclesiastical court.[19] Thomas Max Safley's tally of impotence cases in the Diocese of Constance was 133 for the seventy years from 1551 to 1620.[20] Though they do not point out any trials against impotent women, the work of Ferraro and Safley shows that impotence accusations occurred regularly throughout Europe. More concretely, Darmon's work on impotence trials in eighteenth-century France depicts many cases of female impotence. Monique Cuilleron, studying Paris's high ecclesiastical court for the sixty years before the French Revolution, found that 9 percent of the impotence cases she encountered were against women.[21] Back in Spain, María del Juncal Campo Guinea discovered twenty-two impotence trials between 1584 and 1694 in the Diocese of Pamplona, just northeast of the Diocese of Calahorra and La Calzada. Again, roughly 5 percent of these cases involved female impotence.[22] Most other work on early modern Spanish ecclesiastical courts has also found impotence trials.[23] Additionally, the hundreds of trials accusing witches of causing impotence should also be taken into account. Male and female impotence caused real and widespread anxiety among European peasants.[24]

Many newlyweds, then, might understandably have been concerned about consummating their marriages. But what circumstances might ultimately have led a husband to accuse his wife of being impotent? In three of the cases against allegedly impotent women in the Diocese of Calahorra and La Calzada, husbands initiated the cases for annulment. It was just as likely, however, for a man to accuse his wife of impotence as a counter-accusation to having been accused of impotence himself. Finally, in one extraordinary case—discussed at length below—an entire community charged a would-be-bride with impotence because it was commonly believed that she had been "castrated." The court did not have any special legal mechanisms for dealing with an accusation against an allegedly impotent woman. Supposedly impotent women were subjected to the same proofs and requirements as men. For instance, the court demonstrated no special concern for female privacy or shame as unique from men. This stands in marked contrast, for instance, with how the ecclesiastical court treated married women accused of adultery. In such cases the tribunal took great pains not to reveal the names of adulterous wives. Impotent women, on the other hand, defended themselves against laws and legal procedures more often used to prosecute men. It seems ironic that in order to prove her sexual aptitude, and thus her privilege to marry, a wife had to submit to a visual and physical violation. In effect, a woman's sexual potency was to be proven through her ability to submit sexually to a man, to be penetrated, and therefore violated. This would grant her the right to participate in the marriage sacrament and contract.

The ordeal that men faced, then, women experienced as well. All individuals in such trials would face a loss of reputation and humiliation in their parishes, neighborhoods, and towns. One woman complained about "the shame that [she and her husband] suffered by the village's gossip."[25] The court demanded that women visit the medical experts that would determine their potency within six days after notification. In these medical examinations they put themselves, practically naked, at the mercy of doctors, surgeons, and midwives who proceeded to ask intimate questions, and then poke and prod with fingers and instruments. Whereas men had to demonstrate erection and, occasionally ejaculate, allegedly impotent women had to submit, at the least, to penetration by the fingers of a surgeon and midwife. In other cases the medical expert witnesses used candles or specially prepared phallic instruments. In the course of litigation a woman might have to undergo two or three of these physical examinations. Regardless of all these efforts and embarrassments, the individual might still be diagnosed, quite arbitrarily, as impotent.

Interestingly, however, in at least one case there is evidence that these examinations may also have educated young women and men who were sexually ignorant. In 1735, after the court declared Juachina Cordón impotent and annulled her marriage, she and her former husband, Franzisco Rodríguez, seem to have been enlightened by the separate experiences they had had with medical experts. They concluded that their problem consummating the marriage was something they could overcome. Juachina and Franzisco began working together to remedy what they newly understood to be her abnormally narrow vagina. Franzisco testified that he snuck into her room in her parents' house on several occasions and used his fingers (as the medical experts had done) to stretch her vaginal opening.[26] Eventually Juachina was able to have sex with Franzisco; she soon found herself pregnant by his frequent visits and they then had to petition the court to be allowed to remarry.

Impotence diagnoses were usually quite tenuous. Though medical opinion and testimonies were crucial in determining whether a wife was impotent or not, they were not as decisive as one might suppose. In actuality, lawyers won and lost their cases through rhetorical manipulation and reinterpretation of medical testimonies. When expert testimony was not to their satisfaction, attorneys might petition for second and third medical diagnoses by new experts. They would question the capability or objectivity of medical experts. Attorneys might submit the testimonies of servants, family members, and friends who, in one way or another, had knowledge of a woman's sex life. They would attempt to reassign the blame for nonconsummation to the husband, or argue that with time and sexual maturity a woman would become able to have sex.

Male and female impotence seem to have been equated because the legal proceedings used male impotence as the dominant model. Court functionaries treated women much the same way as they dealt with men in impotence cases because court officials were much more familiar with accusations against men. Attorneys may have changed the genders of the petitioners, but the formulaic legal language was basically the same. In 1681, for example, the complaint against Josepha Díaz de Durana was that she "has not been able to consummate the marriage because she suffers from visible and natural impotence."[27] Word for word this is the same as a charge against an impotent man. The "passive" and "active" roles in the sexual act, so typical during this era, were disregarded or ignored. This is not surprising since the lawyers prosecuting impotent women had many experiences bringing impotent men to court. Attorney Juan de Gámiz, for instance, prosecuted more than fourteen impotent men before trying a woman for impotence in 1704. There was simply no reason why lawyers would take the time to create new legal dialogue and rhetoric to prosecute so few female defendants.

There were, however, issues that complicated the court's sexual scrutiny of impotent women. Foremost of these was sterility. In the court documents it becomes clear that many family and community members were not simply concerned about the defendant's ability to have sex. Rather, some arguments were sidetracked by whether or not a litigant could bear children. This was a question irrelevant to canon law, which clearly permitted sterile individuals to enter the sacrament of matrimony. Still, the fertility of any newlywed couple was much hoped for by families and communities. Once a charge of impotence had been entered, the ecclesiastical judge might be forced to consider husbands' demands to annul marriages to sterile, rather than impotent, wives. Medical experts, too, often responded in their testimonies to reproductive questions outside the strict boundaries of the impotence diagnosis. Indeed, how these professionals and the ecclesiastical institution answered concerns about barrenness shows that the church court could often serve community values outside the scope of, or even in contradiction of, canon law.

The ability to bear children emerged several times as an issue in the case against Magdalena Fernández de Valasco Sáenz, who was accused of impotence by her husband, Pedro Martínez. Of the three cases in which men initiated cases against allegedly impotent women, Magdalena's is the most heartrending. Pedro entered a plea for an annulment from his newlywed wife, Magdalena, in November 1697. He claimed that she was "very narrow in her vulva to the effect that its penetration is impossible as well as [for] the reception of the material that serves for the preservation of the species."[28] In this initial plea Pedro's lawyer already referred to the importance of the "preservation of the species," even though sterility could not legally be an issue. According to his attorney, Pedro had fathered three children in a previous marriage. The fault for the lack of consummation, his lawyer argued, must therefore be Magdalena's. Magdalena's mother had already attempted to open and/or expand her vagina using hands and instruments, demonstrating the importance Magdalena's family placed on the marriage. They wanted to protect the marriage perhaps more than their daughter.

The judge began by ordering a physical inspection of Magdalena by medical experts in Logroño. The first examination testimony described her as short, sixteen years old, and premenstrual. The doctor also discovered that some instrument had been used to mutilate Magdalena's genitalia, making it impossible for her to bear children. She accused Pedro of injuring her, but Pedro argued that Magdalena's mother had done the damage when she attempted to open her daughter's vagina by force.

Young Magdalena, of course, had her own attorney whose aim was to defend her right to the marriage and her status as a wife. He proceeded to attack the much older husband for trying to have sex with a girl of "such a tender age."[29] Magdalena's lawyer argued that she only needed time so she might mature sexually. Using a personal anecdote about a similar case, he argued that eventually Magdalena would be able to consummate the marriage and bear Pedro children. Indeed, a second medical examination of Magdalena found that she was not sixteen but instead seemed to be about twelve years old.

The diagnoses of two medical teams consisting of a doctor, surgeon, and midwife seem to indicate that Magdalena suffered from an imperforate hymen. This abnormality causes blood to accumulate in the vaginal cavity and uterus and, if untreated, can lead to sterility.[30] Everyone agreed that she suffered from some malformation of the vagina: "her parts [are] very closed because having inserted a finger into the orifice [the midwife] could not insert it very far inside and [the midwife] recognized that [Magdalena] had solid tissue and that it seemed to her, for that reason, that [Magdalena] had not had sex."[31] Magdalena began to bleed from the painful and intrusive examination, but the diagnosis was perhaps more painful. The medical conclusions persuaded the court that Magdalena was indeed impotent. Her marriage was annulled and she was forbidden ever to marry again. Pedro was liberated and had the right to remarry as he pleased.

Magdalena's identity as body and as commodity determined her social status and life. Even more than most impotence trials, this dispute between Magdalena and Pedro resembles a breach of contract. When Pedro returned Magdalena to her family it was as if he was returning unsatisfactory goods to a vendor. The young girl, likely forced into marriage by an unaffectionate family, could not meet the sexual and reproductive demands of a sexually experienced man. Rather than console a daughter abused by their son-in-law, Magdalena's mother attempted to make the marriage work by trying to cure Magdalena herself. Only the court provided some defense for Magdalena, providing her an attorney, someone to fight for her interests. Ironically, her economic and social interests were best served by demanding that her marriage to Pedro be recognized, thereby making him responsible for supporting her.

As in many impotence cases, the court made its decision on the basis of doubtful medical evidence. In fact, the medical diagnoses were ambiguous enough to provide the court with a great deal of leeway. In this case the court determined that Magdalena was impotent, even though her sterility was the more crucial factor. Her vagina "could not permit the introduction of the material that serves for reproduction"[32] After being penetrated in one way or another by her husband, mother, and medical experts, Magdalena's defect was no longer whether she could engage in the sexual act; rather, her fault was that she could not have children. So even though the court understood in this case and others that sterility could not be used as a formal plea to annul a marriage, sterility could, nonetheless, become the decisive issue.

But female impotence cases cannot be understood as simply the treatment of women's bodies as reproductive commodities. Much of the language of impotence arguments reveals that early modern Spaniards connected the female sex to social harmony. For centuries Catholic theologians had recognized that women's sex, though it created and encouraged sin, was also necessary in creating and maintaining social order. Because the church agreed with Paul in 1 Corinthians 7:8–9 that for most Christians it was "better to marry than to burn," the maintenance of stable monogamous unions needed to be guaranteed by regular marital sex; according to this logic, the mutual conjugal debt needed to be fulfilled by sexually able and willing wives.[33] Sex inside marriage was supposed to prevent spouses from seeking sexual gratification elsewhere. One of the greatest fears was that a husband would commit adultery with someone else's wife, creating many possibilities for illegitimacy, dishonor, hatred, and violence. Englishman William Gouge conveyed the predominant view of the era when he stated that "impotent persons cannot yield due benevolence." Implying that affection in marriage was expressed through sexual intercourse, he argued that "though procreation of children be one end of marriage yet it is not the only end." For Gouge and many others in early modern Europe, sex in marriage existed to satiate sexual appetites that otherwise proved to be socially destructive.[34]

The threat of adultery, and the scandals that adulterous affairs invariably caused, undergirded the justification for annulments based on impotence. The court, as well as most early modern Spaniards involved in these cases, assumed that anyone married to an impotent spouse would eventually pursue their sexual satisfaction illicitly. Uncontained lust and illicit sex would then potentially tempt other community members, particularly married women. Once the chastity of married women was threatened, the cornerstone of social order was disturbed, male honor was lost, violence erupted, and the community's future was compromised by the birth of illegitimate children. Canon law assisted in the protection of women's honor, then, by allowing for some marriages to be dissolved that could not maintain the socio-sexual order.

And yet female sexuality was connected to even less tangible powers than the social ordering of small communities. Women's sex was thought to be susceptible to unseen supernatural forces. Clearly, European misogynist traditions had linked female sexuality to evil for centuries. One aspect of this was the story of the "Fall of Man." Eve's seduction by the devil and her subsequent temptation of Adam had obvious sexual connotations. Ethnographer Stanley Brandes provides us with a twentieth-century Spaniard's perspective on women and sex that echoes the traditional misogynist belief that "woman is of the devil": "She was that way from the very beginning, and she has been trying to tempt and dominate man ever since."[35] Impotence trial testimonies reflect a similar opinion among peasants that women were more susceptible to sex and magic than men. Early modern Spaniards understood women's genitalia as being connected to and able to influence magical forces. Magical spells, for instance, often focused on genitalia.[36] Witches allegedly communed with the devil by having sex with incubi.[37] For commoners, supernatural forces were especially connected with the female sex organs and its products: menstrual blood, pubic hair, the umbilical cord, and placenta.[38]

Medical and ecclesiastical authorities recognized the supernatural connections between female sexuality and magic as well, though they usually understood them as negative.[39] Women were traditionally described as dirty and impure during menstruation, a view supported by the many prohibitions of Leviticus.[40] Scholastic medicine also championed this misogynistic biological point of view. When older women ceased purging themselves of poisonous blood through menstruation, according to Pseudo-Albertus Magnus writing in the late thirteenth or early fourteenth century, they developed the power of the "evil eye." The fear of the "evil eye," or "fascination" as it was termed, was prevalent throughout early modern Spanish society. Two Castilians authored books on the phenomenon. Diego Alvarez Chanca published *Tractatus de fascinatione* in 1499, followed by Antonio de Cartagena's *Libellus de fascinatione* a generation later in 1530.[41] The "evil eye" was a unique power only women had and resulted directly from women's unique biology.

It is not difficult to imagine the circumstances that allowed magic spells to affect male potency: A man would fear that curses or spells would make him impotent, on his wedding night, for instance, and the resulting anxiety would cause the impotence he feared so much. Female potency would seem to be unsusceptible to such curses, from the modern perspective, because psychological blocks cannot prevent simple sexual intercourse. Yet, one wife and her lawyer tried to persuade the court that she had indeed been made impotent by an evil spell. In 1691, in Calahorra, Joseph de Arostegui accused his wife of four years, Antonia Garrido, of impotence. He demanded an annulment of their marriage. The husband's lawyer claimed that "my [client] has never been able to consummate the matrimony because [the wife's] vagina is narrow and she does not have her parts like other women."[42] The court summarily sent Antonia to a medical examination by a team of experts who had been recommended by the husband and his legal counsel. The doctor, surgeon, and midwife all submitted statements to the court in which they agreed that Antonia had physically deformed genitalia. The medical team declared her absolutely impotent.

But Antonia fought her husband's attempt to escape their marriage and label her impotent. In response to the first medical determination (there were to be others), Antonia's lawyer, Thomás Pérez de Baños, suggested that her vagina was bewitched, that she had been made impotent by evil spell: "my [client] has fervent suspicions that in the doubtful case that [she] has some [type of] impotence, it is by evil spells and witchcraft."[43] Pérez argued that, because the impotence was caused by a curse, it was not permanent and therefore could not justify an annulment. He reminded the court that the Catholic Church had spiritual remedies and exorcists to rescue and help people affected by such magic spells.[44]

The fact that a woman's potency and genitalia could be cursed as easily as that of a man provides an insight into how early modern Spaniards conceived of impotence spells. Witchcraft was not simply an early modern explanation for what would later be described as psychological phenomena. Magic was also a power that was thought to physically transform people and things. Impotency spells on men were often described as castrations by which men lost their penises or, more often, the penises were stolen and kept by the offending witch or demon.[45] This was a magic by which people were thought to be able to physically transform themselves into animals or be able to fly. Considering that early modern curses and spells were often described as causing real physical transformations, then, we can understand how Antonia's lawyers could argue that her vagina had been deformed by malicious spells.[46] Magic, therefore, could not only be used and controlled by, but also affect women's sex. Eventually, Antonia was able to win a second vaginal examination by a medical team that she and her lawyer considered to be less biased. They determined that she was completely potent. Still seeking an annulment, however, her husband then claimed that *he* was impotent. The church court did not acquiesce to Joseph's machinations; they eventually ordered him to return to "a married life" with Antonia. We do not know if this judgment, however, actually resulted in Joseph accepting life with Antonia as his wife.

Antonia Garrido and her lawyer had appealed to the rhetoric of sexual magic, but even outside the spiritual and magical realms early modern Spaniards believed that the vagina held hidden powers. Doctors ascribed to women's sexual organs great physical powers, such as a peculiar spermatic magnetism. The purported ability of a woman's uterus to draw a man's semen into itself without having sex is an important example of how even medical doctors, using quasi-scientific explanations, accorded extraordinary powers to the feminine sex. The idea that vaginas had this ability originated from the great traditional European medical authorities, and most principally Averroës. One example is the following description of the magnetic, and voracious, uterus from *De secretis mulierum* (*On the Secrets of Women*) attributed to the Pseudo-Albertus Magnus and published widely throughout Europe in the sixteenth and seventeenth centuries: "Averroës said . . . [II *Colliget*] that a girl from his neighborhood once confided to him, swearing that she was telling the truth, that she had never been impregnated by any man, and nevertheless she was pregnant; and she asked him to help her. Averroes carefully examined the case to determine the cause, and he found that she had been bathing in tepid water in a bath and suddenly was impregnated by attracting male semen, for a man had ejaculated in this bath and the female member on its own power extracted as much semen from the bath as it could."[47] Later in the same work we also find a description of the uterus as a magnet: "when the woman conceives, her womb attracts the male sperm with all its power, just like a lodestone attracts iron."[48]

The idea that vaginas had this hunger and ability to obtain the male seed was popular throughout Europe (more than seventy editions of *De secretis mulierum* appeared in Europe during the sixteenth century).[49] The Spanish manifestation of this concept appeared in the trial of Ana María Sáenz against her husband, Juan García, in San Román de Cameros in 1687. Their complicated drama would result in Ana María Sáenz pairing off with one Francisco Sáenz, while Juan García married a second Ana Sáenz. Not only does it demonstrate the currency of the notion of the "magnetic uterus," this case shows how the court would use casuistry to fit canon law to convoluted domestic disputes.

Ana María and Juan had been married for eight years before suing for an annulment. They both claimed that during the entire span of their marriage they had never been able to have sex. Although Ana María had initiated the litigation by filing an impotence charge against her husband, the court took Juan's counter-accusation that his wife was the impotent partner as the more credible indictment. After examining them both and finding Juan to be entirely potent, medical experts unanimously agreed that Ana María was impotent, adding that any attempt to open her vagina surgically would pose a threat to her life. The court decreed the marriage annulled; it allowed Juan to remarry at his leisure. The judge found Ana María was absolutely impotent and for that reason barred her from any future marriage. The case had taken less than two months from beginning to end, and its conclusion would have been rather simple if it had not been followed by two pregnancies.

Not only was Ana María inexplicably pregnant six months after the court's verdict that had deemed her completely impotent, but her former husband, Juan, had successfully impregnated his new wife. When Ana María sought to marry Francisco Sáenz, the man whom she claimed had impregnated her, the ecclesiastical court was forced to review its previous decision. While Ana María had had nothing to show after eight years of marriage, and had allegedly never had sex with her husband, a few months as a single woman had resulted in her pregnancy. More perplexing for the court was the fact that her first husband had already apparently proven his virility in his new marriage to Ana Sáenz. Apparently he was not impotent either. The tribunal's most pressing question was how a medically certified impotent woman had become pregnant.

To answer this question and explain how they could have made such a mistaken diagnosis, Dr. Gregorio Fernández de Villemayor and surgeon Juan Baptista Martínez de Garijo invoked the magnetic powers of the uterus. They speculated that Ana María's vagina, which they believed was definitely too narrow to accept a penis, had magnetically attracted Francisco's semen, "as is clear from many stories and every day it is seen that women become pregnant without the penetration of the vagina, only by the actual magnetism of the uterus."[50] We cannot be certain whether Dr. Fernández de Villemayor and surgeon Martínez de Garijo actually believed in the magnetic powers of the uterus. They may have been trying to maintain Ana María's impotence diagnosis while explaining her pregnancy. It was important to defend the court's first decision, that Ana María was impotent, because if she was not impotent then her first marriage was still valid. Ana María would have to return to Juan García, and he, in turn, would have to abandon his second, pregnant wife, and return to the first.

But despite the fantastic magnetic ability that these medical experts rhetorically attributed to Ana María's vagina in their declarations, her own explanation for her pregnancy was less extravagant. According to Ana María and Francisco Sáenz, he had sneaked into Ana María's house after dark overcome with a resolution to enjoy her sexually. After secretly watching Ana María undress, he made himself and his intentions known to her. Ana María claimed that she acquiesced to his demands, but only after he swore to marry her (part of another rhetorical formula, one of seduction).[51] After two nights of sexual attempts their determination resulted in successful, and then successive, copulation. Ana María found herself pregnant, and single, several months later. According to his lawyer, Francisco Sáenz then approached the church court for permission to marry Ana María to "restore her honesty and reputation."[52]

The court's final solution was pragmatic and inventive, disproving stereotypes of canon law as inflexible and church courts as oppressive. The court used jesuitical reasoning to appease the parties and find a verdict that suited the communal demands for social order and legitimacy. The ecclesiastical court reviewed its earlier ruling and found that Juan had been impotent, but only in respect to his first wife, Ana María. According to the medical team, Dr. Fernández de Villemayor and surgeon Martínez de Garijo, "Juan García, in respect to Francisco Sáenz, is not as potent because [he] . . . has a virile member with a fatter head than the said Francisco Sáenz."[53] This curious medical opinion helped the tribunal justify the annulment of Ana María and Juan's marriage and their remarriages to two other people. After her encounter with Francisco Sáenz, Ana María was no longer impotent and, according to canon law, should have been returned to her first marriage with Juan García. An affirmation of the first marriage would not only have returned two individuals to an unhappy union, but would have resulted in the creation of two illegitimate children because the two women had become pregnant. Instead the tribunal invoked the explanation of respective impotence, allowing it not only to annul the first marriage, but also to order that the pregnant Ana

María Sáenz marry Francisco Sáenz and Juan García marry the pregnant Ana Sáenz.

The court also demonstrated its responsiveness to community interests when it considered the single case of a "castrated" woman in the Diocese of Calahorra and La Calzada. This case against a "castrated" woman also illuminates the inadequacy of gendered vocabulary in the early modern period. Though extraordinary, there were precedents in canon law and European folklore for the female "castrate." Canon law referred to the *mulier eunuchissa,* the woman eunuch, to mean a women who was or had been made sterile.[54] Legal theorists consequently encountered problems with Pope Sixtus V's proclamation *Cum frequenter* of 1587 that prohibited eunuchs from marrying.[55] Did this mean sterile women, female "eunuchs," were also prohibited from marrying? Though it took several centuries to answer this question definitively, in practice sterility did not bar any person from matrimony. As we have seen, nonprocreative sex served matrimony's second purpose, satisfying and containing lust; only *impotentia coeundi,* sexual impotence, rather than *impotentia generandi,* sterility, was an impediment to marriage.

The "castrated" woman can also be found in European misogynist folklore explored by Louise Vasvári in which "taming" a wife was sometimes likened to "castrating" her.[56] One version of the female castration tale is told in the French *De la dame que fur escouille.* This account depicts the "castration" of a domineering mother-in-law. After getting hold of a pair of bull testicles, a new son-in-law forces his mother-in-law onto a table, makes incisions in her abdomen, and, through surgical slight of hand, removes the testicles. The mother-in-law, thinking she has been castrated, thus readily accepts her son-in-law's authority. To this day in certain parts of Spain, a forceful woman is said to have testicles; she is called a *cojonuda,* or "big balled woman."[57] In the early modern period the "castration" of overbearing women was desired by men so as to reestablish what they understood to be the natural patriarchal social order. The important characteristic of these "ballsy" women was that, though their husbands may have been cuckolded, they themselves were anything but lacking.[58] The application of male anatomical vocabulary to women—castration, "balls"—reveals the instability of gender boundaries in early modern Europe.

A vagueness regarding gender was not only part of the court's legal language. Since many testimonies came from villagers and parish priests, gender ambiguity was clearly also a part of the language of sex outside the court. In the parish church of the Basque town of the Gardelegui, a village close to and ruled by the provincial capital of Vitoria, three banns announced the aproaching marriage in the spring of 1711 of Thomas de Yabala to María Ana de Harana. Before the couple legally wed, however, the town priest discovered that María Ana "[was] impotent because the gelder had cured her on both sides [of her groin]."[59] Apparently, as an infant María Ana had undergone an operation to cure an illness. A hernia surgeon, often referred to as a castrator or gelder, had operated on her groin. In boys these hernia operations often involved the removal of one or both testicles.[60] Several uses of ambiguous terms show that Spaniards conceived of female sexuality in exclusively male terms. Because they used male sexual terminology, clerics, lawyers, and other people involved in these cases often conflated several sexual distinctions that might be made in our own age between women and men. The community of Gardelegui imagined that María Ana was, in fact, a castrated woman. The priest who brought the couple to court, and undoubtedly others of the parish community, suspected that María was sterile rather than impotent, *impotentia generandi* rather than *impotentia coeundi.* The confusion between sterility and impotence was one of many errors in terminology that litigants made in this case. The case first reached the court when María Ana's fiancé, Thomas, sought permission from the bishop's court for María Ana to marry. In the development of canon law, after centuries of theological debate, the Catholic Church had resolved that the sterile, as the parish of Gardelegui supposed María Ana was, were permitted to marry.[61] But the ecclesiastical court in Logroño, rather than grant María Ana license to marry as canon law dictated, reflected the concerns of the community by beginning an investigation into whether she was or was not castrated.

Fortunately for Thomas and María Ana, her surgeon, Martín de Burgos, was still alive to set things straight. The hernia surgeon had operated on María Ana as well as on boys who had later come before the church court asking for marriage licenses. On March 29 the vicar and ecclesiastical judge of the town of Arnedillo took Martín de Burgos's testimony about the operation that he had performed on María Ana decades earlier. Martín explained that roughly twenty-three years earlier he had "cured and castrated" María Ana of two intestinal hernias. She was only about seven months old at the time. According to Martín the "castrations" he performed on girls had nothing to do with actual sexual castration: "the said cure does not prevent the use of marriage nor ability to procreate in [María Ana] nor in other women castrated on both sides, because in females the testicles are not castrated."[62] Immediately after receiving Martín's testimony, the church court gave María Ana permission to marry Thomas.

Everyone involved used many ambiguous terms. For example, the misapplication of the word "to castrate" (*castrar*) by Martín de Burgos was, in large part, the reason María Ana had to appeal to the court in the first place. The surgeon applied "castrate" to any cutting or tying of intestinal ligaments in an operation rather than just to the sexual neutering that most people understood the word to mean. María Ana was the victim of popular and medical concepts that confused female sexual anatomy with male genitalia. Equating female with male genitalia did not stem from any inherent ignorance among rural Spaniards; instead, such imprecision had a long tradition in European medicine, deriving in part from Aristotle's opinion that women were, ultimately, imperfectly formed men.[63] The seventeenth-century surgeon Paolo Zacchia, whom many northern Spanish doctors cited in their medical reports to the court, also used male vocabulary when describing female sexual anatomy.[64] Even in Martín's informed and professional testimony, he refers to María Ana's organs by male terms, calling ovaries "testicles," for example.

People used and were misled by several other ambiguous terms in this case. *Impotente, potrero,* and *castrar/castrada* were all thought by different people to mean different things. The most persistent confusion surrounded castration. As we have seen, Martín's use of the term "to castrate" could include any operation that manipulated ligaments in the groin, regardless of dictionary definitions that exclusively defined castration as sexual emasculation. Nearly every curative groin operation performed on young children during this time, executed by hernia surgeons, was assumed to result in castration. In fact, these surgeons were often bluntly called "gelders," a term more often connected to lopping off animals' testicles. Thus it is not surprising that because Martín had operated on María Ana's groin, her neighbors and family thought that she had been "castrated," as many boys who underwent hernia operations were. And, following this assumption, if she was "castrated," she must be sterile. The typical operation to cure a hernia at this time in northern Spain involved the removal of, usually, one of a boy's testicles and the relocation of the second testicle inside the inguinal canal. The boy would therefore not exhibit any testicles in his scrotum, causing many community members to question whether he was or was not a full castrate. Several male impotence cases were fought over this very question in the diocese; most were resolved with an explanation of the procedure by a hernia surgeon. This confusion in the use of the term *castration* led to many boys, who had not been completely castrated, being called "castrates." This occurred, for instance, in the impotence case of Juan de Aleson and María de Lagaria, in 1685 (see chap. 5). He was commonly known in his village as "el capon" because it was thought that he had been castrated as a child during a hernia operation.[65]

Curiously, perhaps by confusing female with male sexual anatomy, the language of the court reflected a respect for an inherent potency of women's sex vis-à-vis men's sex. Vaginae, vulvae, and clitorides, after all, were not treated as the "other" in this language, but were understood by all concerned as the "same"; the same as men's genitalia, that is. And it should be emphasized here that documents occasionally did refer to women as sexually "potent" in the same sense as the word applied to men. In Arnedo, in 1735, for example, after examining Juachina Cordón, Dr. Adrián de Muro argued that "if it were possible to find a competent man with a member as narrow as the cervix or vagina of the said Juachina, she would be potent."[66] Furthermore, men who were not impotent, rather than simply being called "potent" were often referred to as "viripotent," a term that combines the Latin word for man, *vir*, with power, *potente.* Did the use of this male-specific term assume, then, that women were "gynecpotent"?

The answer would seem to be that early modern Spaniards did see women's sex as potent, a source of power for them as individuals. But this focus on women's sexuality would also mean that women were understood as sexual entities more exclusively than were men. In Spain, genitalia were thought to contain many real, not merely symbolic, sorts of power: material, social, and magical. Women were not devoid of a sex or simply the object of sexual desire, a perception more reminiscent of Victorian England; early modern texts spoke of female "parts" and "members," often in a male vocabulary, that were just as integral to sex and reproduction as penile potency.

The decisive factors of female sexual power were the elemental ability to reproduce and the capability of maintaining the socio-sexual order. In early modern Europe the sex organs in and of themselves, of course, held the key to the creation of a legitimate human legacy. Without this generative aptitude, every other aspect of the replication of everyday life from decade to decade—familial, economic, political—would have failed. Impotence trials revealed widespread anxiety over being able to have children. But this concern over human reproduction was not only an everyday worry for peasants, for whom it was, partly, a matter of economic survival; reproduction became a serious concern for state ministers in Spain and France worried by the depopulation of their respective kingdoms.[67] Don Diego de Saavedra Fajardo, for instance, propounding solutions to Spain's problems, explained in 1631: "the Roman censors used to formulate penalties, so that, sterility being reviled, they encouraged men toward matrimony, privileging as well the propagation and multiplying of children. Spain needs even more this attentiveness [to propagation] because of the expulsions that it has made of peoples, because of those that have been consumed in its sundry wars, and because of those who have left to populate the Indies and other kingdoms."[68]

The central role of the sexual organs in the creation of the human future connected them to several types of unseen powers. As we have witnessed in these impotence trials, women's genitalia were seen as the sources of invisible magical and magnetic forces; they offered people a next generation, the continuation of the family name, and, ultimately, the kind of immortality that even peasants could achieve.

Rather than simply repress sexuality, as the Catholic Church recommended, the people in small communities, as the rhetoric used in female impotence trials reveals, linked social harmony with the correct use—or exploitation—of female sexuality. Amity and harmony, though rarely obtained, were prized by small European communities above all else in daily life. In court documents, for instance, one finds constant complaints about the public "scandals" caused by sexual misconduct and marital strife. A great deal of sexual scandal was best prevented by confining *men's,* rather than women's, lust to the marital bed: avoiding scandals like fornication, adultery, masturbation, male sodomy, bestiality, as well as the social evils of illegitimate children. As these female impotence trials make clear, wives were expected to be sexually able. A wife's sexuality was important because it allowed her to fulfill the conjugal debt and maintain social order, containing her spouse's sexual lust. The early modern community's ideal of marriage, then, could not include wives who were impotent.

Of course, part of the power of women's sex was that it could clearly provoke conflict as well. Misogynist clichés linking women's sex to human destruction abounded: Helen was blamed for the deaths of thousands in the Trojan War; Delilah's sexual appetite consumed and destroyed Samson; and Eve's dalliance with Satan in the Garden of Eden, according to Saint Jerome and other patristic writers, cursed humankind to suffer from sexual lust.[69] Into the twentieth century, rural men in Andalusia still believed that too much sex with one's wife progressively debilitated a husband; while, through the same act, a wife would gain vitality, sapping her husband's strength: "Well water and a naked woman / Lead men to the grave."[70] Monogamy, as a strategy for sexual regulation and social harmony, was often expressed as the solution to the female appetite. Rather than drawing attention to the possibility that men's lust needed to be satisfied in marriage, early modern writers focused on women's dangerous and destructive sexual covetousness that had to be gratified and controlled by marriage. When they described women as the lust-driven gender, then, they hypocritically foisted on the female sex the sexual hunger with which they grappled themselves.[71]

Drawing on many different rationales, then, medical, magical, and economic, rural women in early modern Spain derived a great deal of power from their sexuality. These were powers, however, that would be forgotten, lost, or taken away in the cities and towns of the nineteenth- and the twentieth-century Western world. Female magical powers were eventually debunked, even among Europe's peasants. Midwives lost their monopoly to know and treat the female body to male medical experts.[72] As Thomas Laqueur has argued, male scientists discovered that the female orgasm was superfluous to reproduction. Consequently, female sexuality was robbed of an important aspect of its potency. Although now a cliché, the sexually inert, frigid Victorian woman became a clear bourgeois idealization of womanhood. Middle-class women had lost their sexual powers, leading to their symbolic "castration" by Freud at the end of the century.[73]

But the point of this study is that two centuries before Freud, local church courts reflected the popular belief that women had considerable potency in their "parts": generative, magical, and social. They did not lack sexual organs in any sense; instead, texts described women as *having* sexual "members." Because women had inherent—and sometimes unique—sexual powers, they could therefore lose them, and be found impotent in court and legally deserted by their husbands.

4: The Prosecution and Sexual Persecution of Impotent Men

> El querer y no poder es más antiguo que el peer.
> (To want to and not be able to, is more ancient than the fart.)
> —Spanish saying[1]

Traditionally, Catholic Church courts have been blamed for the persecution, exposure, and humiliation of impotent men. Few events in early modern courts seem as alien to modern sensibilities as impotence trials. These legal procedures can strike the modern reader as violations of individual integrity and sexual privacy. Historian Pierre Darmon, for instance, does not hide his consistent horror when he writes about how Parisian judges probed and exposed the intimate lives of husbands and wives under France's ancien régime: "the questions of the Church judge during the cross-examinations had the cutting edge of a scalpel, and the incisions made so carelessly into the already scarred past of the couple were clearly an exercise in mental torture."[2] Darmon's blunt anger is the product of our own age. His clear respect for sexual privacy clashed with the early modern sentiments he read in the court documents. Unlike Darmon, the common person in the early modern period understood sex to be a public concern. Institutions and individuals of early modern Europe yearned for a well-ordered society, a society in which change was rare and everyone acted according to their place in a well-defined hierarchy. The rights and privacy of an individual were of secondary concern. When sex was not enjoyed in its legitimate place—the marital bed—and by spouses with one another, it could always cause social disorder. Illegitimate pregnancy, violence, bigamy, and venereal disease all disrupted the Christian peace that Spanish communities idealized but obviously never achieved. The sexual function ordered marriage, placing husband over wife and parents over the sexual product: children. So even though charging men in public with sexual incapacity may appear bizarre or barbarous to modern readers, the impotence trial was a logical part of early modern institutional efforts to ensure that only legitimate individuals entered into unions that would, in turn, create future legitimate individuals.

Even though we cannot say that impotence litigation was common in early modern Europe, it clearly was common knowledge that impotent men should not marry. The famous Martin Guerre case demonstrates that nearly everyone knew a sexually unconsummated union could be annulled. As already mentioned, the Basque Martin Guerre was impotent during the first eight years of his marriage. Urged on by her family, Guerre's unsatisfied wife nearly went to court to press for an annulment. Clearly Guerre's in-laws expected the marriage to be consummated, and when it was not, they knew enough about canon law to suggest ending it.[3] Ever more evidence shows that impotence trials were not rare. The earliest law code allowing divorce on grounds of impotence can be traced back to Justinian.[4] Catherine Rider has recently demonstrated that several famous medieval impotence trials, especially that of Philip Augustus of France in 1198, likely increased the use of the impotence plea to gain annulments.[5] She has also documented twenty-two cases of magically induced impotence between 800 and 1450.[6] For the early modern period, Thomas Max Safley counted 133 impotence trials between 1551 and 1620 in the Diocese of Constance.[7] Guido Ruggiero and Joanne Ferraro have both documented several impotence cases in early modern Italy.[8] María del Juncal Campo Guinea found twenty-seven cases of annulments based on impotence in the Diocese of Pamplona during the sixteenth and seventeenth centuries.[9] According to Darmon, the years between 1730 and 1788 yielded twelve Parisian cases, but these were only those extraordinary cases appealed to the high court in that city.[10] There were more than eighty-three cases between 1650 and 1750 in my own study of the Spanish Diocese of Calahorra and La Calzada. Considering the number of documents that have survived over the centuries, escaping fires, wars, mildew, worms, and premeditated destruction, it becomes apparent that even though impotence trials were not everyday events, they also were not rare.

Any study that focuses on annulment cases brought on grounds of impotence must overcome the morbid curiosity they provoke; the very word "impotence" elicits, to paraphrase Foucault on sex, a response of either shame or ridicule. The mere mention of impotence remains a taboo today, especially in the company of men, despite the publicity and popularity of the anti-impotence drugs of Pfizer Pharmaceutical and others. And yet the rich documentation of impotence trials reveals for the modern historian intimate lives and mentalities long forgotten, *if* we can overcome the timidity or nervous laughter that typically surrounds discussion related to the penis. Because these cases contain frank testimonies about the bedroom politics of spouses and lovers, they provide the social historian with exceptional means to understand early modern sexual behavior, gender constructions, marital expectations, and the effects of ecclesiastical law on society. They also include in-depth medical testimonies that inform other types of historical investigation, especially in the history of medicine and law.

How do we explain the frequency of impotence trials? What motivated church officials, lawyers, and litigants to spend so much money and time investigating genitalia? Traditionally historians have accepted a conception of a repressive early modern society in which the elites of a hierarchical society meddled in the personal sexual lives of commoners. It is Darmon's conviction that such intrusive, and what he sees as malicious, investigations of peoples' bodies, of their vaginas, uteruses, testicles, and penises, were motivated by the voyeurism and licentiousness of a powerful and corrupt judicial and clerical elite. He sees the impotence trial as a way that the clergy dominated the laity. Foucault takes a similar top-down approach in his explanation of the early modern Catholic Church's sexual discourse.[11] Yet neither Darmon nor Foucault's approaches, both of which focus on the church and its power over everyone else in early modern society, convincingly explain the causes and the characteristics of impotence trials. They are both part of an anticlerical tradition that has long been particularly strong in France, a point of view made famous by Voltaire's indictment of the church and clergy as the cause of the social injustices of his age. Such an opinion of the Catholic misrule has been a powerful force in historiography concerning church courts. Yet, women were the primary actors in these cases. Though church courts provided the venue and mechanisms for persecuting impotent men, these trials were initiated by and fought between spouses; the church court simply provided the battleground, set some rules, and kept score.

Generally, aside from the cases of female impotence discussed in chapter 3, it was women who sued husbands in impotence trials. The domestic hierarchy of male authority over female was the key issue in an impotence trial, and all rhetoric in the cases related to it. The clerical-lay relationship was never debated. Though domestic politics in these cases was interpreted and mediated by canon law, the dispute was about masculine authority in a household, not ecclesiastical power. And women were charging that such authority could not exist without male sexual virility. Legal combatants often used words, phrases, and ideals outside the church's own ideological discourse. Litigants and lawyers drew their rhetoric from deep-seated cultural beliefs about virility and power.[12] Sexual potency ultimately legitimated and set the conditions for a husband's right to dominate his wife. In impotence litigation the connection between power and the phallus was literal and plain; a woman challenged the legal authority of her husband to rule her, "correct" her, administer her dowry, money, and person by exposing his inability to get an erection. The direct link between virility and power was obviously a traditional cultural value that had preceded Christianity but become a part of canon law on marriage during the medieval period (see chap. 2). Ecclesiastical judges found themselves confronted by dissatisfied wives, and it fell to them to determine whether men were or were not impotent. The role of the church court, then, was more one of an interested third party rather than of the primary persecutor of impotent men. So, unlike the Inquisition's activities in, for instance, finding and burning sodomites, the church court in these cases was not the repressive boogeyman so clearly portrayed by the French philosophes of the Enlightenment.[13]

Detailed sexual investigations by agents of the court worked to resolve issues of potency and maintain the domestic political and gender hierarchy. Matrimony, the economic and legal foundation of seventeenth-century society, was based on what appear to be trivial physiological questions: Could a man achieve an erection? Did a bride have an intact hymen? All the probing questions and brutally thorough medical examinations were simply part of a logical quest to determine the truth of apparently basic sexual questions. A condemnation of church courts for the persecution of impotent men, then, has already been done. Instead, this chapter aims to explain the circumstances, motivations, and means by which spouses entered and were affected by "impotence trials."

Eighty-three impotence cases came before the court during our period. In addition to these trials, several allegedly impotent men came to the court for marriage licenses. All these cases that involved charges of impotence lead to important conclusions. First among them is the fact that ecclesiastical tribunals considered sex in marriage to be everyone's business. It can be safely said that a majority of Spaniards, men and women, idealized marriage and hoped to enter the adult community of husbands and wives, however much they joked about the poorly married. Entrance into matrimony, after all, usually coincided with a man entering a profession, gaining rights to participate fully in society, and often obtaining a great deal of property. For a woman, marriage was occasionally as loathsome as it was elevating: though a wedding would confer on a woman a certain amount of power and respect in and from her community, as a bride she would be forced to leave the comfort and protection of her family's house; often she would have to leave the town of her birth. Sex was integral to the making of marriage. Church officials understood copulation as the definitive act that perfected a marriage, and took to logical extremes its investigations into whether bride and groom had had sex or not. Impotence and the divorces that resulted from it robbed individuals, most often men, of this important married status. The charge of impotence, conversely, provided many women with a means to end, in a formal way, marriages that they detested. The physical examination of impotent spouses by church officials was simply a rational attempt to ensure the legitimacy of marriages and annulments. Modern divorces and annulment cases can still incorporate an accusation of impotence, although with the ease of secular divorce such charges are no longer common.[14] Early modern tribunals differed in the fact that they forced the prosecuting wife to prove medically that her husband was impotent.[15]

Frequently an accusation of impotence was a ruse to win a divorce. A great deal of documentation reveals many husbands and wives who fraudulently used the impotence charge as a loophole to annul marriages they no longer found convenient. There was good reason to choose the impotence accusation. In the diocese of this study, pleading sexual nonconsummation was the only way that litigants successfully won annulments. The few people who tried other pleas, like arguing that their spouse was a relative or that they never freely consented to the marriage, all failed. In a time in Spain when no one was permitted to divorce their spouse and remarry, a new love was always illicit. The charge of impotence was the only option that would allow someone to legally leave their spouse and begin a new life with someone else.

Yet, the accused rarely agreed to these de facto divorces by annulment. Only in a few odd instances did wife and husband work in collusion to annul a marriage, using the charge to effect a mutually desired divorce. Instead, the accused usually denied that he was impotent. Unsurprisingly, allegedly impotent men fought the charge of impotence, and in countercharges demanded that the court force their wives to return home and live "a married life" with them. One spouse was always trying to escape the presence of the other. These cases usually ended with a clear victor and clear loser, the stakes being rather high. A wife who won an annulment would regain control of her dowry. With her husband proved impotent, she would also have proved herself a virgin. Both these possessions, a dowry and virginity, would give her good prospects on the marriage market. The husband who lost such a case would be barred from any future marriage; he would lose access to the dowry. Worst of all, he would have to live with the public humiliation of being sexually deficient, of not actually being a man.

The Litigants

The bishop's court of this study attracted litigants from every corner of its expansive jurisdiction. Three geographic realities affected litigiousness (see map). First, and most obvious, impotence litigation arose in the smallest of communities as well as in the larger towns. Couples from many tiny rural populations throughout the mountainous diocese had recourse to the church's justice. Second, the court's greatest impact was on the people in and around Logroño. Six couples were residents of Logroño, and twelve more were within a day's journey. The bishop usually preferred life in Logroño; it was closer to the road to Madrid, larger, and centrally located. Ignoring most demands from the residents of Calahorra or Santo Domingo de la Calzada that he reside in those towns, he usually kept the tribunal in Logroño. Third, more court business came from the southern, Castilian half of the diocese than the northern, Basque portion. Only twenty cases, about a fourth of the eighty-three impotence trials, came from the mountains and seacoast that lie north of the Ebro River valley. Certainly, the distance and rough terrain of the Basque country must have prevented many couples from beginning trials in Logroño. The journey from Durango to Logroño, for instance, was a trek of nearly one hundred miles along the winding roads that descended from the foothills of the Pyrenees down to the Ebro. Few ordinary peasants would have wanted to seek justice from so far away. Travel difficulties, however, cannot completely explain why fewer Basques than Castilians failed to make use of the court's jurisdiction. The southern half of the diocese was also full of mountains, only rockier and less verdant than those in the Basque country. Castilians in the south may have preferred the court's justice because it was culturally their own. Even though many Basques spoke Castilian, and the court provided translators for those litigants who spoke only Basque, the cultural difference may have resulted in jurisdictional remoteness.

One of the most important facts of any type of litigation, not just impotence trials, was who initiated the case. Clearly the people who began these disputes had something to gain from them. Wives brought the great majority of charges to the court, forcing their uncooperative husbands to defend their virility publicly and in court. Although men, and their sexual organs, took center stage in most impotence trials, women were the chief actors because they were the plaintiffs and primary beneficiaries. Yet there were many impotence trials that deviated from the usual case that pitted a wife's accusation of impotence against a husband's piteous denial. Jesuits, parish priests, fathers, husbands, and couples acting jointly all initiated cases at one time or another. Evidence in the documentation occasionally reveals that initial accusations were prompted by someone other than the accuser prima facie. A wife who began a case may have conspired with her husband or her father or perhaps a lover to try to have an unwanted marriage annulled.

Any study that so centrally involves early modern church courts must describe and question the role of the church and its interests. Both Pierre Darmon and María del Juncal Campo Guinea emphasize the zeal and power of the clergy in the prosecution of annulments on grounds of impotence. Though I believe both these authors overstate the importance of the church in prosecuting impotent husbands, the actions of clergymen, priests, confessors, and court functionaries could indeed be decisive.

Occasionally the role of the local clergy, especially the couple's confessor, was crucial in beginning or preventing litigation.[16] Some wives learned of the legal options open to them under canon law only when they told their intimate marital problems to their confessor. Confessors were clearly not of one mind regarding the breakup of wedded couples. Confronted with the marital problems of couples in their parishes, some clerics may have chosen to advise tolerance and patience and the maintenance of marital unions. Once a wife informed her confessor that her husband was impotent, it is possible he counseled her to wait. Canon law demanded in impotence cases that a couple wait three years before suing for an annulment. This legal stipulation seems to explain why so many impotence trials began only after couples had been married longer than three years.

Some confessors were determined to separate couples who could not consummate matrimony; after all, if a cohabiting man and woman were not married, then they were living together in sin. A number of clerics ordered individuals to annul marriages that they believed would never be consummated. A trial originating in Nájera in 1685 serves as an example of how confessors caused cases to proceed to the ecclesiastical court. In a declaration to the court, husband Juan de Alesón said "[his] confessor did not want to absolve him until he told the said priest [about his impotence] and that in the meantime he separate from living with the said wife."[17] In this case, Juan's confessor used a common coercive practice among clerics: he withheld absolution as a means to compel a layman to do as he dictated. In another case, in Calahorra, in 1704, after four years of marriage Isabel de Gurrea and her lawyer, Balthasar de Blas, credited a confessor with inspiring the case for annulment: "and my client, for her own modesty and because of modesty and the shame that so filled her, had concealed [the impotence] a long time until, having spoken with her confessor, she was warned as to the bad state that she would be in if she persisted [in the marriage]."[18]

In both these cases, and in others like them, the confessor played an important role in monitoring the sexual lives of married couples and driving cases to trial. If couples were not consummating their marital unions, as in these two cases, a confessor could urge litigation for an annulment and/or separate the couple. Yet, aside from perhaps a need to create new business for the court, there is little evidence that the church had an interest in promoting the prosecution of impotent men. After all, the church court began and tried ex officio only three impotence cases. The motivations that clerics could have had for separating married couples were far outweighed by the interests of families and spouses directly affected by unfruitful unions. Clerics might have simply hoped to break up unconsummated unions as a measure to prevent sexual misconduct and public sins; wives with impotent husbands were thought to be more sexually susceptible to extramarital affairs because they were not being sexually satisfied/controlled by their husbands. It is difficult to imagine what clerics or the church court could gain by encouraging women to accuse their husbands of impotence. The church had little to profit from impotence trials, and the overall lack of participation by confessors and priests in litigation reflects the church's passive role in these trials as an interested third party.

In the above case, Isabel de Gurrea clearly had her own motivations for litigating against her husband. She had waited four years to approach the ecclesiastical tribunal because of shame, not ignorance of the law. She must have known that her marriage was not valid unless she and her husband had had sex. And there is little reason to disbelieve her lawyer's claim that Isabel refrained from litigation only because of the shame that she felt. Having entered a sterile union, Isabel suffered disgrace in a community that believed children were part of the natural order of domestic life. As the wife of an impotent man, she could not identify herself with one of the two respectable statuses open to a woman not in a convent. Publicly she could not claim respect as a marriageable virgin. Privately she could not consider herself a married woman.

The cleric's function in initiating litigation, then, could occasionally be crucial. Priests and confessors advertised the court's jurisdiction in what Richard Kagan sees as a competitive judicial market in early modern Spain. Spaniards could choose the court and jurisdiction that would serve them most favorably. Even though the bishop's court was distant from most small towns in the diocese, its presence was represented by local clergy. Parish priests would have been able to inform individuals about the legal possibilities available to spouses who wanted to escape a bad marriage.

Members of the church could initiate annulment proceedings if they suspected individuals of impotence. The canonical innovation in matrimonial law that allowed third parties to accuse and proceed against impotent spouses, as noted in previous chapters, occurred only in the middle of the sixteenth century and referred specifically to Spain. In 1587 Pope Sixtus v claimed that the women in Spain "do willingly marry men that, usurping the title of 'husband,' hold up to ridicule the sacrament of marriage."[19] To eliminate these "false marriages" to castrated men, Sixtus v decreed that clerics could proceed against couples who were living in unconsummated unions.

When an impotence trial was initiated by a third party, the court's prosecuting attorney or, occasionally, the visiting magistrate officially prosecuted the case ex officio. Even if a member of the couple's community or family made the principal accusation of impotence against a man, that accuser would not enter the case as a litigant. Instead, the interests of that individual accuser would be represented by a functionary of the court, in nearly all cases the prosecuting attorney. Because it often acted with encouragement by a community and prosecuted couples on behalf of community interests, the church served as a voice of the public. It enforced communal interests, not simply those of the church. Here again, the actions of the prosecuting attorney were ambiguous: he could either be the church's zealous and oppressive enforcer of Tridentine sexual morality, or he could be a legal agent, informed by and acting on behalf of the community's offended sensibilities and making use of canon law.

One such impotence trial, begun by a third party and tried ex officio, was that of the prosecuting attorney against Juan Martínez and Barbara Diez. In July of 1714 the prosecuting attorney of the Diocese of Calahorra and La Calzada, Don Bernardo Mangado, sent a letter to the priest of the small village of Lasanta. The cleric was to inform Juan Martínez and Barbara Diez to separate. The prosecuting attorney claimed that it had come to his attention that after five years the couple had yet to consummate their marriage because Juan was impotent. Unfortunately we do not know who brought Juan and Barbara to the tribunal's attention. The prosecuting attorney's letter also ordered that until the end of the litigation Barbara was to reside with her parents. The court instructed Juan to see a doctor to confirm that he was, in fact, impotent.

After pleading poverty and obtaining funds from the tribunal to pay for the medical fees, Juan visited Dr. Don Gerónimo de Herse y Portillo and the barber-surgeon Miguel de San Martín in Logroño. Their judgment was ambiguous: "he is incapable of consummating matrimony with virgins . . . but we also feel and declare that he will be sufficiently potent and able [to have sex with] widows, because it is known that this act is less arduous."[20] The ecclesiastical tribunal relied on medical opinion in making its judgment. They found that Juan was "relatively impotent" (impotent relative to virgins, but not widows, nonvirgins). It annulled Juan and Barbara's marriage. Barbara was free to remarry. Juan could also remarry, but only a "widow" (which implied any nonvirgin). The prosecuting attorney ordered the parish priest of Lasanta to inform Juan and Barbara of its decision and make sure that it was carried out.

This short narrative reveals how impotent husbands could trouble tight-knit Spanish communities. Impotence was not a private concern that simply afflicted the marital pair. Juan and Barbara's unconsummated marriage disturbed at least one person in Lasanta for it to come to the far-off attention of the ecclesiastical court. Perhaps this third party was the parish priest, or from the couple's family or neighborhood. Whoever the informant was, the ecclesiastical court was obviously urged on and aided in its effort to end Juan and Barbara's marriage. The prosecuting attorney's concern to maintain public order is evident in his warning that Juan and Barbara's unconsummated marriage posed a "very grave danger and harm to their souls."[21] Therefore, in this case the tribunal of Calahorra and La Calzada aimed to annul a marriage that it and the community of Lasanta considered a threat to social stability.

This case further shows us how a wife's virginity could unsettle the sexual order of a community. After all, Juan was not declared impotent with anyone other than his virgin wife. The threat to the community was not that Juan could not have sex, but that he could not have sex with his wife. According to this mentality, Juan's sexually unsatisfied wife invited an adulterous affair that would cause scandal in the community.

Just as in cases for separation, in-laws were often important actors in the litigation of impotence trials against men. (Of the few impotence trials against women, wives were never denounced by third parties for being impotent.) In French cases, Darmon argued, mothers-in-law in particular were the cause of several cases against their daughters' husbands.[22] In northern Spain, Darmon's observations are only partially borne out. A wife's parents were undeniably important in their support against her husband. In a small number of cases the parents were obviously behind litigation against their son-in-law. But unlike in abuse cases where a woman's mother sometimes intervened, no evidence from these trials could lead us to emphasize the actions of mothers-in-law in impotence cases. There was no instance in which a woman's mother specifically accused her son-in-law of impotence.

There were cases, however, in which fathers initiated litigation against their sons-in-law on behalf of their daughters. A son-in-law could often find himself dependent on his wife's father. As noted previously, men without means could hope for a better life by marrying into a wealthier family and a large dowry. Such men might tolerate the dominion of a father-in-law if it meant a large dowry and promising inheritance. Joseph de Quintana, father of Catalina de Quintana, and a resident of Santa Cruz de Campezo, approached the ecclesiastical tribunal in 1676 and accused his son-in-law of impotence. His son-in-law, Joseph de Gorguín, lived under Joseph de Quintana's roof and off of his income. Although the marriage was eventually annulled because Catalina decided to continue the lengthy litigation in her own right (the case continued for three years), the trial began strictly as a battle between her father and her husband.[23] An impotence trial, therefore, could simply serve as a means to resolve disagreements caused by jealousy and mistrust, and the squabbles over money, land, and power that so often pitted in-laws against one another. But a truly impotent husband could, clearly, be a disappointment to family members who expected progeny from their children. Regardless of which parent was the main actor, it is clear that a wife's family, if she was fortunate enough to have surviving immediate family, was her main bastion of financial and moral support. A woman's parents rarely sided with her husband against her.

Wives brought sixty-three of the impotence cases to trial, or 85 percent of eight-three annulments. Members of a wife's family directly initiated only 1 percent of the cases. Though it may seem surprising that women generally acted alone to commence litigation, such independence is noted in other studies of marital litigation. Linda Guzzetti, for instance, in her study of marriage separations in Renaissance Venice, finds that after marriage wives acted quite independently of their families in court.[24] The ecclesiastical tribunal also encouraged wives to act apart from their families, though separating a daughter from the support and influence of her family was undoubtedly difficult. In the case of Catalina and her father, the court on several occasions supported her husband's demands that she, as the wife, live in a house with her husband apart from her father. As explained earlier, the church court generally proceeded in trials between couples by weeding out the interests and influences of immediate family members. The church considered matrimony, after all, as a sacrament that involved only two individuals and God. In any case, the interests of family and the community were extremely important. However, from the church court's perspective, such interests were legally superfluous and often caused undesirable complications.

A clear example of how the ecclesiastical tribunal labored to separate parents' interests from those of wife and husband was Francisco Merino's attempt to annul the marriage of his daughter María Merino with Diego Texada. According to Francisco, his daughter had planned to enter the religious life as a nun and not marry. But before she could take her religious vows, the father claimed, one night Diego Texada broke into their house in Ausejo, entering through the window, and raped María. However, María, in a curious response to such allegedly violent treatment, fled with Diego to his parents' house, where they soon announced plans to marry. The court's response to this conflict, one that was truly between father and daughter, was to attempt to remove María from the influences of the two interested parties in the hopes that she would voice her own will. The court therefore ordered that María leave Diego's house and be placed in the care of a third party, a cleric. The tribunal then ordered that her deposition be taken. Her telling of the events was very different from that of her father. María told the court that she was not raped by Diego, that she had never wanted to become a nun, and did indeed want to marry Diego. Her father, in response, urged the court to consider that María was young and foolish. The court allowed the banns for María and Diego's wedding to proceed to be read.[25] In this case it is clear that the church court often went to great pains to separate children from their parents and spouses to ascertain what their individual desires actually were.

By the end of the eighteenth century, with Charles III's Real Pragmática, Spanish parents would win more powers to control the marriage choices of their offspring. Because of the relatively antipapal orientation of Charles III's enlightened legislation, church courts would lose some of their jurisdiction in marital cases. The secular courts would gain more rights to make judgments in marital disputes. The Real Pragmática of 1776 recognized the interests of parents in the marital choices of their offspring and required parental consent for sons and daughters younger than twenty-five.[26] But until then, and for the period of this study, the church persisted in policies that tried to separate individual interests from those of affected family members.

Only five cases, or 6 percent of impotence trials, were brought to court by husbands, either against their impotent wives, or in two curious cases, against themselves (see table 5, appendix A). In one obvious ploy to win a mutually agreed divorce, a husband and wife cooperated in an appeal to the tribunal for an annulment based on impotence. The great majority of cases, though, were begun by women, and so their interests and motivations are the most crucial to understand. Who were these women and what circumstances brought them to assert their rights against husbands and finally make their way to an often distant ecclesiastical court? No woman gave an unmediated, detailed account of her candid sentiments or motivations.

Initial petitions in the ecclesiastical court rarely provided the ages of wives trying to escape matrimony. While the years of marriage were usually part of a formulaic petition for annulment, the ages of the litigants were apparently not as important. This is unlike witness testimonies, which always provided the witness's age at the end of the deposition. Lawyers and notaries in northern Spain did not include such vital information in demands and responses to the court. The main reports that on occasion mention the age of litigants were those resulting from the physical examinations of wives and husbands that the court ordered to corroborate charges of impotence and claims of virginity. Other documents that also provide the age of litigants are the marriage certificates that were sometimes entered into evidence by the tribunal and official declarations. Judging from the handful of cases that revealed the ages of women in trials for annulment, though removing one case brought by a sixty-four-year old woman, the average age of wives who brought impotence cases to trial was twenty-five. If we subtract from this average the four years most women had waited before beginning annulment proceedings, the average age at which these women married was twenty-one, an absolutely typical age of marriage for women in western Europe.

Generally, these couples had been married for many years before petitioning for annulments based on impotence. The husbands and wives had been married, on average, for close to four years before litigating for an annulment. Several older wives claimed that they had not yet consummated their marriages of ten to nineteen years. Years of marriage and cohabitation set these cases apart from suits for breaking betrothals, which were themselves serious contracts between couples. From our contemporary perspective, four years may not seem a long period before petitioning for a divorce. Yet we need to keep in mind that the length of marriages in early modern Europe rarely extended to the decades that many husbands and wives can expect in the twentieth-first century. The early death of spouses made second and even third marriages common. The ecclesiastical court consequently often distrusted the motivations of women who had waited a decade or more before asking for an annulment.

Many factors could lead a wife, who had allegedly discovered that her husband was impotent soon after marriage, to suffer four years of cohabitation before seeking an annulment. First, she may have simply awaited patiently a remedy for her husband's affliction. As seen earlier, it is also quite possible that such women had been advised, by local clerics or lawyers familiar with canon law, to wait the requisite three years before seeking an annulment for her husband's impotence. Such advice at the local level avoided bothering the tribunal, which often ordered women who charged their husbands before three years of cohabitation to return and fulfill the *triena.*

Another conceivable reason men were accused only after several years in an unconsummated marriage was that the charge of impotence served as a simple pretext to end an already troubled marriage. In one possible scenario, after years of unhappiness had failed to bring about an acceptable marital situation, a wife finally sought an escape from marriage by charging that the man she wed truly held no rights over her. Impotence could also have been a pretext for ending a sterile union, a marriage in which the couple had sex but was unable to have children. In either case, a wife would assert that she was still a virgin, thereby defending her prospects for a second marriage. The four-year average delay between these marriages and subsequent annulments therefore probably reveals little about what actually motivated wives to bring impotence cases to court. In sum, many things could explain the four-year delay.

We also have little information about the occupations of litigants. A small number of cases involved wealthy aristocrats, such as the voluminous 400-folio case of Doña María Michaela de Albelda y Vazen against her husband, Don Antonio Francisco Vélez de Ydiáquez y Guevara, knight of the Order of Santiago.[27] At the other end of the spectrum, there were many litigants who identified themselves as "poor." Overall it is dangerous to attempt a general description of the occupations of people involved in these impotence trials. Many of the litigants described themselves as day laborers and, lacking literacy, could not sign their name on court documents. Others were urban professionals: a merchant, a tailor. Many more were wealthy and/or came from the high nobility.

The great variety of backgrounds of people in Spanish impotence trials contradicts the findings by Darmon for France. Darmon found a great singular occupational trend: "the socio-professional breakdown of litigants yields at least one certainty: the absence of any representation from the peasant population . . . rural society was quite simply excluded."[28] Litigants before the court of Calahorra and La Calzada, on the contrary, were not predominantly from any one social status or economic level, and did include rural participants. Richard Kagan famously described Spain as a litigious society, a society in which the great majority of citizens could look to courts to resolve their disputes without spending inordinate amounts of money. His conclusion seems to ring true for the diocese of this study. Rich and poor individuals, nobles, peasants, and vagabonds all appeared in the ecclesiastical court to plead their cases.[29]

Several general characteristics of La Rioja and northern Spain help explain how people from many social backgrounds could have participated in ecclesiastical and other courts. Because there was a large petty nobility (hidalgos) that some authors claim constituted nearly 50 percent of the population, the rift in status between noble and peasant was perhaps less pronounced than in Darmon's France. The customary laws and rights (*fueros*) of the Basques, for example, asserted that every Basque was noble. Town governments and ecclesiastical authorities and their mechanisms of justice were accessible to a large spectrum of Spaniards because, especially south of the Ebro, the vast majority of people lived in towns, not rural homesteads. Most life in northern Spain was town life. In the Ebro River valley, for instance, with its characteristically Mediterranean way of life, agricultural cultivation was centered around inward-looking and urban-centered villages.[30] Furthermore, unlike the Paris that produced many of the impotence trials Darmon discusses, the small cities and towns of northern Spain did not possess a class of urban bourgeoisie that monopolized the mechanisms of municipal or church justice. But perhaps the main explanation for Darmon's conclusion that the French peasantry did not enter into this type of marital litigation was that he investigated only impotence trials that had been appealed to the Parisian high court. Though poor couples often did begin impotence trials, unlike their social superiors they rarely ever appealed the initial decision of the local ecclesiastical court.

Litigants who petitioned to be represented by the court's charity usually defined poverty as a life reduced to nondescript and various manual labor. With their toil, their lawyers argued, they could barely sustain themselves and their families. Occasionally, plaintiffs successfully avoided court and medical fees by proving that they were poor. However, we should be as distrustful of poverty claims as the tribunal was. It is difficult to gauge how poor individuals were who hired lawyers to prove it and had friends attest to their indigence. But clearly impotence trials were open to couples of little means; these cases were not battles limited to the wealthy or merchants in the cities. Very few women began their cases with a claim of poverty. Instead, costs that arose during the trial eventually brought litigants to claim poverty. Medical bills were the most common and prohibitive cost. A doctor, surgeon and/or midwife often made their declaration to the court contingent on payment for the examination. One indicator of economic level was case paperwork. The link between occupation and number of folios in these cases reveals, not surprisingly, the economic hierarchy of litigants: poor litigants averaged cases of only 14 folios, day laborers 26, shepherds 38, porters 47, tailors 55, farmers 57, and nobles and the obviously wealthy 169.

The humbler professions were well represented in impotence trials. Day laborers (*labradores*) and cattle herders (*pastores de ganado*) were at least 14 percent of those charged with impotence before the tribunal (see graph 3, appendix B). Cattle and sheep herders seemed especially susceptible to the impotence accusation because their professions took them far from home for much of the year.[31] A nomadic livelihood like herding made marriages difficult and provided little time for couples to conceive children; at least these were the complaints of Francisco Martínez, who, during thirteen years of marriage to María Jiménez, spent eight months of each year driving livestock to Estremadura. Obviously frustrated, whether owing to the impotence of her husband as she claimed or simply his continual absence, in 1699 María charged Francisco with impotence to gain an annulment.[32] A similar case occurred six years earlier, in the town of Aldeanueva de Cameros (La Rioja). María

Lonbardo filed a case for annulment against her husband, cattle herder Joseph Fernández. Here again, absence, the wife claimed, had impeded consummation. It is just as likely, if not more so, that in these two cases perpetually absent husbands finally drove their wives to search for a way to divorce. In an interview before the court, María Lonbardo's counsel explained that "every year he had gone to the province of Estremadura where he resided nine months of the year in his profession as cattle herder, and the three months that the said Joseph Fernández lived in her place he also went absent watching the livestock so as to have cohabited with her only eight nights."[33] Of the fraction of litigants that revealed their livelihood, six were itinerant livestock herders, and another was a traveling merchant. Considering how often the traveling professions were represented in impotence trials, the absence from the sample of sailors from Bilbao and Spain's northern coast is curious. Still, only six cases originated from the northern coast, and it was rare for occupations to be revealed.

As with women, the average age of husbands in impotence trials was rather young: twenty-nine. The overall youth of the allegedly impotent men in these trials concurs with Darmon's findings for French cases. The youthfulness of these husbands many surprise us, because impotence has often been associated with old age. But these cases did not include even one case of a stereotypical spring-autumn marriage. Among these impotence trials there were no dissatisfied young wives married to wealthy older men. Husbands were generally only three to four years older than their wives. Instead of age, when litigants and doctors stated the possible causes of the impotence in question the factors included illness, shame, an imbalance in body humors, congenital deformity, castration, witchcraft, and youth.

Reputed Causes of Impotence in Men and Women

Accusations made by wives and written by their lawyers were formulaic and mainly concerned with asserting the wife's rights and proving that the woman was not culpable for the nonconsummation of marriage. Therefore wives generally did not specify the reasons for their husbands' alleged impotence. Such specifics were left to medical experts and defense attorneys. Several conditions were recognized as temporary; as such they would not justify an annulment. Youth was more often considered a liability to potency rather than an advantage. Several medical declarations concluded that allegedly impotent young husbands, usually still in their late teens, were only temporarily impotent and would eventually "grow out of it." Diet was an additional factor alleged to cause temporary impotence. Experts suggested that good nutrition, especially a daily dose of wine, could invigorate lifeless virile members. In 1699, Dr. Diez de Ysla, for instance, explained that Antonio Ruiz, from Logroño, was able to deflower a girl seven years after he had been proven impotent because he had recovered "with [his] transformation of age, change of climate, quality of sustenance, and continual use of wine."[34]

Though seventeenth-century physicians and court functionaries lacked the terms used by modern psychology to explain the relationship between an individual's state of mind and impotence, they were neither ignorant of it nor ignored the link. Experts on occasion recognized that shame prevented an otherwise healthy man from experiencing an erection, especially during a medical examination. The tribunal's prosecuting attorney argued on behalf of Antonio Ruiz, for example, that often potent men do not experience erection "owing to the great sense of shame that naturally occasions said inspection . . . as experts are accustomed to declare in similar inspections."[35] The majority of Spaniards likely admitted some belief that witchcraft, curses, or spells could cause impotence. After all, as Keith Thomas has argued, what psychology later claimed to explain in the nineteenth and twentieth centuries, witchcraft did in the seventeenth century.[36] Though a small number of individuals told the court that they had in fact been bewitched, such explanations for impotence were never suggested or given any credence by the church court personnel or any of the medical experts. Though Darmon argues that impotence by evil spell was a popular plea in annulment cases, this was not the case in the Diocese of Calahorra and La Calzada.[37]

The greatest effort by a defendant to convince the court that he had been bewitched, and then successfully cured, came from Antonio Francisco de Idiaquez Vélez Iqueziara in Fuenmayor, 1678. Late in a lengthy battle to clear himself of his wife's charge of impotence, Antonio claimed that he had been cured after visiting an exorcist in the Basque town of Azcoytia. There Antonio was exorcised by the priest Martín Pérez de Heredia, who made the following diagnosis: "And it is certain that the witness [Martín Pérez] from the first exorcism to the last recognized that the said Don Antonio had been cursed for the use of matrimony because [Antonio] always replied according to the demon or demons that aid the spell for the use of matrimony in accordance with the exorcism, seventh folio one hundred ninety four in the treatise *Fustis demonum.*"[38]

With lengthy descriptions, of which the above is only a short excerpt, Antonio, his exorcist Martín Pérez, his friends, and lawyer rhetorically used witchcraft to explain why he had been unable to consummate his marriage. Impotence by evil spell was a versatile defense because such spells could be cured. And Antonio's particular curse, his legal defense claimed, had been cured. Martín Pérez recalled the moment that Antonio expelled the impotence demon: "[while Antonio] continued trembling and vomiting that said day there came from his mouth a toadlike figure about the length of a pinky finger and girth of a sheepskin and on the said figure the witness [Martín Pérez] recognized patently a head, feet, hands, and tail although he did not find it to be alive."[39] According to Martín Pérez and Antonio's cadre of supporters, then, the exorcism restored his potency.

Not only had the exorcism expelled Antonio's troublesome impotence toad/demon, further spiritual investigation by Martín Pérez revealed who had bewitched Antonio in the first place. Pedro Ignacio Vélez de Idiáquez y Guevarra testified that Father Pérez questioned the spirits regarding the impotence spell. The spirits allegedly informed Father Pérez that some woman had used food to bewitch Antonio, thereby preventing him from consummating his marriage. The witness did not know or mention whom the spirits implicated, whether it was Antonio's wife, mother-in-law, or some other woman.[40] But whoever it had been, Martín Pérez and his communing spirits alleged that Antonio was not at fault for his impotence and someone of the opposing party probably was. But Antonio and his lawyer attempted to use the rhetoric of the impotence curse still further. They argued to the court that the couple could consummate their marriage only by performing a similar exorcism on his wife, his accuser, María Michaela de Albelda y Vazen. If she agreed, she would have been placed in the hands, once again, of her husband and his family outside the court of Calahorra and La Calzada's jurisdiction at their home in Navarra. Neither the tribunal nor María Michaela agreed, however, to further exorcisms. Rather than entertain more discussion of witchcraft, the court sided with dozens of medical declarations against Antonio and annulled the marriage.

However, very few impotence trials made any mention of magic, curses, spells, or witches. All descriptions of witchcraft were in defense of impotent individuals, one of them being a woman. Doctors and surgeons never diagnosed impotence as being caused by an evil spell. The court overall disregarded claims of magic in impotence trial proceedings. Yet in the case of Antonio, his wealthy family, friends, and attorney not only believed that an impotence curse could serve as a credible defense, they may have actually been convinced that the spell was real.

It is likely that the majority of Spaniards gave some credence to the belief that impotence could be caused by evil incantations. Certainly exorcists like Martín Pérez, priests famous for their ability to cure men possessed by impotence-causing demons, existed. In the three cases in which exorcisms were described, the men had made pilgrimages to small Basque towns tucked away in mountain valleys to visit exorcists. The existence of witches in the Basque areas of the diocese has become notorious since Gustav Henningsen's history of the Logroño Inquisition's trials against the Basque witches of Zugurramurdi.[41] Witness Pedro Zorzano recalled having journeyed "to the place of Arbayza where there was a priest who, with his prayers, warded off spells and he exorcized them from the witness on one occasion."[42] Research by Darmon, Campo, and historians of early modern witchcraft concludes that Spaniards, as well as peoples throughout Europe, commonly used and/or feared spells designed to render men impotent.[43] According to Darmon, in France such spells often involved tying knots in ribbons and repeating incantations during the wedding ceremony.[44] For the Diocese of Calahorra and La Calzada, however, the only description of a person working a magic spell to make a man impotent describes the use of a magic potion.

Although witchcraft was rarely mentioned in impotence trials, there is every reason to believe that impotence spells were feared, especially by newlyweds, in northern Spain. Witchcraft was likely not referred to for several reasons. First, a spell was not permanent, and the prosecution needed to prove that a spouse was permanently impotent. Second, educated Spanish medical experts did not acknowledge magic, which had been defined by the church as superstition. Third, such impotence curses no doubt were mainly used by a third party against a couple, not by a wife against her husband.

An imbalance in Galenic fluids was also a common reason given for impotence. Rather than account for hidden causes of impotence by suggesting that magic spells had been cast, litigants and medical professionals explained otherwise inexplicably flaccid genitalia in terms of humor imbalances. The doctor-surgeon team of Juan de Salinas and Lucas de la Fuente clearly identified a physiological problem rather than magic as a cause for Juan Martínez de Muro's impotence: "Another cause could be witchcraft about which the [doctor and surgeon] cannot affirm anything, and in so much as the matter touches upon their art as doctor and surgeon they affirm that the said impotence is caused by a cold imbalance of the instruments that serve for procreation as Mercado refers to it in his treatise on male sterility."[45] Medical professionals generally considered heat, associated with blood and yellow bile in the Galenic paradigm, necessary for copulation. Several doctors associated such heat with sexual appetite and the ability for penile erection. Joan Cadden, in her description of medieval cures for overactive adolescent libidos, explains that medieval doctors believed that heat was a cause for, and product of, sexual stimulation. The doctors in the seventeenth-century Diocese of Calahorra and La Calzada, like many of their medieval predecessors, resorted to Galenic humors to diagnose sexual afflictions. In the case of impotence there was a lack of heat, a condition associated with melancholia (cold and wet).[46] Therefore, a ruddy complexion, associated with heat, aided in a positive potency diagnosis.

For doctors and the people their weighty opinions influenced, humors clearly played an important role in a culturally subjective definition of virility. Many doctors described certain physical characteristics as more virile than others, thereby constructing an ideal of virility. Many of the characteristics associated with virility were based, understandably, on male secondary sexual traits such as facial, body, and pubic hair and a deep voice. However, other purportedly "virile" traits, such as a darker skin complexion and an aggressive disposition, were not necessarily secondary sexual characteristics. Again, the traditional Galenic explanation for virility stated that male heat produced these masculine traits: a deep voice, hair, and broad shoulders.[47] Impotence diagnoses by doctors in northern Spain were clear manifestations of traditional European medical discourses on sex differences.

A pallid, tall, thin redhead like Juan de Salazar did not fit the virile phenotype preferred by medical experts in impotence cases. From their examination of the subject, the doctor-surgeon team of Juan Baptista Martínez de Garijo and Matheo de Urrondo determined that Juan was a phlegmatic-sanguine man. They discovered several phenotypical characteristics that revealed the cause of his impotence. He was not muscular and he was of a pale complexion. Furthermore, according to the medical pair, Juan was "gentle and slow to anger."[48] They also complained that he lacked a robust sexual appetite. Worse yet, so far as it impinged on his virility, Juan was in possession of a sizeable penis. Dr. Martínez explained: "as Aristotle says, those with a large plume cannot have too great [of an] erection."[49]

Penis size was rarely mentioned as bluntly as in Dr. Martínez's description as a cause for impotence in court transcripts. The overall opinion of medical experts was that penis size was capricious and was clearly not connected to virility and masculinity. In the words of a Dr. Muñoz of Vitoria: "We see every day small men with large members, and large men with small ones."[50] In the few instances when the issue was submitted as a cause for nonconsummation, large penis size was generally considered a hindrance. According to canon law a man could be deemed impotent with respect to (*impotente respectiva*) a woman if their sexual organs could be proved to be incompatible.[51] If a man's penis was too large for a woman's narrow vagina, for instance, she could claim him impotent vis-à-vis her and seek an annulment. This sexual incompatibility was the charge leveled by Josepha Díaz de Durana against her husband, Juan de Llaranza, in Castillo in 1681. Her attorney Juan de Gámiz Hidalgo stated that his client "is not obligated to undertake the grave risk of a cure, and if she is capable of consummating matrimony, [it is] with a person that does not have the virile member of the magnitude of the aforementioned [husband]."[52] Several medical experts agreed with the sexual incompatibility of the couple and substantiated the wife's fears. The court ultimately decided, though, that Josepha's sexual organ was to blame, not her husband's. The tribunal annulled the marriage, judging Josepha, not her husband, impotent.

A very small virile member, however, occasionally accompanied other signs of failed sexual maturation such as a lack of pubic hair and a high voice. Litigants and court functionaries recognized these characteristics to be those of castrates. In a surprisingly large number of cases, castrates of one form or another defended marriages that they had made, a curious issue that will be explored in the following chapter.

The Determination of Impotence

As discussed in chapter 3, accusations charging women with impotence were relatively easy to verify medically. Proving that a man was impotent was more difficult. The burden of proof clearly fell on the impotent man. The court relied on scores of medical declarations, testimonies, citations, confessions, and interviews in its mission to determine if a husband was impotent or not. Ultimately, endeavors to prove impotence or potency produced more paperwork than credible proof. Such debates wasted amazing amounts of time and money; the average impotence trial lasted one and a half years, but many lasted four or even seven years.

Medical examinations of men invariably resorted to one main physical test, the hot and cold water genital bath, already described in the exemplary case in chapter 1. The medical team would expose the genitalia of the accused to hot and then cold water and observe the dilation and contraction of the organ. It is unclear whether they expected an erection from the test or simply a reaction from the man's penis and scrotum. What is obvious, however, is that some doctors had much higher criteria for potency than others. Many attorneys recognized the limited ability of the hot and cold water bath to determine impotence and attacked the procedure accordingly.

The medical discourse and legal context of these impotence tests found nothing objectionable in acts that could be seen as homosexual because they were part of permissible medical procedure. Rather than enlist "wise women" as medieval English church courts did to test men's genitalia, Spanish church courts trusted the sexual expertise of male surgeons to stimulate a penis to erection.[53] For instance, an additional method that doctors used to discover if a man was impotent or not was the genital massage often administered by surgeons to bring about an erection. Medical declarations commented on this practice only obliquely, however, providing few details. Surgeon Juan de Zaldierna testified that they "used baths of warm water, rubbing, and other acts" to provoke an erection.[54]

Medical experts in the diocese often used the fact that most men experience erections in the early hours of the morning while asleep to prove that men were potent. The same Juan de Zaldierna above, for instance, persisting in his efforts to prove that Antonio Ruiz was potent, testified that "I took him into my house for the entire aforementioned day, and placed a bed in my room, and went to check in on him at midnight; and finally at three in the morning, on the third visit, with certain acts I saw an erection."[55] These extreme pains taken to determine whether a man was impotent or not may seem ridiculous. One would certainly define many of these actions today as intimate acts between men, but ecclesiastical court officials did not note any repugnance to such procedures because they occurred within a medical and legal context.

Medical examinations frequently created more skepticism than certain answers to the impotence question. Defense lawyers cast doubt with ease on medical declarations; these doubts usually led to more physical examinations by other doctors. Like a succession of medieval glosses, medical authority easily followed medical authority until the litigants exhausted the money to pay them.

On rare occasions the ecclesiastical tribunal employed two other legal methods to determine if a man was impotent or not: the *careo* and the *septima manus.* The careo was an interview, literally a confrontation, between the wife and the husband questioned together. In this hearing, conducted directly by the tribunal or one of its agents, the interviewer aimed to bring into the open any discrepancies in the testimonies of the wife and husband. Court officials hoped that the truth would emerge by forcing the parties to confront one another. The court used the careo in only four cases. The careo was likely used as a way to expose straightaway obvious factual inconsistencies.

Septima manus was a medieval method for determining male impotence. Called "examination by seven relatives" (*examinación a siete deudos*) in Spain, this procedure depended completely on the overriding opinions of seven members of the couple's kin.[56] In our sources, the court resorted to septima manus only once, in an impotence trial from Santo Domingo de La Calzada in 1702 involving Ana de la Cámara and Santiago de Redezilla. In this case the tribunal was troubled by the fact that Santiago was a widower who had had no complaints from his first wife regarding impotence. After medical testimonies and conflicting declarations by both parties failed to satisfy the court, the tribunal called for the testimonies of "seven relatives." Several members of the husband's family confirmed that he was indeed impotent and the court annulled the marriage.[57] Unfortunately for Santiago, he had not had any children during his first sixteen-year marriage. Generally when a man could prove that he had fathered children from a previous marriage, or that his wife had had a miscarriage, he ultimately silenced any claim of impotence against him. The issue of miscarriages was important, for instance, in the impotence case against Baptista Ruiz de Alba by his wife, María Beltrán de Guevarra. Baptista ultimately won the case when he convinced the court, with corroboration by witness testimonies, that his wife had had two miscarriages during their marriage.[58]

While the ecclesiastical tribunal itself rarely solicited testimonies to prove or disprove potency, defense attorneys often resorted to eyewitnesses to prove their clients' sexual potency. We've already seen, in the preceding chapter, how crucial and fickle witness testimonies could be in impotence trials. What is more interesting about such testimonies is how public sex and even erections could be. Because sharing rooms and beds was a common practice in early modern Spain, for instance, things that are today private easily became public knowledge in small early modern communities. The fact that Joseph de Zauda and Antonio Francisco de Ydiáquez Vélez Yqueziara shared a bed allowed the former to attest to the latter's morning erection. Antonio's erection gained wider fame when Joseph roused the other men in the house early in the morning to observe it.

When the court had no evidence that a man was impotent—if he proved totally potent before doctors, for instance—the tribunal resorted to the impotence examination's common upshot: the determination of the wife's virginal state. If the couple had consummated the marriage, as the husband often claimed, then the woman would not be a virgin. Because most cases involved young spouses in their first marriages, the nonconsummation that a wife alleged presumed that she was still a virgin. The examination to determine this was usually performed by a midwife under the supervision of a doctor and surgeon. Yet, as Dr. Don Mathias Femat Lobera admitted to the tribunal in 1681: "judging virginity is very difficult."[59] Virginity in women was often as difficult to ascertain as potency was in men. Lawyers just as easily denounced verdicts of virginity as they did judgments of potency. A vaginal examination, therefore, rarely solved the central impotence trial conundrum.

The result of the prying examinations, witness interrogations, and tests was the exposure of a couple's sex life before their parish and community.

However, though the publicity and investigation of Spanish impotence trials exposed the sexual acts and lives of husbands and wives, the tribunal never treated sex nearly as openly to the public as their French neighbors. "Trial by congress," a test in which a husband sexually mounted his wife before witnesses, was relatively common in French impotence trials during the early modern period. Yet the "trial by congress" was apparently a French novelty; neither the term nor its possibility was ever mentioned in documents of impotence trials in the Diocese of Calahorra and La Calzada. Nor did María del Juncal Campo Guinea, in her study of the Diocese of Pamplona, describe the "trial by congress" as ever being used.

Court Verdicts

The church court utilized several options when making its decisions even though there were apparently only two possible rulings. The tribunal could rule the marriage valid and compel the couple to live together, or else the judge could order the marriage annulled. Yet canon law permitted flexible variations of both determinations. Periods of trial cohabitation could be ordered, for instance. Annulments could range from a decision that permitted both parties to remarry, to another that allowed remarriage of the impotent husband only with a widow, to a decision that left one of the spouses socially and sexually ostracized. The court was often forced to rule two or more times in cases that spanned several years. In a case from Santa Cruz de Campezo in 1676, for instance, the court initially ordered the three-year trial period of cohabitation, the triena. The litigation continued, however, after the three-year trial period ended and the tribunal made a second decision allowing an annulment. If a wife was persistent, she could generally successfully annul her marriage to a man she claimed was impotent. Table 6 (appendix A) shows the percentage breakdown of decisions made by the court. Because some cases contained more than one decision, this table does not faithfully reflect the final outcomes of the eighty-three impotence trials.

As shown in table 6, the ecclesiastical court initially allowed 49 percent of couples to annul their marriages, but after trial periods of cohabitation, the court eventually permitted annulments in forty-six of eighty-three impotence trials, or 55 percent of the cases. As explained earlier, the church tribunals could find impotent spouses respectively or relatively impotent. The vicar general ruled only one case of impotence as respective, permitting both man and woman to remarry other individuals. This was the case of Ana María Sáenz versus Juan García described in chapter 2. As you will recall, the logic that annulled their marriage in 1687 rested on medical testimony that Juan's penis was too large for María, especially when compared to the penis of her lover, Francisco Sáenz, which was of more agreeable dimensions. The court ruled that in respect to each other, then, María and Juan did not fit together physically. However, considering the circumstances of the case—especially the fact that both spouses had found other lovers and the two women were pregnant—disaffection rather than disproportion had made María and Juan incompatible. And the court, therefore, demonstrated that it could craft pragmatic solutions for peculiar cases not anticipated by the law code.[60]

In 23 percent of its decisions the court found in favor of the spouse accused of impotence and decreed that the couple "live in the same house, eat at the same table, and sleep in the same bed."[61] The court thereby assumed that cohabitation would solve any problems with consummating the marriage. If the wife demonstrated any resistance to returning to live with her husband, the court would censure and/or excommunicate her until she complied with the court order. Censures generally informed the entire parish of the court's ruling and could therefore place considerable pressure on the wife to return to her husband.

Another common decision, occurring in 19 percent of cases, advocated a trial period of cohabitation. During the allotted months or years, the couple was expected to live, eat, and sleep together and attempt to consummate the marriage. With sex as the goal, the tribunal urged the couple to pray, confess, and attend mass often. The trial period was usually set at three years, the triena already mentioned. However when persuaded by the unique circumstances of different cases, judges could fix the trial period for as little as six months. At the end of a trial period, if the couple still had not had sex and the litigants returned to court, the tribunal would usually allow the wife an annulment.

The court gained further flexibility in its decisions by making wide use of the relative impotence judgment. A decision of relative impotence against a man stated that he was presumed impotent with virgins but totally potent with "corrupted women" or widows. A relatively impotent man could therefore remarry so long as his new wife was not a virgin. A man hoping to remarry after such a ruling would usually have to seek a license from the court, however. He might then order the examination of his prospective wife to confirm that she was not a virgin. The tribunal issued the decision of relative impotence in seven cases. The use of both relative and respective impotence decisions demonstrates how arbitrary church courts could act in annulment cases and how such annulments could approach the criteria of modern divorces.

However, the court also barred many individuals found altogether impotent from remarrying. The men and women that the ecclesiastical tribunal judged to be absolutely impotent were supposed to never remarry. But were they able to remarry despite these verdicts by the court? In his study of French impotence cases, Darmon feels that many impotent individuals did go on to remarry. He argues that the church courts' decisions were often ignored by supposedly impotent men.[62] This may have been the case regarding the wealthy couples he studied in Paris and elsewhere in France, but it seems unlikely that anyone judged absolutely impotent in the Diocese of Calahorra and La Calzada could remarry without deserting the community that knew them. Undoubtedly, for some Spanish men, considering the opportunities of Spain's expansive colonial empire, anonymity in a new town, province, or colony would have easily permitted individuals to remarry. Yet land, money, and family likely tied most women and men to their communities and also to the infamy that impotence rulings had brought them.

Decisions did not change in time because of a change in judges' attitudes. Rather, judgments were much more affected by the activity of the court itself. Annulments were easier or more difficult to obtain over time depending on how accessible the ecclesiastical court was to the public: Was the court near to where prospective litigants lived? Did clerics direct litigants to the court? Were the court offices even open? At least some of these issues were directly addressed by Bishop Pedro de Lepe Dorantes. Again we witness the influence of the reinvigorated tribunal of the late seventeenth century. Because the court was more active in general under the reign of Bishop Lepe (1686–1700), annulments were easier for more couples to obtain. However, the percentage of annulments that the tribunal ultimately granted did not change appreciably between 1650 and 1750 (see graph 4, appendix B). The annulment rate was consistently just over 50 percent of the total number of impotence trials that came before the court for nearly every decade. This fact suggests that the court relied on steadfast criteria for allowing annulments rather than acting on the whim of whoever served as the vicar general. Therefore the frequency of annulments depended on the proximity or activity of the ecclesiastical tribunal, not on any change in the court's attitude to annulments in general.

Litigants dissatisfied with the court's decision, of course, could appeal to a higher court. Appeals to the metropolitan see of Burgos from the Diocese of Calahorra and La Calzada, and from Burgos to the papal nuncio in Madrid, were clearly expensive and lengthy. Only eleven of the eighty-three cases considered here went before the archbishop's metropolitan court in

Burgos. Four cases proceeded to the pope's representative in Madrid. Any impotence trial that was tried in Burgos suffered from the same difficulties that it experienced during its initial hearing, except the metropolitan court case was even more thorough, careful, and verbose in its procedure. The metropolitan court, for instance, would order new medical examinations and more learned medical opinions. In the massive case of Anttonio Francisco de Ydiáquez Vélez Yqueziara, for instance, among many other papers, the metropolitan court received an extensively researched report on the possible causes of the subject's impotence from Dr. Andrés Goméz at the Royal University in Valladolid. There is no clear pattern of decisions on appeal to Burgos. Often the court in Burgos upheld the decisions made in the Diocese of Calahorra and La Calzada, as in the preceding case. Occasionally the original decisions would be overturned. As we shall see in the next chapter, the course of litigation depended less on the court functionaries than on the money and legal schemes of the litigants themselves.

5: Rhetorics of Divorce, Reputation, and the Male Body

> In well-ordered societies a marriage should be reviewed every three years, and dissolved or renewed like a rental agreement. It shouldn't have to last a lifetime and bring everlasting misery to both parties.
>
> —Miguel de Cervantes, "The Divorce Judge"[1]

It should surprise no one that annulments were used as divorces in the early modern period, but the question has actually been often asked and hotly debated. Many authors have asserted that, by the marital impediment of consanguinity for instance, annulments since the Middle Ages in Europe were easily procured and served as de facto divorces. The case for this argument is usually and aptly concluded with the example of Henry VIII of England's first annulment from Catherine of Aragon, which, though it initially failed, was based on affinity. The foremost critic of the opinion that annulments were used as divorces is Roderick Phillips. He ably addresses the question. But in his analysis he assumes that for annulments to have been used as divorces ecclesiastical judges needed to have been corrupt. Phillips implies that by acknowledging that annulments were often used as divorces, one thereby implicates ecclesiastical judges as coconspirators, that they shirked investigating thoroughly the facts of a case. In reference to those cases in which annulments were clearly used as divorces, he writes: "No doubt the ecclesiastical judges can be considered accomplices in these cases."[2] Phillips praises the abilities and character of early modern church judges for their thorough and honest administration of judicial procedures in order to argue that annulments were rarely used as divorces. Though Phillips admits that the cynical abuse of canon law must have occasionally occurred, these cases were rare. Overall, he feels that early modern Europeans were convinced of and complied with the church's laws, on consanguinity and affinity for instance, and behaved according to its mandates. Phillips, then, places great importance on how institutions made and applied law, believing that laws greatly affected the behavior of early modern individuals.

But Phillips's assertion that fraudulent annulments could be caused only by the church court considers just a part of the picture. Church courts and ecclesiastical judges could have easily fallen prey to bright litigants armed with money, good lawyers, and a straw witness or two. As demonstrated below, the court of Calahorra and La Calzada often did fall prey to wily husbands and wives. Furthermore, Phillips's argument that ordinary husbands and wives could not be as cynical about the church's law as these deceptive actions would suggest is also doubtful. It is clear from the cases in this study that the seventh sacrament was often and casually ignored and abused by married couples. As proof that early modern Spaniards dismissed canon law on marriage, consider the fact that in many of the annulment cases in the Diocese of Calahorra and La Calzada the husband and wife had already decided to live separately. The only reason several separated couples came before the court at all was because clerics or the visiting magistrate general ordered them to live together. In a separate study, María del Juncal Campo Guinea found that marriage outside the church was still common in seventeenth-century Navarra.

Phillips's opinion is the product of a perspective that emphasizes the role of the clerical elite, who prevented divorce, and the canon law on marriage that, supposedly, individual husbands and wives were often too timid to contradict. Pierre Darmon, on the other hand, is quite convinced that annulments, especially resulting from impotence trials, were manipulated to be used as divorces. However, he shows a bias similar to Phillips's in that he again focuses on the role of the ecclesiastical judges. Darmon does not see these annulments as divorces but instead as cases of inhumane harassment. Taking a psychoanalytical and anticlerical approach, he argues that the impotence trials against husbands in eighteenth-century France were persecutions of sadly sexually debilitated men by zealous priests: "The trial assumes the form of a sacrifice in the pagan sense of the term, in which the high-priest or judge unburdens himself of his neuroses by transferring them to his victim. This is the deeper meaning of the impotence trial. It is essentially the product of an ill-assimilated sexuality, and the expression of a confused and murky libido. From this came the privileged role of the church in a system devised to channel the impulses of a bruised sexuality and the ragings of unassuaged virility."[3]

Darmon seems to assume that most of the husbands were actually impotent and the Catholic clerics were to blame for their public humiliation. He also makes a caricature of the early modern priest as possessing an "ill-assimilated sexuality." Yet, to judge from synodal decrees and the ubiquitous complaints of early modern Spaniards, Spanish clerics were often quite comfortable with their sexuality and virility, leaving the countryside peppered with single mothers and their illegitimate children.[4] More to the point, however, Darmon is concerned with how impotence trials affected men, what they meant to those condemned impotent and those clerics ordained with arbitrary power. In other words, he sees impotence trials as contests between men. He neglects the perspectives of the women involved. In his brief description of wives involved in impotence trials, they are another persecuted party. According to Darmon, such women had fallen victim to their husbands' sexual dysfunction; they then became despised by society for daring to expose their spouses' sexual deficiencies. However, if we consider the goals of the wives who brought their husbands to trial, we discover a more powerful image. In bringing an end to a marriage, impotence trials had as their first and foremost goal the liberation of the wife. Aside from their goal of ending their marriages, wives who accused their husbands of impotence worked to destroy them publicly and politically. Rather than pitiful victims, such wives were vigorous, often victorious, defenders of their own interests.

What often blinds us to the fact that impotence trials were struggles over women's legal rights are the proceedings' naturally penis-centered charge and procedures. For many wives an impotence trial was a way to gain some power over themselves and what they owned by right. We should not underestimate the fact that women brought these trials to court; clerics rarely brought couples before the tribunal on charges of nonconsummation. Clerics had a significant role in these cases as judges. The ecclesiastical judges in these cases generally acted as mediators in the vicious litigation between the interested parties. The battling spouses had much more at stake than the church. There is little evidence that men accused of impotence were persecuted by the court. When we compare the role of clerics to the those of the litigating wives and husbands and their representatives, we find that church officials spent little money or time in the events of impotence trials despite their supposed "ragings of unassuaged virility."

Annulments, especially those based on impotence, were clearly often used as divorces by Spaniards in the early modern period. There were at least four characteristics of impotence trials in this northern Spanish diocese that demonstrated the close relationship between annulments and divorces. First, these annulments were often pursued and litigated as modern divorces. Court notaries often labeled cases of annulment incorrectly as "divorce," and litigating attorneys and witnesses treated such cases with the same lax terminology. Furthermore, several litigants readily switched their pleas for separation based on abuse to annulment on grounds of impotence. Though canon law might have been specific, in the eyes of married couples the results of a separation and an annulment were nearly the same, especially since these couples were usually already living separately. Second, in the public mind and secular courts the division of the couple's property was the most salient aspect of divorce. Actually dissolving the seventh sacrament was of secondary importance. The church court's decision about whether the spiritual marital bond existed or not, though it could be crucial, was often simply treated as a legal technicality. Third, decisions annulling marriages were flexible, sometimes allowing both husband and wife to remarry. Finally, several cases reveal how easy it was for litigants to lie to and dupe the ecclesiastical tribunal to get the decision that they desired.

Spanish notaries and litigants frequently used the words "divorce," "separation," and annulment based on "impotence" interchangeably. This flexibility in terminology is clearly significant. How litigants perceived their cases must guide an understanding of what these annulments actually meant. An initial 1703 petition to the tribunal for an annulment by María Josepha Pérez Cauallero against her allegedly impotent husband, Pedro Pérez Cauallero, was clearly not a legal suit for separation. Nonetheless, court notaries titled the papers and filed the case as a "divorce." In fact, the accusation that the annulment was going to be used as a divorce was Pedro's primary defense; he charged that Ixea's mayor was behind the prosecution of the case and intended to marry María Josepha after she won.[5] The tribunal made many such filing mistakes, demonstrating a bureaucratic confusion between annulments and separations. These inconsistencies can be explained by either careless organization or lack of legal understanding by the court's staff. But if the tribunal's functionaries misunderstood the meaning of annulment vis-à-vis divorce, then litigants and uneducated Spaniards probably saw no distinction between the two.

A few revealing petitions demonstrate just how unimportant the path to divorce was to many early modern wives. Often a wife's goal was simply to be removed from her husband while maintaining possession of her inheritance, goods, and livelihood. There were preferences, of course. As noted earlier, an annulment was obviously superior to a separation from hearth and cohabitation for wives seeking to remarry. A legal separation allowed no opportunity for a second marriage since that would, of course, be bigamy. Just as in a separation, an annulment allowed for the restitution of a wife's dowry and also gave her half the goods acquired during the marriage. But unlike in a separation, after an annulment a women would be allowed to find a new husband; impotence trials were even more advantageous because they often confirmed a woman's status as a virgin. Occasionally this status was attested to by medical experts. In keeping with the mentality of the era, a bona fide virgin could expect better marital prospects than a woman whose reputation was in doubt.

Perhaps it was the opportunity to remarry that convinced Ysauel Sáenz to first attempt an impotence charge against her husband, Francisco Beltrán, in

1699. But her case against him was weak, so in her petition Ysauel and her lawyer made a secondary accusation. They asserted that her husband also abused her. Ysauel's lawyer, Juan de Gámiz Hidalgo, concluded her petition with the stipulation that "in the case that there is no grounds for an annulment, [we would] place a demand of separation and specify the verbal and physical abuse [by the husband of the wife]."[6] Amazingly, in this case, along with another in 1718, Juan de Gámiz Hidalgo chose to fight alternately for an annulment on grounds of impotence or a separation for abuse based on whichever seemed more plausible to the tribunal. In a similar but even more blatant petition to the church court in 1685, lawyer Francisco López de la Plaça asked for an annulment and/or separation for his client Juana de Ortega.[7] He based his plea not only on the grounds that her husband was impotent and abusive, but also because the wife never gave her consent when she married. López de la Plaça argued that Juana had never agreed to the marriage to begin with. Though such cases do seem suspicious, they do not prove that the wives and their attorneys were deceiving the court. Clearly, impotence could have been accompanied by abuse, and both may have happened to a woman who had been forced to marry. But what these three cases demonstrate is how easily a separation could be exchanged for an annulment and vice versa. Lawyers and litigants considered annulments and separations together as paths to divorce.

Such either/or petitions were rare. Most wives who attempted both annulment and separation pleas to escape marriage were not as candid as Ysauel and her lawyer. Instead, they generally moved from a charge of abuse to one of nonconsummation resulting from impotence only after the first accusation failed. Despite the advantages of annulment over separation, at least two women resorted to a charge of impotence against their husbands only after first seeking separations. In 1708 María de San Juan approached the diocesan court in the hope of receiving a separation from her abusive husband of two years, Gregorio de Astroquiza. Gregorio ignored the litigation against him after the tribunal served him papers to appear before the court. Perhaps aggravated by the husband's apathy, Judge Pedro Oñate y Murillas, María, and her lawyer proceeded with the formalities of a separation. The church court gathered witness testimonies in the couple's town of Meñaca. They continued to petition Gregorio for a response.

Two months after her first petition, however, María changed her plea from separation to a petition for annulment claiming that her husband was impotent and that they had not consummated the marriage. María may have changed her plea because she needed to threaten her husband with more severe consequences than simply living separately in order to force him to respond to the litigation. María complained to the court that Gregorio was already liquidating the goods that the couple owned. The tribunal responded by publicly posting Gregorio's name and the charges of impotence against him in the couple's parish. After four months Gregorio finally responded. He appeared in Logroño to be seen by medical experts, who succinctly judged him impotent. María had successfully used the more drastic charge of impotence to publicly humiliate her husband, force him to respond to the court's legal actions, and gain the freedom from him that she desired when she initially petitioned for a separation.[8] More important for our purposes, María's litigation against her husband shows how a separation could seamlessly transform into an annulment. She did not have to drop her original petition, nor was she forced to begin a new trial against Gregorio. This was because the objective of both charges was the same: divorce.

Dissolution of matrimony was not rare enough in seventeenth-century Spain to have it ignored by marriage contracts. As a demonstration of how widely accepted such de facto divorces were, provisions for annulment were already provided for in many marriage contracts. An annulment stipulation from 1703 that María de Baraya and Juan Baptista de Arriola included in their marriage contract read: "And it is agreed and a condition of both parties that if the Lord our God permits us that this matrimony be dissolved without children, and in case there are if they were to die as juveniles, to each party will be restituted and returned that which each one brought to this matrimony with the declaration that the goods have to be divided according to their use and in agreement with the practice of law."[9]

Such a provision for annulment in a marriage contract may lead us to several different conclusions. It is a wonderful example of how meticulous and thorough early modern marriage contracts were. Notaries designed marriage contracts to ensure that no situation left the ownership of goods, land, and money in doubt. Reading several such contracts may persuade us to believe, as it has many historians, that early modern marriage was primarily an economic institution. Simply because such documents included a stipulation for annulment did not mean that marital dissolution was all that common. But these provisions for annulment do demonstrate that secular law recognized that some marriages genuinely ended, and marriage contracts needed to include provisos for such odd cases. Furthermore, this particular agreement between Juan and María made a condition that the marriage must be dissolved legally; the division of property that the contract outlines would not occur if the couple mutually agreed to divorce outside the laws of church and state. The statement therefore acknowledges the custom of couples divorcing illegitimately.

Individuals involved in the administration of secular law, corregidors, municipal judges, lawyers, and especially notaries, perhaps saw annulments more realistically as de facto divorces. As we have already seen in chapter 2, ecclesiastical synods in Spain had long complained about the contracts devised by notaries that permitted divorces and hammered out the legal and material consequences for the interested parties. In the seventeenth century the church had generally educated secular courts and their functionaries that cases involving the making and breaking of matrimony belonged in the church courts. The church had successfully defended its jurisdiction over marriage. Divorce cases that appeared before the Real Chancillería in Valladolid, for instance, came into the royal jurisdiction only per force—termed *via de fuerza*—on appeal from an ecclesiastical court, and rarely without a legal battle.[10] Yet even though secular law yielded to the jurisdiction of the ecclesiastical courts over separation and annulment, secular judges, lawyers, and notaries continued to regulate the legal provisions regarding the division of estates and payment of legal costs of these de facto divorces.

As a rule, the actual motivations of the litigants in impotence trials were disguised. It is as difficult for us today to guess at a litigant's true motivations for bringing their case to court as it is to trust the claims of their plea. But there were a number of trials in which the motivations of the litigating wife or husband were bluntly stated. Other trustworthy facts emerge in confessions or the reconciliation of the parties. There were occasional examples of annulments that clearly were the de facto divorces that Cervantes described in his *Divorce Judge:* such divorces were the fruits of agreements made between conniving husbands and wives who no longer desired each other's company. The investigation of the court's prosecuting attorney in Bilbao in 1678 uncovered one of these ruses designed to fool and use the ecclesiastical court.

The Bilbao corregidor for Charles II, Domingo de Uribarri, understood that only the church could adjudicate separation and annulment cases. But for the corregidor and one couple who were mutually eager to divorce, Juan de Jaugregui and Francisca de Renteria, an ecclesiastical annulment was a mere technicality and an afterthought. According to the accusation of the tribunal's prosecuting attorney who discovered their true intentions, "they are asking for an annulment of their marriage more for their particular earthly interests than for the service of Our Lord God."[11] On September 10, 1678, Juan, his parents, Francisca, and her father stood together with the corregidor and ratified a contract that would split the couple's goods and restore the wife's dowry once they annulled their marriage. The couple also agreed to split the court costs of the ecclesiastical trial for annulment that they would have to argue before the church court in Logroño. Two months later Francisca appealed to the ecclesiastical court for an annulment based on the impotence of her spouse. Her husband dutifully refused to respond to the allegations of impotence. Francisca's lawyer, Juan de Gámiz Hidalgo, then argued that, seeing that the husband failed to reply to the charges of impotence, the annulment should be allowed.[12] Had the prosecuting attorney not discovered the couple's ruse, they would have handily won an annulment; no decision completed the case, and so whatever the couple ended up doing, they did not win an annulment from this court.

No case demonstrates the ability of ordinary Spaniards to manipulate the ecclesiastical court and its decisions for their own purposes better than that of Francisco de Dueñas against his wife, María de Henériz. On the May 6, 1699, Francisco appeared before the court in Logroño declaring that after being married to María for the past three and a half years, he had been unable to consummate the marriage because he suffered from the "natural impediment of absolute impotence."[13] He then asked to be seen by medical experts to confirm his impotence. Francisco was in a rush. Only three days later and before the ecclesiastical court could officially accept the case and inform his wife, Francisco had already been examined by Dr. Don Francisco Diez de Ysla of Logroño. The doctor succinctly declared him impotent, finding that the supposed twenty-three-year-old was "thin, limp, and of a humid temperament in all parts of the body and in those that serve for procreation . . . he is missing the right testicle and there is some weakness in the other testicle."[14] The ecclesiastical court declared the marriage annulled and sent their verdict to Francisco's wife.

By the time news of Francisco's petition and annulment reached his wife and she could respond, it was already August, and she was seven months pregnant. María had been staying with her father after a fight with her husband in May. Her father, Dr. Juan Martínez de Henériz, gave angry testimony before the ecclesiastical court in Logroño on September 25 regarding the results of their hasty decision: "And with the said decree [of annulment] the said Francisco de Dueñas, her husband, ran off to the city of Seville, and from there embarked to the Indies."[15] María's father went on to explain to the court that even though Francisco had only one testicle, he was notoriously virile: he "would have an erection and ejaculate and . . . had declared as much to different people, talking about the complaints of his wife and of how my daughter is presently eight months pregnant."[16] By the time his father-in-law presented this evidence to the court, Francisco was gone. María gave birth to a daughter on October 10. Her lawyer fruitlessly continued to file motions for Francisco to appear before the court. Eventually María and her daughter went to live in the protection of a nearby convent in Cañas.

This second case tells us much more about impotence trials than the majority of cases whose decisions were never reviewed or reversed. It demonstrates that impotence trials were a well-known stratagem to gain a divorce. Ordinary Spaniards, not just clerics and lawyers, knew that impotence could serve as a means to escape marriage. Francisco not only knew that he could get out of marriage by faking impotence, he pretended impotence for the medical examination and moved his case through the court quickly and adeptly, getting a letter of annulment in a matter of days. Francisco and María's case clearly shows that claims of impotence might hide various other causes of marital breakdown. Francisco's reasons for entering a plea of impotence included a disagreement with his wife and the impending birth of a baby. Francisco also easily convinced a university-trained doctor and a barber-surgeon to declare him impotent. Whether this was enabled by a bribe or the fact that he lacked a testicle is not significant. More important is the fact that, even by contemporary standards, medical testimony was highly ambiguous and contradictory. Finally, Francisco's case also reveals the public character of sexuality in seventeenth-century Europe; according to his father-in-law, Francesco's virility was notorious in the town.

Judicial decisions in impotence trials varied significantly. Judges were undoubtedly greatly influenced by political factors when they declared who was impotent or not and who would remain married or be freed. The fact that decisions widely contrasted with one another was not simply due to the different circumstances of each case or the innate ambiguity of the resting penis's hidden potential (no doctor, surgeon, or judge really knew how a well-formed pudenda and testicles, inexplicably quiet, might perform under the right circumstances). Canon law itself was incomplete, unclear, and easily manipulated by judges who had to make specific choices. Ecclesiastical judges, in fact, were often forced to make decisions because they could not know the secrets of a couple's sex life. Their doubtful decisions could easily be appealed by the litigant who lost. The ecclesiastical court could not refuse to allow appeals to proceed to Burgos (though, as we shall see, by failing to give a decision the court could effectively end a plea). Given enough money the case could play for months, maybe years before the metropolitan tribunal of Burgos. Several more doctors, surgeons, and midwives would testify before the tribunal. If the ecclesiastical court in Burgos finally made its tenuous decision, the case might even go before the papal nuncio in Madrid. For those litigants who had them, money, political influence, and time were the most important deciding elements of impotence cases. The existence of the impotence in question was rarely a provable and determining factor.

Unlike their French neighbors, Spaniards could not, or at least did not, avail themselves of the infamous "trial by congress." The trial by congress was never mentioned in impotence trials before the bishop's court of Calahorra and La Calzada, the metropolitan tribunal in Burgos, or the papal nuncio's court. The church court was well aware that male litigants could suffer from what would be called today "performance anxiety." Spanish doctors and jurists often noted the chilling effect that shame caused in men during medical examinations.

But despite its flaws, the French trial by congress did have the benefit of being unambiguous: the husband could do it or could not. Unfortunately, Spanish judges could not avail themselves of the finality of a trial by congress. The actual potency or impotence of the accused remained concealed. However, ecclesiastical judges could pronounce several ambiguous decisions, neither annulling a marriage nor completely finding for the allegedly impotent husband. To provide a further test of a marriage, ecclesiastical judges could decide that a husband and wife must cohabit for a trial period. Often this trial period could be the typical three years, called a *triena* in Castilian, *triennium* in Latin. As early as Emperor Justinian, Roman law in Europe had provided for such a trial period when a spouse was accused of impotence.[17] While Pierre Darmon found only two decisions allowing a triennium in France for all of the seventeenth century, in the Diocese of Calahorra and La Calzada alone judges resorted to this solution on no less than eleven occasions.[18] In other cases, however, judges called for a shorter trial period of a year. As we shall see below, perhaps the easiest solution for the ecclesiastical tribunal in a distasteful or ambiguous case was to make no decision at all, allowing litigation to exhaust itself when the litigants ran out of money, time, or patience.

Christian Sexual Rhetoric in Impotence Trials

When litigants, lawyers, and witnesses made statements about sex in the context of an impotence trial, they revealed various sexual attitudes held by Spaniards in the early modern period. For the most part statements made by Spaniards in these impotence trials confirm much of what we already know about early modern sexual discourse and sentiments. Legal documents treated lust as a feared and powerful element of social disorder. Court officials always pointed to women as the source of this social disorder. The authors of legal petitions described sex in marriage as the possession and control of a woman by a man. Also in full accord with the sexual attitudes of western Europe, court documents time and again described virginity not only as a pure and perfect state but as a powerful one as well. On the other hand, medical reports and witness testimonies depicted women who were not virgins in terms that conveyed mainly disgust. Legal petitions characterized impotence in the marital bed not as an illness or a lamentable condition but as a deception perpetrated by a fraud.

These discreet and various attitudes dealt with many different sexual circumstances. But all such attitudes, whether they concerned a pregnant girl or an impotent husband, sprang from a perspective that early modern Spaniards shared regarding the place of sex in the order that God gave to the universe. One constant in this sexual universe was the role played by physical lust. To understand the threat that impotent husbands posed to the social order that the church worked to create, it is essential to understand the contemporary concern over lust.

The authors of court documents portrayed lust in impotence trials as a natural, ubiquitous evil. It was natural because it was part of God's established order. In other words, the church did not consider heterosexual lust a perversion, as it did homosexuality.[19] Lust led to fornication, which court officials treated as a lamentable but understandable outcome of desires that were part of the divine cosmological order. That is to say, fornication was an *illegitimate* use of a Godly ordained act, heterosexual sex. Though it may seem strange that descriptions of coitus appeared in impotence trials, witnesses often gave explicit testimonies that contained descriptions of acts of fornication, as when wives had affairs with men other than their impotent husbands.

Lust between man and woman was treated as an understandable evil because, though fornication was a sin, it formed part of the Catholic Church's cosmology that was ultimately based on Aristotelian symmetry. According to Aristotelian concepts of order and the universe, male balanced female, hot with cold, dry with wet, and so on.[20] The bodily union of man and woman was a symbol of the unification of Christ and the church, whether it occurred between spouses or not. One indication that the church treated sex as a divine act in itself was the fact that canon law decreed that an "affinity" existed between any man and woman who had had sex; this "affinity" entered into the calculations of consanguinity that ultimately determined if a couple could marry without a dispensation.[21] In a hypothetical circumstance, then, if José had sex with Josepha, an affinity was created between the two. If José then planned to marry Josepha's daughter, the affinity between him and the mother would pose an impediment. In the eyes of church canonists, extramarital sex created a spiritual connection that transcended the sexual act itself. Still, to have heterosexual sex outside of marriage was to abuse this symbol of Christ's union with his church. Church fathers had come to base the canonical view of sex on interpretations of several biblical scriptures. One of these important passages was Saint Paul's instruction to the Corinthians: "Or do you not realize that anyone who attaches himself to a prostitute is one body with her, since *the two,* as it is said, *become one flesh.*" Though church dogma never approved of sex that caused social disorder, when a man and woman succumbed to pleasures of the flesh they were rarely described in court documents in derisive terms. Instead such incidents were treated as tragic, understandable human failings.

This tolerance for sexual weakness was reflected in many of the documents in impotence trials. Sex outside marriage between a man and a woman, a priest and a maid, was often attributed to weaknesses of the flesh. The language used by court functionaries lessened the culpability of these poor victims of the flesh. According to her lawyer, such was the plight of María de Ocana in Haro at the end of the seventeenth century. During seven years of marriage to her allegedly impotent husband Matheo del Campo, she, "carried away by the fragility of the flesh, had carnal relations with [name crossed out] from the town of Haro, who deprived her of her flower and Virginity by which she became pregnant and gave birth to a girl that was apparently from the said cleric."[22] Here the anonymous cleric and María's carnal weakness were understandable results of his and her unfulfilled sexual desires; his weakness was amplified by a vow of chastity, hers by an impotent husband. Of course this was a weakness emphasized by the rhetoric of the woman's defense attorney, which was ultimately successful (she received an annulment and permission to remarry).

A further example of the tolerance that the court showed for weaknesses of the flesh was the confession of Melchora de Olazabal. In a declaration that related her amorous Christmas Eve encounter with a priest, Melchora told the tribunal her personal reenactment of the Fall: "He carried with him nearly four dozen apples . . . and of these he gave some to [me] . . . and [I] accepted them with good will. . . . I took the said fruit and began to eat of it, and immediately I recognized having at that time a certain uneven pulse and sensual movement, brought on by the love for the said Don Francisco."[23] The priest then pursued Melchora and ravished her in a nearby garden. Don Francisco consoled Melchora that "as they were young they would not die so soon and that they would have enough time to confess with the passage of time."[24] They repeatedly fell victim to temptation several times over the following days and weeks. Neighbor and witness Catharina de Azazeta refused to condemn the couple. After all, she said, "they have always kept it secret until the present occasion and in the eyes of the neighbors of this town they have not encountered any scandal whatsoever."[25]

What these two cases demonstrate is not necessarily a leniency by the court when it considered punishing sex outside of marriage; instead they reveal a widely held assumption that defined lust, elicited by and directed at women, as a pervasive temptation that had to be guarded against at all times. As such, these northern Spanish concerns exemplified a centuries-old European misogynist tradition. European religious authors who vehemently criticized women as the root of social disorder were motivated by men's fears that they would fall victim to the female body. In northern Spain, apprehension over the sexual power of women warranted, in the eyes of diocesan officials, rules and laws whose purpose was to control women and contain their sex. An example of such precaution was the pronouncement of the diocesan synod of 1698 limiting female servants in clerical housing to those who would, supposedly, not be as sexually tempting: "We permit that women can enter with the food, being over forty years old or younger than twelve."[26] If patriarchal authority at home and matrimony were the first lines of defense in the church's battle to control female sexuality, then having priests avoid women who could get pregnant was the second.

The ecclesiastical court did not attempt to regulate sexual behavior vis-à-vis the honor code. The discourse of honor did, of course, appear in court documents; but questions of honor were always tangential issues that were never debated or investigated by the court. Recent investigations into the early modern Spanish code of honor have demonstrated that it was a secular means to control sexual behavior. Ann Twinam's studies of the honor code in the Spanish colonies have shown how female honor was relative, not absolute, and that honor was a public, not private, quality. Perhaps a useful way to conceptualize the use of honor in Spain, which some authors depict as an unwritten code of law, is instead as a public economy of repute. Honor could be gained or lost depending on public reputation. Like money, one could be born with various amounts of honor. In the early modern period honor could be bought and sold.

Perhaps the most important aspect of honor in relation to impotence trials was its public nature. Honor was never private but instead was based on public reputation. So long as a person took measures to keep dishonorable behavior concealed from a community, and maintained their reputation, honor went unharmed. As Twinam has expertly demonstrated, women could create two separate identities by tending to their public reputation regardless of their private realities.[27] One identity was public and based on an honorable reputation. The other was private and based on their behavior behind closed doors. Though questions of honor could drive some individuals to homicide and suicide, the honor code was actually quite flexible, and individuals often did act contrary to the dictates of honor. Church courts were not primarily concerned with the honor code because their jurisdiction was the private and spiritual lives of individuals. The Diocese of Calahorra and La Calzada made provisions to protect the reputation and honor of women only in certain circumstances. One type of instance in which the court demonstrated concern about honor was that in which a married woman was indirectly implicated in adultery. In such cases the ecclesiastical court would strike the names of the adulterous wife from witness testimonies *por el honor del santo matrimonio.* And even here it was the honor of the sacrament, not the individual, that the tribunal aimed to protect.

As part of this effort to order society sexually, the church needed to help communities define who was and was not a man. Hermaphrodites, those who were patently between sexes and often derided as monsters, presented church courts with urgent and difficult cases of sexual ambiguity. In the Diocese of Calahorra and La Calzada we have the case of Juan/a de Leyda. In 1711 the tribunal of the diocese began an investigation into the question of whether Juan/a de Leyda was able to marry or not. Juan/a's sexual ambiguity began to worry family and community members when, at the age of twenty-one, s/he showed obvious interest in sex and marriage as a man. Juan/a engaged in "an illicit exchange" with a girl of his parish with whom s/he had also discussed marriage.[28] Court physician Dr. Lucas de Salas physically examined the young individual in the city of Calahorra on April 16, 1711. Dr. Salas displayed his disgust in a medical report to the court. With the considerable weight of his learned opinion he denied Juan/a any claim to a gender: "There being the virile member (if it even merits that name) . . . that nature (which always is parted from one) divided to make two instruments from what should have been one; two were made, and both with total imperfection."[29]

Without a gender, Juan/a lost considerable opportunities in the community. The tribunal did what it could to sexually quarantine Juan/a. The judge aimed to protect the village of Salinillas from what he considered a horrific sexual anomaly. Juan/a was ordered not to leave Salinillas, not to enter the service of the church, not to have illicit sexual contact with anyone, and s/he certainly was not to marry. The fact that Juan was not permitted to enter the clergy highlights a curious and important point regarding how the body was connected to sanctity, order, and sexuality. The canon law that required clerics to be physically intact dates back to the Council of Nicaea.[30] Juan/a was considered a sexual monster and therefore had neither the rights of a man nor a woman, lay or cleric. Yet outwardly, Juan/a was expected to reinforce and conform to the strict division of genders that ordered society, even though it could not apply to her/him. The court mandated that s/he dress as a man, and commanded the local parish priest to doctor Juan/a's baptismal record. They changed her/his name at birth from "Juana" to "Juan."[31]

With the preceding case in mind, it should be noted that members of the community, not the church court, often brought people who might cause sexual disorder to the attention of authorities. Direct accusation to the court, or quiet denunciation to neighbors, a bailiff, or a local priest were the usual paths to judicial scrutiny. The church court, in other words, did not search for and destroy sexual reprobates; rather, it relied on the active participation of the community. Members of the community were anxious about individuals in their midst who did not merit the rights pertaining to manhood: rights of inheritance, local political rights, and social stature. Womanhood, usually marked by entrance into marriage, was also guarded by ritualistic communal standards.[32] Furthermore, even though the church court required Juan to remain celibate, he/she could not join the ranks of the clergy in the service of God. Those chosen to serve Him needed to fit into His perfectly ordered creation. Despite some early modern literature that suggested a place in creation for the hermaphrodite, at the local level Juan/a was considered an anomaly, a monster, and his imperfect soul was revealed by his imperfect body.[33] But sexual imperfection and illegitimacy was to be found in other conditions as well, such as in eunuchs and monorchids.

Manhood in Spain has long been associated with *cojones,* "balls," (testicles). Ethnographer Anton Blok, perhaps, explains this connection best: "*Hombría* [manliness] implies a direct reference to the physical basis of honour: those who live up to this ideal have *cojones* (testicles), while those who fail to show fearlessness are lacking in manliness and are considered *manso,* that is, castrated, tame."[34] Into the twentieth century Basque mothers fed their boys rams' testicles in soup ("Rocky Mountain oysters") to ensure they would grow into men. Charles II, that last, sterile, pitiful Hapsburg who left Spain without an heir, was fed bulls' testicles, again in soup, in the hope they might conjure his own virile spirits. Cases in which castrates appeared in court reveal better than any litigation communal anxieties about manhood, marriage, and gender status. Castration in Spain has a long history. Historians interested in the development of musical castrati in Europe often point to Islamic Spain as the source of early castrates and the medieval practice of castration. Spain, however, cannot be singled out as the originator of European castration, at least according to musical historian Richard Sherr, who points to the long tradition of castrates in northern France as well.[35] For the purposes of this investigation, what can be stated more concretely is that in the early modern era the removal of either one or both testicles from young boys was, apparently, not entirely rare in Spain.[36] Whether they lost testes to cure a hernia, become a castrato singer, or for another purpose altogether, several men appeared in court lacking testicles. It should be of no surprise that common health problems regularly left many early modern Spanish men lacking testicles. Referring to Italy, Valeria Finucci has found a similar situation: "Castration was hardly uncommon in the Renaissance, and not so much because there were castrati singers, I would argue, but because at any given day a number of men circulated in the streets with somewhat suffering or damaged genitalia."[37] The presence of men who lacked one or both "cojones" (testicles) in small communities meant that manhood had a discernable physical component; no one could take it for granted that all men were, indeed, sexually intact.

One entertaining example of the sentiment that the possession of testicles was sometimes to be doubted comes from the seventeenth-century comedy *The Examination of Suitors.* In search of an appropriate husband, Marquesa Doña Inés interviews several male candidates. During one of the examinations a servant turns to the audience and says, "What a beautiful thing, a melodic and subtle voice, from a man with such a beard!"[38] The implication is that, given his soft voice, there was the possibility that he might be a castrate. In this instance, all doubt was removed by the suitor's full beard.

Physically emasculated men, often pilloried by communities in small villages as "capons," provided important foils against which masculinity could be defined. Regardless of their infamous local reputations, or perhaps to restore them, these castrates occasionally attempted to marry. They were determined to claim masculine status in court, thereby proving to their communities and families that they were men. Of these married castrates, some were taken to court and thereby entered the historical record (see table 3, appendix A).

As an initial example we have Juan de Aleson, who, in 1685, was forced to separate from his wife of twenty years, María de Lagaria, because their families claimed Juan was a castrate. Why the families decided to denounce the couple to court after so many years of marriage is unknown. Perhaps inheritance issues came into question; maybe the community had simply gradually grown intolerant of the couple as an anomaly. Both were residents of the town of Nájera, a small town that lies in the dry northern plain of Old

Castile, just south of the Ebro River, in the modern province of La Rioja. Aware that as a castrate Juan was unfit for matrimony, family members took the case to the bishop's court in Logroño to annul the marriage.

In beginning its investigation the court first ordered Juan and María to separate. The court discovered that Juan had long been widely known in the community as a castrate—further proof that manhood required both cojones and a reputation for having them. Not only had many people known him to be a castrate, but even Juan had often candidly admitted that he lacked testicles. In one of the many stories that witnesses recalled about Juan's reputation as the local eunuch, a man named Juan Izquierdo junior began a fight with Juan de Aleson. During the squabble Juan "el capon" allegedly impugned Izquierdo's masculinity by saying that he regretted "that he didn't have balls to give him."[39] Yet despite his well-known reputation as "el capon," Juan de Aleson had been married to María de Legaria for twenty years. There seemed to have been some alarm at the time of their marriage. According to the testimony of their neighbor Bernabe de Arriaza, when Juan's older brother asked María de Legaria why she married a castrate, she replied "that that way she would be free from dying in childbirth."[40] Though the marriage was undoubtedly unusual, no one of the family was concerned enough about the marriage initially to bring the couple to court. Only when María, failing to avoid the dangers of childbirth, begat a child did family members finally interfere and work to bring an end to her false marriage to Juan. The child might have kindled family anxiety about claims to their estate. They may have needed to demonstrate that the child could not have been Juan's and therefore had no right to his property and theirs.

Community and family members' litigation to end Juan's marriage illuminates the social issues that castration most affected. The community was asserting its belief that manhood in their society should not be claimed by anyone who was not physically capable of penetrative, reproductive sex. A neutered man could not reproduce, could not have a lineage, and therefore should not marry and maintain a household. Exclusion from these institutions resulted in being barred from local politics because only heads of households could fully participate in municipal government. Sexual capacities were the foundation for gender distinctions and rights. The Catholic Church had long before defended this widespread concern for communal sexual order in Spain. Pope Sixtus v unequivocally prohibited marriage to castrates in 1587 when he responded to the Spanish papal nuncio's question about several women in Madrid who had married eunuchs.[41]

The prevalence of castrated men was a crucial factor if we are to attempt to understand the discourse of early modern sexuality. Did the discussion of sex and gender assume that there was a population of physically emasculated males? Certainly more boys were castrated during the seventeenth century in Spain than we might expect. Castration often guaranteed an individual an education and thereafter a livelihood singing in cathedral choirs. Such an income would not only have benefited the castrato but, more importantly, the family that castrated him. The obvious conclusion that many historians have drawn from the pervasiveness of castration in early modern Spain, then, is that it was a means of social mobility for impoverished peasant families. Poor Spanish peasant families, the scenario goes, with too many mouths to feed, eking out a living farming the infertile soil of the Spanish central plateau, saw the castration of a son as a means to better their material condition. Castration would win for him an education, and an income, and thus provide the parents with a means to escape poverty. If particularly talented, a young castrato might hope to win entrance into the Royal School of Boy Singers.[42]

Of more than 250 marital litigation cases in the church court of the Diocese of Calahorra and La Calzada between 1650 and 1750, there were nineteen cases of castrated men. Thirteen had had one testicle removed, and six lost both. Admittedly, this is not an overwhelming number of castrates and monorchids (monotesticular men); and it should not be surprising to find such people involved in impotence trials. Yet several characteristics of these suits demonstrate that such castrations were more common than we might expect. In one seventeenth-century French parish, Patrick Barbier claims to have discovered more than five hundred boys castrated under the pretext of hernia operations.[43] Outside of the many documented cases that I have found in Spain, the court often treated missing testicles as ordinary rather than extraordinary. The many men who were castrated but did not attempt to marry, and therefore did not appear in the court records, can only be guessed at. But by all accounts castration was common enough to be a characteristic of early modern society that we would not recognize today. Michael McVaugh has demonstrated the popularity of castration in Italy beginning in the fourteenth century and clearly linked it to hernia surgery.[44] The fact that *hernista,* "hernia surgeon," was a profession unto itself speaks to the prevalence of castration throughout Spain. Up until the mid-eighteenth century hernia surgery usually involved the removal of testicles.

Several musicologists have argued that hernia operations in the early modern period were often pretexts for castration.[45] Some contemporary Spaniards held the same opinion. One eighteenth-century Spanish surgeon painted a grim picture of the dishonest hernia surgeon: "The day being selected, the parents abandon the house because they lack the courage to listen to the cries of their son: some of the assistants are disturbed, others are troubled, and no one looks clearly at the actions of the surgeon, in this manner giving approval to what he does. He carries out his bloody show, pulling out the balls, while pretending to have left them inside [the boy]."[46] According to this same author, one particular gelder had a hungry dog on hand to which he would slip the severed organs during the operation, thereby destroying the evidence.[47] The above scenarios generally placed the blame for castration on deceptive hernia surgeons and on the church, which created a demand for castrati voices. Such literature was, of course, part of typical eighteenth-century anticlerical polemic, but the main thesis of such descriptions rings true: the popularity of castrati necessitated the invention of common pretexts for castration. Hernias were a common pretext.

A couple of cases in the Diocese of Calahorra and La Calzada corroborate the implication that at least some hernia surgeons purposefully castrated boys in early modern Spain. Agueda Yzquierdo, for instance, could recall the castration of Juan de Aleson, the full castrate who later married María de Legaria. Agueda testified, somewhat matter of factly, that Juan's father "arranged to castrate the said [Juan de Aleson] his son and the gelder or hernia surgeon was in his house to perform [the castration]. As she was a neighbor, the witness passed by the house and saw how the said surgeon castrated and gelded of both sides the said Juan de Aleson."[48] Unfortunately the witness never stated exactly why Diego castrated his son. In another case a witness claimed that, because the hernista was conveniently in the village operating on his own boy, another man arranged to have his son castrated too.[49]

Family members, more often than the church itself, worked to publicize the genital deficiencies of their kin. In 1689 José Ruiz de Çorçano petitioned the church court for a marriage license because family members were allegedly preventing him from marrying: "Some of his relatives, for hate and ill will and for other personal ends have informed [the priest] that he suffers from . . . impotence . . . [because] they removed both [of his] testicles."[50] José argued that this was simply a lie, that he was fit for marriage, and asked the court to interview the surgeon who had performed to operation. The tribunal did just that, and brought master hernia surgeon Joseph Matute before the court to testify. The hernia surgeon confirmed José's claim, making it clear in his testimony that he had left him with one healthy testicle. After a physical examination of José, a separate doctor and surgeon team concurred, and the ecclesiastical court gave the young man permission to marry. He was confirmed in his manhood.

Four months later, however, José's older brother, Juan Ruiz Sorzano, hired a lawyer to contest his younger brother's right to marry. He urged the court to reverse its first decision. Juan begged the court not only to forbid his younger brother a marriage license, but to make him pay the court fees and order José to be forever silent on the subject of any future matrimony. Juan, the older brother, justified this meddling into his brother's life "because my complaint is legitimate and legal to contradict [my brother] because it looks to the defense and service of God."[51] Not only was Juan interested in stopping a castrate from polluting what was a holy sacrament, marriage, he also asserted "that [my complaint] prevents serious inconveniences that would occur if it would happen that [José] marries."[52]

This case shows how important full masculine status could be for a family and community. Both brothers' pleas to the court reveal a family feud over money, land, and possibly even petty political power in a small community. Their clash was not just about this one marriage. Juan and the family, in fact, wanted José never to marry. Therefore the case did not arise because this particular bride was a bad match for José. If José ever married, he would apparently ruin an overall family plan. Why? The motivations are only hinted at in the petitions and the trial. José claimed that his family was preventing the marriage because of hatred, ill will, and with "other personal goals" in mind. Juan argued that a marriage by José would cause "serious inconveniences." Economic motivations are the most likely cause of the dispute. Juan, as an older brother, may have wanted to preserve the family's estate, keeping it for himself and his own children. An unmarried brother would have lived off the estate, but would not have been able to alienate any part of it to his own wife and children. There was little to worry about if one's younger brother was a reputed castrate. Perhaps the castration of his younger brother had even been planned; though gruesome, this would not have been such a bizarre practice and was not unknown in other parts of Europe. According to Patrick Barbier, in Naples peasant families with four or more sons were permitted to castrate one for the benefit of the church.[53] With his brother's marriage, Juan would also cede some of the family's political standing in the community. José, for his part, would become an independent vecino with a voice in the community, as well as gain a family and household of his own. The castration of José, then, was perhaps a way to prevent the alienation of the family's estate.

Two years earlier the court witnessed a similar quarrel from the town of Villar del Rio. In this case Domingo de Viana was being prevented from marriage by his father, Matheo de Viana. The seventy-year-old Matheo personally warned the local priest that his son, Domingo, at the age of twenty-seven, was a castrate. The priest was thereby forced to stop the banns for Domingo's approaching marriage. In testimony to the court the priest stated that when Domingo's father announced Domingo's lack of manhood, the son "for having been prevented [from marriage by his father] . . . placed hands on [his father] and treated him very badly."[54] Domingo had been "castrated" at the age of two, and again a year later (the word used was "castrated," but these were apparently hernia operations). His father believed that these two operations had left his son fully castrated. Matheo had supposed that the hernia surgeon left only one testicle within Domingo "for appearances."[55] He had been content to know that his young son had been left unmarriageable. Perhaps the father in this case, so late in life, was intent on preventing the marriage of a son because he hoped to keep an inheritance intact, perhaps in the hands of another son. In any case, manhood was to be denied Domingo, as it would be denied those who were impotent.

As demonstrated in the case of castrates, manhood clearly depended on physical attributes: being a sexually intact male. The social-sexual order that the ecclesiastical court attempted to create and defend demanded physical standards for men and women based on traditional European assumptions about human sexual nature. Many sexual acts also breached the sexual order of the Christian cosmogony. In several impotence trials, for instance, wives accused their husbands of illegitimately using fingers or instruments to penetrate their vaginas. The lawyer for Josepha de Echabarría demanded that she be placed in a safe house "owing to the real fear that . . . the said Antonio Ruiz . . . plans to break the Virginal Seal with his hands."[56] Lawyers for wives in impotence trials made their pleas according to a conception of sex that permitted only one true sexual interaction: coitus. Plaintiffs portrayed other acts by husbands as violent, deceptive, and cowardly. From such a view of sex, there was but one legitimate tool to penetrate the vagina: the penis. An impotent man could not be a husband because he could not have legitimate sex.

In the estimation of medical experts, the sexual act of consummation, when it occurred, was a mere physical act. Yet the rhetoric that surrounded that sexual act in the language of impotence trial pleas was far from plain. Litigants and their lawyers always described the nuptial consummation in highly ceremonial and symbolic language. A wedding was an act of taking possession of the bride by the groom; marital sex was the control of the wife by the husband. The possession of a newlywed wife occurred when her husband took and deprived her of her virginity. The initial sexual act was invariably described in words that either conveyed a women's sense of loss—"remove," "deprive," "lose," "get" (*quitar, privar, perder, lograr*)—or her ruination—"break," "violate," "deflower" (*romper, violar, desflorar*). What a woman was supposedly losing on her wedding night, though much debated in impotence cases, was her hymen.

The words that lawyers used to describe the virgin vagina emphasized its perfection and power. Doctors often diagnosed men as impotent relative to virgins in the belief that only the most virile penis could penetrate the hymen. Court functionaries alternately called the hymen the "virginal cloister" (*claustro virginal*) or the "virginal seal" (*sello virginal*). It is important to note that notaries always capitalized "Virginal Cloister" as they did other words that conveyed respect or power, such as "Matrimony" or "Justice." Of course virginity has long been intertwined with religion and spiritual purity, something Ann Twinam calls a "cult of virginity," which reminds us of the role virgins played in the maintenance of pre-Christian Roman temples.[57] Saint Jerome's praise of virginity is an example of the early Christian adoption of this enduring sentiment.[58] The worship of the myriad of incarnations of the Virgin Mary continued the veneration of virginity in Spain. All the hallowed respect and power accorded to virgins was lost to a woman upon marriage.

When we compare how early modern Spaniards described the two sexual organs, we again see the similarities, though in opposition, between potency and virginity. According to early modern descriptions, the vagina lost its perfection upon its use, while the penis was perfect only *in* its use. As seen in the vaginal examinations already described, the existence of the hymen was as fundamental to virginity as penile erection was to a man's potency. While on the wedding night the virgin "lost" something and was "broken," sex from the perspective of the man, as depicted by these documents, was exactly the opposite. The husband was to "take from her" (*privarla*) and "take pleasure in her" (*gozarla*). In sum, sex in the language of the court was a discourse of sexual subjection; impotence cases were based on showing that this submission of woman to man had not come to pass.

Medical professionals and lawyers characterized the penetrated vagina as something imperfect and spoiled. Court documents commonly used the term "corrupted women" (*corruptas*) for all women who were not virgins. A doctor, surgeon, and midwife who examined Martina de Robres determined that she was not a virgin because the parts of her vagina "lacked the perfect Union," were "darkened," and the vagina "was missing its natural heritage."[59]

Studying the elite of Spain's trans-Atlantic colonies, Twinam has found that a woman's sex was either considered controlled or "out of control." According to her, women whom witnesses considered to be in control were virgins, cloistered religious women, wives, and chaste widows. Society considered any other woman as out of control, sexually and otherwise. Sex was one obvious means by which men could dominate women. For the church, marital sex was the most important method by which it could contain feminine sexuality. Marriage, even in the canonists' pedantic musings, was based on coitus.[60] According to the church's conception, then, sex was meant to control the lust and disorder that women generated in society. This control by use of sex was fulfilled by the conjugal debt, thereby supposedly assuaging a woman's libido. Diego Yzquierdo claimed that he was not able to pay his conjugal debt and control his wife's sexual appetite, for which reason he petitioned for a divorce in 1692. In his petition his lawyer complained: "[She] is foolish and frequently, being in the conjugal act, such a madness tends to come over [her] that all my strength and greatest spirits are needed to restrain her and protect her from the rigors of this passion."[61] The sexual control of a wife by her husband was often equated, by lawyers before the court, with the sexual consummation of a marriage. An impotent man could not be expected to control his wife if he could not sexually subjugate her. His rights and powers literally rested in his phallus. This relationship between power and sexual ability is the central theme of the early modern rhetoric of impotence.

A man charged with impotence was often described by his accusers as an imposter. By posing as a virile man he had illegitimately laid claim to a holy sacrament, a woman, and all that came with marriage: dowry and money. Canon law provided for fines for men found to have married knowing that they were impotent. It was on this basis that the tribunal of Calahorra and La Calzada fined Blas de Espinossa, a castrate who had dared to attempt to marry in Baños in 1680.[62] However, the court rarely fined impotent men, because the deception, marrying with the knowledge that one was impotent, was difficult to prove. In any case, the loss of marriage and of dowry and the public humiliation were certainly punishment enough for a man the court found to be impotent. Prosecutors generally portrayed the impotent husband as a desperate and pathetic man, lacking honor, defrauding an honorable woman.

Impotence Trials in Public and the Emasculated Man

The legal documentation that has survived from impotence trials gives us few clues about what it meant, socially, to be deemed impotent in a personally interdependent community of seventeenth-century Spain. Certainly men exhibited, in the words of a Dr. Adrián de Muro from a report on an impotence examination, a "shame and blushing to be accused of impotence."[63] There are a few obvious facts of which we can be sure. An individual would certainly not be considered fully a man if he admitted being impotent. Hence the phrase so often repeated by wives of allegedly impotent husbands: "He was not [to be taken for] man." In many senses a man's honor was as dependent on his virility as a woman's honor was on her virginity. While a virgin's honor was a state and rested in her unpenetrated vagina; a man's honor had to be proven time and again by the sexual performances of his penis. A man had to win and maintain his honor sexually along with the many other acts that brought him honor, such as dueling and keeping his word. When a local cleric publicly announced that an individual was impotent, that man's reputation would be undermined. His business and political standing would suffer enormously. We can expect that an impotent man would be treated not simply as a cuckold, but worse, as a castrate or eunuch. And though some castrates attained wealth and fame, such as the castrato vocalist Farinelli in the court of Philip v, according to Darmon, early modern individuals viewed castrates with increasing derision.[64] For these reasons, few husbands probably ever admitted to being impotent even after the most public and damning decision by the ecclesiastical court.

According to the pronouncements of the 1698 synod, the only trials that were to be administered secretly by its court were those accusing priests or married women of maintaining licentious affairs. Such secrecy was more than anything an effort to protect the reputation and standing of the church and the sanctity of matrimony. Men accused of impotence were not afforded any privacy by the ecclesiastical tribunal. As in France, Spanish impotence trials took place before an ecclesiastical court that permitted a public audience. In eighteenth-century Paris these public impotence trials gained a large popular audience, especially when trial briefs were copied, published, and widely distributed. In the much smaller rural towns of northern Spain, impotence trials surely garnered less notoriety than in cosmopolitan Paris. But the very fact that Logroño, Bilbao, and Calahorra were small cities must have made the impotence trials well known by a large percentage of their populations.

In most cases a community was already aware that a man was allegedly impotent before a wife charged him before the ecclesiastical tribunal. Rumor and gossip were extremely effective mediums of communication in small and close-knit communities. Litigants not only pled their cases before functionaries of the ecclesiastical court, they fought an equally important battle in the court of public opinion. Both wives and husbands needed to make use of gossip to defame one another while attempting to keep their own reputations intact. While a man worked to refute the assertions of his wife, perhaps boasting to neighbors that he was clearly potent, a wife might assure those around her that she was lamentably, but honorably, still a virgin. The opinions of neighbors and friends could become pivotal. Neighbors could be called to testify, like the relatives in the case of Gerónima and Diego in the first chapter. A priest testifying in the case of Antonio Francisco Vélez de Ydiáquez and María Michaela de Albelda in 1678, for instance, relied on the gossip that he had heard from a maid named Agustina who had told him that Antonio was indeed impotent, or so *she* had heard.[65]

The manipulation of public opinion was extremely important for the effectiveness of the ecclesiastical court as well as for the success of a wife's trial against her husband. If a husband could convince the local mayor, for instance, that his wife's case against him was false and malicious, his wife might find it difficult to have court mandates carried out. She might not be able to take fundamental actions such as reclaiming her dowry and the money that her husband owed her. Local officials could easily sidestep edicts of the ecclesiastical court if they felt they were illegitimate. In an impotence case that was independently prosecuted by the abbot of Nájera, for instance, the town notaries simply refused to follow the ecclesiastical judge's request to serve papers on the accused husband, Melchor Sanchez. Town officials clearly did not consider his wife's litigation against him legitimate. The abbot proceeded to excommunicate officials in the husband's town who had supported him and had refused to take actions against him. His wife's lawyer complained that "the vicar of the church of the said village of Asencana . . . and other people do not behave as they should and ask for the said censure; rather with note and scandal and in scorn of [the censure] they go about together and do business as if without [being censured] or being posted in placards, nor do they pay attention to the excommunication."[66] Political allegiances were fundamental in small communities, and hearsay was a basic source of information in any local social and political network. If the court could not convince local officials of its legitimacy, its orders could easily be rejected.

More often than not town gossip went against husbands publicly accused of impotence. Neighbors and even friends constantly questioned men's virility. Protecting one's sexual reputation was extremely important in a society in which virility and virginity could easily come into doubt through gossip. Virility and virginity often had to be publicly proven. Public tests of men and women's sexual statuses most spectacularly occurred on the nights of and just following a wedding. One such proof, known throughout Europe, was popularly called in Spain *cencerrada.* In a cencerrada a couple would be harassed on their wedding night by a crowd of loud, we can assume intoxicated, well-wishers who urged on the consummation of the wedding with lewd language while banging pots and pans or ringing cowbells. We know that this was a common tradition in the Diocese of Calahorra and La Calzada because the prosecuting attorney complained about its popularity in the town of Autol in 1751: "They go out at night . . . people of all classes, and together at the house of the newlyweds utter extremely immodest, denigrating, and obscene words . . . that cause great hostilities between one or another family due to the faults, that being found, fail, or being hidden come out into the open . . . that from this arises, that because of such pernicious harassment they hinder . . . the celebration of many weddings."[67]

In his condemnation of the ritual, the prosecuting attorney here insinuates that the pressure placed on the newlywed husband by the cajoling crowd sometimes caused impotence, preventing the sexual consummation of the marriage. The cencerrada brought "out into the open" those "faults" that were previously "hidden." The cencerrada was therefore the first test of a husband's potency. The groom had to perform sexually before a crowd.

Communities further confirmed the consummation of a marriage, and that the wife had been a virgin, by the traditional display of bloodstained sheets from the nuptial bed the morning after the newlyweds' first night together. Though the custom clearly employed a flawed method, family and friends took the proof that a bride had bled upon the consummation of her marriage as a sign that she had been a virgin. Displaying the sheets publicly was an ancient and widespread custom in France, Italy, and Spain. In many nations throughout the Mediterranean similar traditions whose purpose is to prove that a bride was a virgin on her wedding night persist to this day. Darmon quotes a witness of the early modern Spanish custom: "The Spaniards, that are great observers of ceremony, on the day following the wedding do have matrons show the sheets of the nuptial bed in public with great acclaim, to parade the stains of defloration, crying out all the while from a window: *Virgin la tenemos* [we've got a virgin]."[68]

This ritual not only supposedly proved that the community did indeed "have a virgin" but also that her husband had had her—that he was not impotent. Of course such tests were easily passed using various wedding night tricks. Such deceptions were important in order to maintain that a bride had been a virgin and that the husband was not impotent and had consummated the marriage. In 1677, María Michaela de Albelda y Vazen complained that her husband "wanting to disguise the impotence and defect that he suffers . . . wounded the said Doña María Michaela on the outside of her vagina. . . . She was compelled to admit [this] to a maid and to Doña Antonia de Etulain, her mother, and by the great amount of blood that there was on the sheet she realized that it was not from copulation."[69] Sex between husband and wife was a public concern, and occasionally, as we see here, a public event. Gossip and rumor were the lifeblood of this public interest in individuals' sexual statuses.

The church, too, had ways to influence public opinion. One example of the publicity power of the early modern church was the customary reading of banns before a wedding. Because of the church's concern over clandestine marriages, canonists at Trent considered it imperative that parishes be made aware of an individual's sexual conditions. By reading banns in the respective parishes of bride and groom, clerics informed the laity that the sexual statuses of two members of the community were about to change from single and available to married and forbidden. The church could confer or deprive people of respect by publicly displaying information about them. When churches displayed the penitential robes of men and women convicted by the Inquisition, for instance, they were constantly publicizing the shame connected with their families. Such infamy besmirched the honor of families for generations.

An effective and direct method of publicity in the parish was the church's placard (*tablilla*). Placing a person's name and accusation on parish placards was a drastic and powerful tool for local church authorities to control people. Tribunal officials treated it as such a drastic measure that orders to use placards against an individual often accompanied an order for his or her excommunication. A community once informed of the goals of the diocesan tribunal could further aid in the apprehension of the accused. By referring to the placards the laity also had the opportunity to denounce the offender to parish authorities. One example of the power of the church placards comes from the city of Vitoria in 1673. Antonio Ruiz de Garibay came before the court only after his wife had convinced the tribunal to place his name on placards. She wanted to force him to live with her in Vitoria rather than in the distant capital, Madrid, where he resided. Use of the placards was often successful at forcing unresponsive men to appear before the court. In his petition, Antonio before all else pleaded that his name be taken down from the church placards.[70]

The use of banns and placards did not spare the impotent. One of the most damning ways to frighten and gain the attention of a husband accused of impotence was to place his name on the local parish's placards. If a husband accused of impotence fled, could not be found, or simply refused to respond to his wife's charges, his name and the claim against him would be displayed for the entire community to see. Such publicity might appear in several churches if more than one parish were involved. The tribunal's first order when it began an investigation into whether a husband was impotent or not stated that if the man did not reply to the accusations, they would "publicize [the charge] and declare [the charge] and place it on placards"[71] The court would shame the accused into submission. Such public humiliation was often a more powerful method of control than even the sequestration of a man's money and property. If the tribunal impounded a husband's home, he might still ignore court orders by depending on friends or family for support. But it was impossible to escape or ignore the ubiquitous shame caused by posters announcing that one was impotent.

Even if an individual responded promptly and quietly to the court's initial letter ordering him to appear before it, the proceedings of an impotence trial were far from secret. The simple administrative business of the court alerted the local parish priest and local notaries and perhaps other officials to take testimonies and do its bidding. Often the local priest, who acted as the provisional judge (juez de comisión), needed to hire a local doctor and surgeon to perform the medical examination of the accused. The majority of people accused of impotence were fortunate in that they were able to have their hearings held far from the towns in which they lived. There were, of course, several men called before the court who lived in Logroño. Their neighbors presumably could casually attend the proceedings of their trials in which the most intimate details of their sexual lives were revealed.

If the church courts never attempted to keep impotence proceedings a secret during the trial, after the trial an impotent person's situation became much worse. Once the court reached a decision, it made sure to publicize its judgment. The ecclesiastical tribunal needed to make decisions regarding impotence public so as to prevent further scandal, illegitimate marriages, and subsequent litigation. When church officials were informed that a man or woman was impotent, they considered it imperative that the community be warned about the individual in question. Following the church's reasoning, parishioners needed to know that a person was sexually defective and not apt for a married life. An example of the tension caused by these public announcements was the assault on priest Matheo de Grijalba by one of his parishioners when he attempted to read the pronouncements of the tribunal of Calahorra and La Calzada in La Guardia in 1705.[72]

All these ways for the public to learn about, and participate in, impotence trials made it impossible for men to avoid the shame and alienation that accompanied impotence. This fact demonstrates that the charge of impotence was not merely a means to an annulment. The social stigma that went along with impotence made such accusations more powerful. When a woman announced to her community and church that her husband was impotent, she not only began a fight for her dowry, independence, and rights, she necessarily attempted to destroy her husband's standing in that city or town. Few men presumably acquiesced in the destruction of their reputation.

The futures of men whose marriages were annulled on grounds of impotence were probably not as bleak as we might imagine. In the great majority of trials, husbands vigorously fought the claims made by their wives. Regardless of the results of medical examinations and court decisions, many men maintained that they were potent and most likely continued to do so even after their marriages were annulled. So long as an allegedly impotent man could convince the important friends and relatives who supported him, all was not lost. An adamant refusal to admit impotence, for instance, was the stubborn disposition of Don Antonio Francisco Vélez de Ydiáquez y Guevara, knight of the Order of Santiago. He was as constant in asserting his potency, in fact, as he was in his repetition of his lengthy title. For four years Don Antonio fought his wife's claim that he was impotent. Examinations of his genitalia perplexed a score of doctors and surgeons, some claiming that he was impotent, others that he was quite likely virile. Antonio was able to bring before the court several individuals who had witnessed the exorcism that supposedly cured him; several men also attested to having witnessed Antonio's penis erect when they shared a bed with him. Joseph Fort, a cleric in Logroño, testified before the court that "he slept in a bed a long time with the said Don Antonio Francisco de Ydaiaquez before he contracted the said matrimony and on many and repeated occasions the witness saw that the aforementioned used to have an erection of the virile member."[73] Even though Don Antonio eventually lost to his wife, by persistently maintaining that he was virile Antonio likely succeeded in convincing his retinue that he was indeed still potent. After all, men could be vindicated after having been declared impotent. For instance, Darmon repeats the famous French case of the Baron d'Argenton. The Baron d'Argenton had lost a high profile impotence trial to his wife in the late sixteenth century. He was, however, vindicated upon his death when, per his request, surgeons extracted from his cadaver's groin two hidden testicles, thereby proving that he was not a eunuch, but a virile man.[74]

The charge of impotence, then, was serious, powerful, and not uncommon. Impotence litigation in the seventeenth century was also not a canonical anomaly. Church courts simply made decisions on the premise that sex and sexual capacity were ultimately necessary elements in marriage formation and a crucial factor in the ordering of society. If impotence trials seem antimodern, it is not because of some of the embarrassing proceedings of Spanish courts. We need look no further than actions of U.S. lawmakers in the Clinton/Lewinsky scandal to realize that even modern courts can expend vast amounts of money and time in fruitless attempts to discover sexual truths.

But unlike courts in early modern Spain, today's courts consider impotence a private concern. It was, perhaps, the conceptualization of private and public interest and where sex fit into those spheres of interest that was so different three hundred years ago. The tribunal of Calahorra and La Calzada considered a husband's impotence a danger to public peace and therefore a public matter. Impotence was a potential threat to social harmony and could encourage sins of fornication and adultery. Therefore it was necessary that the parish be made aware of impotent individuals so they would not attempt to marry again. Priests were instructed to announce the decrees against impotent individuals to the local parish. Impotent spouses could hardly have hoped to escape reckoning with the public's interest in their sexual ability and behavior.

Conclusion

> Quien hizo el casamiento hizo el apartamiento.
> (Whoever made marriage made divorce.)
> —Spanish saying[1]

When scholars explain the development of modern loans at interest, they rarely neglect its roots in Catholic Europe even though the Catholic Church disavowed interest and punished usury as a sin. In Spain, good Catholics earned interest on loans by, among other ruses, utilizing the *censo al quitar.*[2] The censo al quitar allowed a borrower to temporarily sell land to a creditor and then lease it from him for a predetermined period of time at a price usually 14 percent higher than his selling price. The land would revert to the original seller at the end of the lease. Catholic separations and annulments form a basis for the history of modern divorce in much the same way that the censo al quitar does for the history of credit. The Catholic Church banned divorce as it did usury, but separations and annulments fulfilled the common need for divorce just as the censo al quitar satisfied people's need for credit.

The development of modern divorce is most often portrayed as revolutionary rather than evolutionary. Lawrence Stone, for instance, engages in clear exaggeration to show the vast difference between divorce in old-regime Europe and contemporary divorce: "Eight hundred years ago, in the Christian West, the highly restrictive moral code of the medieval canon law made divorce virtually impossible, except for the very rich and powerful. . . . By way of contrast, a few years ago a judge in America casually granted one woman no fewer than sixteen divorces in eleven years."[3] Recent studies have treated divorce as a modern phenomenon that appeared first with the Reformation and became consolidated with the social changes that resulted from the Enlightenment. In this progressive history of divorce, affection and disaffection are the new modern factors that propelled demands for divorce and remarriage in the nineteenth and twentieth centuries.[4] This focus on affection places a great importance on adultery as the primary motivation for divorce. The preoccupation with love-based marriages also assumes that remarriage is the proper and principal goal of divorce. In this "revolutionary" history of divorce, several historians define Protestant divorces as the only true divorces in the modern era. "Real divorce," writes Beatrice Gottlieb, "legal dissolution and permission to remarry during the lifetime of the first spouse—was written in the laws of Protestant countries."[5] Catholic divorces become ignored rather than being included as an important model for modern divorce.

Sixteenth-century reformers loudly derided Rome's refusal to allow divorce and remarriage; however, their concerns were almost entirely over adultery and, most importantly, the ability of men to divorce women. Reformers like Calvin wanted to ensure that men be allowed to divorce and remarry on grounds of adultery and severe disaffection.[6] Religous reformers generally ignored wife battery as grounds for divorce; Calvin himself denied divorce to an abused wife who had lost an eye, and sent her back to live with her husband.[7]

However, the Protestant fight with Rome over divorce need not be the central event in the history of modern divorce. Not only did sixteenth-century reformers ignore abuse as an important motive for divorce, but they wrote from a male perspective because they were principally concerned with disaffection and extramarital affairs as reasons for divorce. Rarely did men, after all, file for divorce because they were physically abused. Rather, men were and are more likely to divorce a first wife in search of a second. Most divorces today, however, are begun by women. And a large percentage of women who seek divorce do so out of disaffection, to protect themselves and their children from abusive husbands.[8] Early modern Catholic annulments, which had as their aim the ending of marriages, were clearly predecessors to many modern divorces that share these goals. As Jeffrey Watt stated so well: "The separation of body and property [the separation from hearth and cohabitation] should be viewed as a logical step in the evolution of divorce."[9]

Roderick Phillips has refuted the assumption of a generation of historians of marriage who considered annulments as a means of de facto divorce in medieval and early modern times. According to the earlier view, annulments based on consanguinity were easy to procure in medieval Europe and served medieval Europeans as the equivalent of modern divorce. Phillips has pointed to research that suggests annulments were, in fact, not easily obtained, especially on the pretext of consanguinity. My own research indicates that Phillips is correct in part; annulments based on *consanguinity* were rarely successful. The paucity of annulments based on kinship may have resulted from the fact that consanguineous marriages in Spain were quite common. Marrying one's cousin only required the customary ecclesiastical dispensation, which the church happily granted for a fee. However, as this study has shown, other pretenses for annulment, particularly impotence, could often succeed in church courts. This study supports, then, the earlier view and not Phillips's opinion. Whether actually the result of impotence or of hidden motivations such as disaffection or adultery, annulments did serve early modern Spaniards as de facto divorces.

The most important characteristic of Catholic annulments was that they were usually litigated by women against men. Catholic divorce was a surprisingly powerful legal device for Spanish women who were otherwise subject to male domination. A husband's authority over his wife was vulnerable to two convincing rhetorics: that of sexual debility and of physical cruelty.

Male power was subject to a public reputation of sexual ability. In Spain, exactly as Elizabeth Foyster has found for seventeenth-century England, "the responsibility for household control [rested] on male sexual potency."[10] A virile husband helped contain female sexuality; an impotent husband, conversely, had no legitimate authority over his wife. Though I hate to invoke such overused terms as patriarchy, the body, and the phallus, all these issues were unavoidably a part of impotence trials. Women and their lawyers in impotence trials attacked the authority of their husbands by asking the court to examine his body, and chiefly his penis. The phallus here was not some nebulous Freudian symbol of male authority like Roman fasces, a king's staff of justice, or the Washington Monument. The actual legal power of these husbands over their wives depended on their genitalia. From the perspective of Spanish communities and the church, a virile man was as crucial to a legitimate marriage as was a virgin bride: both helped to ensure social order and legitimate offspring. According to the thinking of early modern Spaniards, a woman whose husband was impotent was susceptible to extramarital affairs and resulting illegitimate pregnancies. The community and church's concern about a husband's potency, then, was in part an interest in preventing public scandal and promoting legitimate citizens.

Another characteristic of litigation before the church court was the prominent role of reputation and widely held communal opinions. Women who complained that their husbands were impotent needed the support of their communities to win in court. Without neighbors, family, and local officials to support, or at least condone, her litigation against her husband, a wife's case would quickly flounder. Women, therefore, had to have some political influence in their communities. Gossip was the most important form of propaganda that spouses used in small towns to marshal support to their legal cause. As another social historian of early modern northern Spain has noted, "Gossip could come to be a conviction."[11] Recent studies of sexuality in seventeenth-century England have emphasized the great influence that women had over the reputations of men by making use of gossip.[12] This fresh appreciation for the political importance of gossip is just as fitting for the small

Spanish towns of this study as it is for England. Casting doubt on a man's sexual potency was easy in early modern Spain. Witness Christobal Garzes de los Hayo in Préjano in 1704, for instance, recalled that María de Escolana "always said and says publicly that . . . her husband is not a man."[13]

It may seem strange that many clerics questioned the legitimacy husbands as heads of households. After all, the church has long been depicted as a bastion of patriarchal power. The secular church, that part that dealt with the laity, was composed of and governed completely by unmarried men, and it is not difficult to find clerics who wrote extremely misogynist literature. Historians have assumed that this misogyny extended to clerical attitudes about relations between husbands and wives. Yet here again we find an inconsistency between normative literature and individual opinions. These cases frequently reveal local clerics who defended wives against their husbands, and even encouraged marital annulments. There was, in the first place, a great difference between the overall conceptual opinions of the Catholic Church toward women and the ordinary daily actions of local parish priests. The attitudes of local priests toward women varied considerably from cleric to cleric. This study demonstrates that historians cannot assume that clerics held any general opinion for or against the rights of women in marriage. Instead, it seems that patriarchal institutions did not support one another, did not cooperate, in their domination over women. In many Spanish towns, religious and secular institutions competed with one another for power, money, and influence. Local clerics may have increased their influence vis-à-vis secular institutions by supporting the rights of local women against husbands, thereby weakening local secular powers.

Impotence trials, most importantly, provided Spanish women of the early modern period a legal method for gaining power over their own persons and property. Church courts allowed women to fight their husbands in court, destroy them publicly, and then often permitted them to lead physically and economically independent lives. In church courts, at least, women actually had plenty of legal powers at their disposal and litigated on their own behalf, a fact that forces historians of law in Spain to revise earlier assumptions that "women of any age . . . could not litigate on their own behalf" and had to be represented by a husband, father, or brother.[14] Instead we find that women could litigate, and directly accuse, the patriarch in their lives. Lawyers always litigated in the name of their female client. But was some male family member standing behind all the women that came before the ecclesiastical court? All evidence suggests not: male family members were usually not involved in these women's suits. And when male kin were involved, in cases where wives' fathers demanded to participate for instance, the church court forced them to hire a separate lawyer from their female kin. As further evidence, powers of attorney clearly transferred what was distinctly a woman's own legal authority to her lawyer. The rights of men over these women were rarely noted. Spanish women had more legal options at their disposal than is often imagined.

The impotence trials of the Diocese of Calahorra and La Calzada, then, reveal interests related to reproduction rather than salvation, divorce rather than sex, magic rather than honor, and social order rather than the strictures of canon law. And though it may surprise readers accustomed to descriptions of church courts as agents of sexual oppression, the local church court, at least in matrimonial issues, responded to the demands and concerns of the individuals who approached the judge *seeking* solutions to their sexual troubles. That a church court would be responsive to its social context should not be astonishing. Joanne Ferraro has described a similar ecclesiastical court in the "Serene Republic" of Venice.[15] The church court, then, served the public as well as embarrassing the impotent. It satisfied spouses needful of divorce as much as it castigated men and women who could not perform sexually.

APPENDIX A. TABLES

TABLE 1: *Vicars General of the Diocese of Calahorra and La Calzada, 1650–1750*

Vicar General	Year(s)
Martín Acuela Velasco	1652–54
Juan de Eucaz	1653
Diego Ruíz de San Bizentte (consultant to the Inquisition)	1654–56
Gaspar de Salasar	1660–62
Pedro Manciles	1672–75
Cristoual de Uruñuela (consultant to the Inquisition)	1675–80
Gabriel de Esparia	1676
Licentiate (canonigo doctoral) Joseph de Texada y Guardia	1680–84
Bernardo de la Mata	1684–1701
Miguel Lopez de Espinoza	1686
Dr. José Lavidiantre	1702–6
Pedro de Oñate y Murillas	1708–12
Licentiate Balthasar de Lezaun y Andia	1711, 1712, 1713, 1715
Bartolomeo Trevino	1714
Licentiate Pedro de la Quadra y Achiga	1718–30
Gerónimo Joseph de Santerbas y Bergara	1730–39
Bernabe Antonio de Brocomante	1740–47
Juan de Gueñes	1750–53

TABLE 2: *Cases of Female Impotency, 1676–1735*

Year	Cause	Town	Decision	Age M	Age F	Profession	Defendant	Prosecution
1676	Annulment	Santa Cruz de Campezo	Cohabit for three years	?	?	?	Husband	Father of wife
1681	Annulment	Castillo	Annulled	?	?	Porter of goods	Husband	Wife
1687	Annulment	San Román	Annulled	29	22	?	Husband	Wife
1691	Annulment/ separation	Calahorra	Cohabit	?	?	?	Wife	Husband
1697	Annulment	El Rasillo	Annulled	?	16	?	Wife	Husband
1704	Enforce cohabitation/ annulment	Préjano	Separate	25	?	Poverty/ day laborer	Wife	Husband
1716	Annulment	Munilla	Annulled	28	?	?	Husband	Wife
1735	Annulment	Arnedo	Annulled	26	26	Pastor de ganado	Husband	Wife

TABLE 3: *Alleged Castrates Before the Diocesan Court of Calahorra and La Calzada, 1680–1718*

Year	Cause	Town	Decision	Age M	Age F	Profession	Defendant	Prosecution
1680	Marriage license	Baños	Not given, fined	?	?	?	*	Man
1681	Annulment	Logroño	Annulled	?	?	Tailor	Husband	Wife
1685	Annulment	Nájera	Annulled	?	?	Day laborer	Couple, lover	Ex officio
1687	Marriage license	Villar del Rio	License given	?	?	?	Man	Local priest
1688	Annulment	Gamileo	Cohabit	?	25	?	Husband	Wife
1689	Marriage license	Nalda	License given	?	?	?	Man	Brother
1692	Annulment	Logroño	Annulled	20	?	?	Husband	Wife
1693	Annulment	Taniñe	Annulled	?	?	Pled poverty	Husband	Ex officio
1693	Marriage license	Cornago	License given	?	?	?	Couple	Ex officio
1695	Enforce cohabitation	Almarza de Cameros	Cohabit	25.5	?	Shepherd	Wife	Husband
1698	Annulment	Logroño	Annulled	16	?	?	Husband	Wife
1699	Annulment	Albelda	Annulled	23	?	?	Husband	Wife
1702	Annulment	La Calzada y Grañon	Annulled	40	29.5	?	Husband	Wife
1705	Marriage license	Redezilla del Camino	License given	?	?	?	Man	Ex officio
1710	Marriage license	Arnedo	License given	?	?	?	Man	Ex officio
1711	Marriage license	Gardelegui	License given	?	24	?	Couple	Ex officio
1718	Enforce cohabitation	Dima	Cohabit	?	?	?	Wife	Husband

TABLE 4: *Impotence Trials in the Bishop's Court, 1650–1750*

ACDC/Legajo	Year	Town	1st decision	2nd decision	Age M	Age F	Profession/ status	Defendant	Years of marriage	Duration of case
27/628/1	1655	Rodezno	Unknown	—	?	?	Tailor	Husband	1.5	1.25
27/589/55	1673	Oñate	Annulled; absolute impotence	—	?	?	?	Fiscal general	10	0.25
27/656/57	1676	Santa Cruz de Campézo	Triena	Annulled; absolute impotence	?	?	?	Husband	0.75	3
27/345/31	1678	Fuenmayor	Annulled; absolute impotence		?	?	High nobility	Husband	1.5	2
27/334/7	1678	Erandio/Bilbao	Cohabit		?	?	?	Husband	5	0.4
27/650/2	1679	San Román	Cohabit	Cohabit	?	?	?	Husband	0.5	3
27/494/23	1681	Logroño	Annulled; absolute impotence		?	?	Tailor	Husband	19	1.2
27/222/2	1681	Castillo	Annulled; absolute impotence		?	?	Porter	Husband	4	6.5
27/710/11 (see 27/710/14)	1683	Villamediana	Unknown		22	?	?	Husband	1	0.1
27/494/36	1683	Logroño	Unknown		?	?	?	Husband	3	0.2
27/284/43	1685	Derio	Triena		?	?	Farmer	Husband	6	0.5
27/214/2	1685	Carcamo	Triena		?	?	?	Husband	6	0.8
27/566/40	1685	Nájera	Annulled; absolute impotence; fine, exile		?	?	Day laborers	Couple and male lover	20	0.8
27/314/22	1686	El Ziego	Triena	Annulled; relative impotence	22	?	?	Husband	1.5	4.5

27/650/4	1687	San Román	Annulled; absolute impotence (against wife)	Annulled; respective impotence	29	22	?	Husband	8	1.25
27/284/52 (see 27/284/43)	1687	Derio	Annulled; respective impotence		?	?	Farmer	Husband/ priest	6	0.1
27/373/2	1688	Gamileo	Cohabit		?	25	?	Husband	7	0.5
27/495/2	1690	Logroño	Annulled; absolute impotence		?	?	(Wealthy)	Husband	?	0.75
27/274/5	1690	Cornago	Cohabit one year	Cohabit one year	?	?	?	Husband	7	1.5
27/710/14 (see 27/710/11)	1690	Villamediana	Annulled; absolute impotence		30	?	?	Husband	8	0.2
27/187/38	1691	Calahorra	Cohabit		?	?	?	Wife	4	0.5
27/9/16	1691	Agoncillo	Triena		?	?	?	Husband	?	0.25
27/403/1	1692	Huercanos	Cohabit		?	?	?	Husband	4	0.15
27/82/4	1692	Arrancudiaga/ Llodio	Unknown		?	?	?	Husband	1	0.16
27/309/1	1692	El Rasillo	Triena		30	?	Livestock herder	Husband	3	4.2
27/495/6	1692	Logroño	Annulled; relative impotence		20	?	?	Husband	2	7
27/710/15	1692	Villamediana	Cohabit	Triena; mutual absolute impotence	23	18	?	Husband	0.25	6
27/710/16	1693	Villamediana	Cohabit		18	?	Poverty, day laborer	Husband	0.02	0.04

continued

TABLE 4 *(continued)*

ACDC/Legajo	Year	Town	1st decision	2nd decision	Age M	Age F	Profession/ status	Defendant	Years of marriage	Duration of case
27/21/14	1693	Aldeanueva de Cameros	Annulled; absolute impotence		?	?	Livestock	Husband herder	11	0.5
27/662/40	1693	Taniñe	Annulled		?	?	Poor	Husband	?	0.25
27/571/52	1693									
27/389/14	1693	Haro	Cohabit	Annulled; absolute impotence	39	25	Day laborers	Fiscal general	7	8
27/379/3	1694	Grávalos	Annulled; absolute impotence		?	?	?	Husband	2	0.2
27/450/1	1694	Jubera	Annulled; absolute impotence		31	?	?	Husband	1.75	1.6
27/513/5	1694	Lumbreras	Cohabit		?	?	?	Husband	4	0.2
27/6/10	1694	Abersturi	Annulled; absolute impotence		?	?	?	Husband	4	0.1
27/80/19	1695	Arnedo	Triena, four months	Annulled	38	?	?	Husband	4	5
27/562/44	1696	Murillo de Rio Leza	Annulled; absolute impotence		?	?	Poverty	Husband	2	0.4
27/80/14	1697	Arnedo	Cohabit		?	?	Wealthy	Husband	2	0.25
27/309/3	1697	El Rasillo	Annulled; absolute impotence		?	16	?	Wife	0.5	0.4
27/526/52	1698	Margarita	Annulled; absolute impotence		?	?	Poverty	Husband	11	0.25

27/495/29	1698	Logroño	Cohabit	Septima manus; annulled; absolute impotence	16	?	?	Husband	?	15
27/274/3	1699	Cornago	Unknown		23	?	?	Husband	3	0.1
27/495/42	1699	Logroño	Triena		22.5	?	Day laborer	Husband	0.2	0.75
27/15/19	1699	Albelda	Annulled; absolute impotence		23	?	?	Husband	1	0.6
27/29/5	1699	Alescanco	Annulled; absolute impotence	Cohabit	19	?	?	Wife	3.5	0.5
27/658/46	1699	Sarnago	Annulled; absolute impotence	Husband allowed to marry	43	?	Livestock herder	Husband	13	2
27/649/21	1699	San Pedro Manrique	Cohabit		25	?	?	Husband	0.75	0.25
27/457/25	1702	La Calzada y Grañon	Annulled; absolute impotence		40	29.5	?	Husband	0.2	1.6
27/439/7	1703	Igea	Annulled; absolute impotence		32	22	?	Husband	9	1.5
27/188/26	1704	Calahorra	Annulled; absolute impotence		36	?	?	Husband	4	0.1
27/611-17	1704	Préjano	Separate/ cohabit		25	?	Farmer/ day laborer	Wife	?	1.25
20/165/06	1704	Helorio	Triena, one year		?	?	?	Husband	3	0.2
27/438/83	1705	Ibrillos	Cohabit	Cohabit	?	16				

continued

TABLE 4 *(continued)*

ACDC/Legajo	Year	Town	1st decision	2nd decision	Age M	Age F	Profession/ status	Defendant	Years of marriage	Duration of case
27/328/17	1706	Enciso	Annulled; absolute impotence		18	18	Shepherd	Husband	1.5	3.3
27/538/54	1708	Meñaca	Annulled; wife can marry		33	?	?	Husband	2.3	2
27/188/38	1708	Calahorra	Annulled; relative impotence		21	?	?	Husband	5	0.1
27/476/34	1708	Lasanta	Annulled; absolute impotence		27.5	?	?	Husband	1.25	0.25
27/222/4	1708	Castillo	Triena		44	?	Day laborer	Husband	4	0.1
27/562/53	1710	Murillo de Rio Leza	Annulled; absolute impotence	Triena	32	?	Royal secretary in Avila	Husband	0.1	4
27/691/37	1710	Viana	Annulled; absolute impotence		50	?	?	*	4.5	0.1
27/312/8	1711	Villarreal de Álava	Annulled; absolute impotence		?	?	?	Husband	1.5	0.1
27/555/23	1712	Munguia	Triena, one year		28	18	Day laborer	Husband	3.5	1.1
27/660/12	1712	Sotes	Triena, one year		21.5	?	?	Husband	0.25	1.1
27/657/26	1712	Santa Cruz de Yanguas	Annulled; absolute impotence		?	?	?	Husband	2	0.05
27/328/19	1712	Enciso	Triena, six months		25	20	?	Husband	4	1.8

27/551/19	1713	Munilla	Annulled; relative impotence	?	?	Poor	Husband	4	0.05	
27/476/35	1714	Lasanta	Annulled; relative impotence		29	22	?	Couple	5	0.08
20/164/02	1716	Munilla	Annulled; both can remarry		28	?	?	Husband	3	3
20/150/13	1718	Dima	Cohabit	Cohabit	?	?	?	Wife	8	1.2
20/164/06	1720	Torre en Cameros	Annulled		?	?	Sheepherder for mesta	Husband	3	0.1
J 965/3	1720	Nájera						Husband		
27/819/41	1724	Santa Olalla	Cohabit		?	?	?	Husband	5	2.5
20/164/09	1729	Garayo	Unknown		?	?	?	Husband	16	1.5
20/164/12	1732	Murillo de Rio Leza	Triena		?	?	Poor	Husband	0.3	0.75
20/164/08	1733	Soto	Unknown		57	64	?	Husband	4	0.2
20/164/04	1734	Entrena	Annulled; wife can marry		26	21	Day laborer	Husband	4.25	0.33
20/164/05	1735	Arnedo	Annulled	Cohabit	26	26	Livestock herder	Husband	3	1.25
20/164/10	1739	Vitoria	Annulled		?	?	?	Husband	0.25	0.25
20/164/16	1741	Aramayona	Unknown		33	?	?	Husband	7	3.5
20/145/14	1745	Bilbao	(Mutual reconciliation)		?	60	Wealthy merchant	Husband	12	0.5
20/164/07	1751	Villafranca	Unknown		?	?	?	Husband	0.33	0.1

TABLE 5: *Who Brought the Charge of Impotence to Court*

Wife	85%
Husband	6%
Prosecuting attorney	4%
Couple together	4%
Wife's father	1%

TABLE 6: *Impotence Trial Final Decisions*

Marriage annulled	49%
Couple ordered to live together	23%
Couple ordered to live together for a trial period	19%
Decision unknown	9%

APPENDIX B. GRAPHS

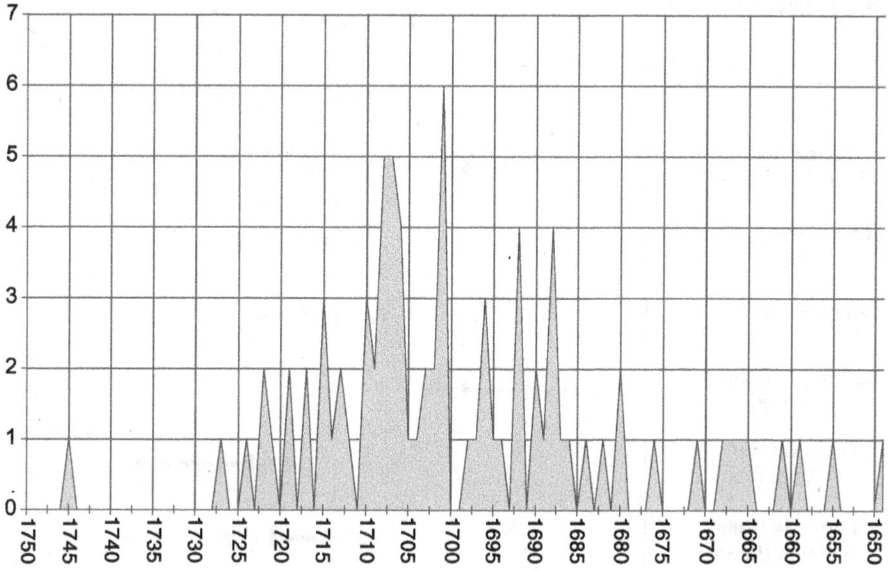

1. Number of public adultery (*amancebamiento*) cases per year, 1650–1750

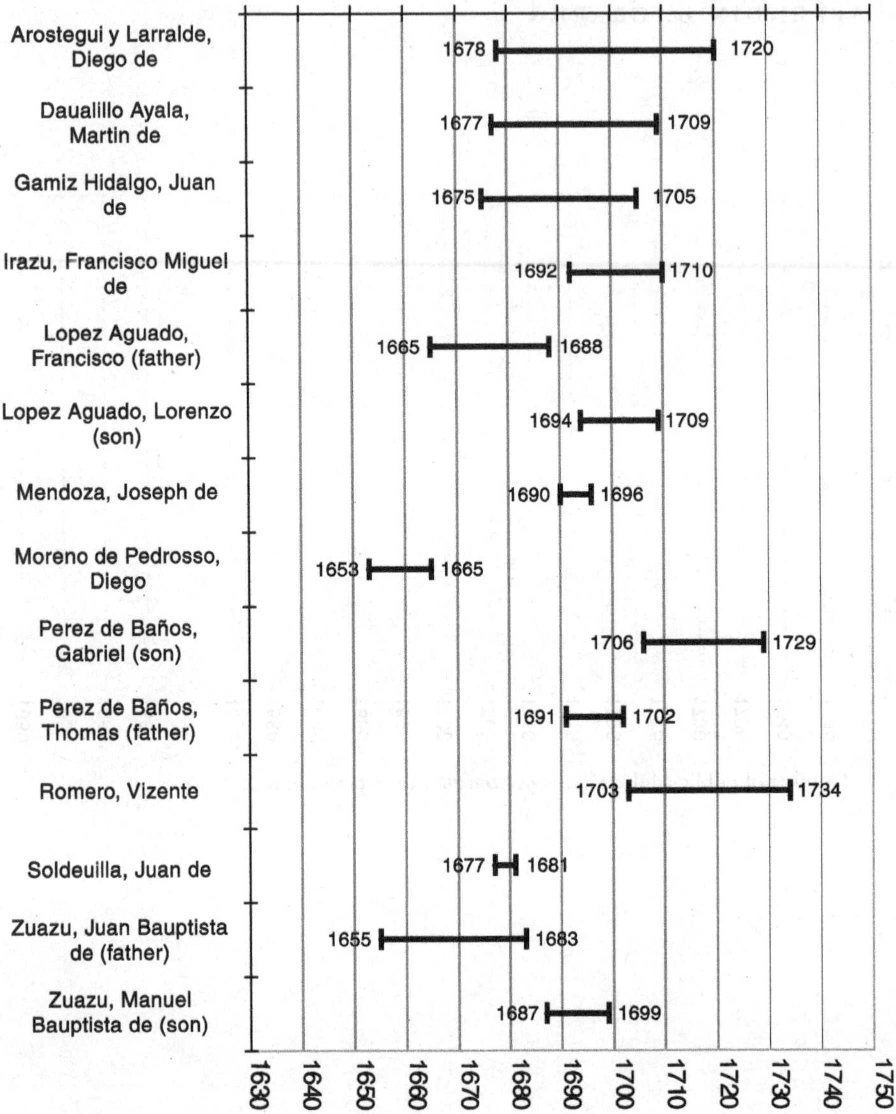

2. Attorneys of the church court

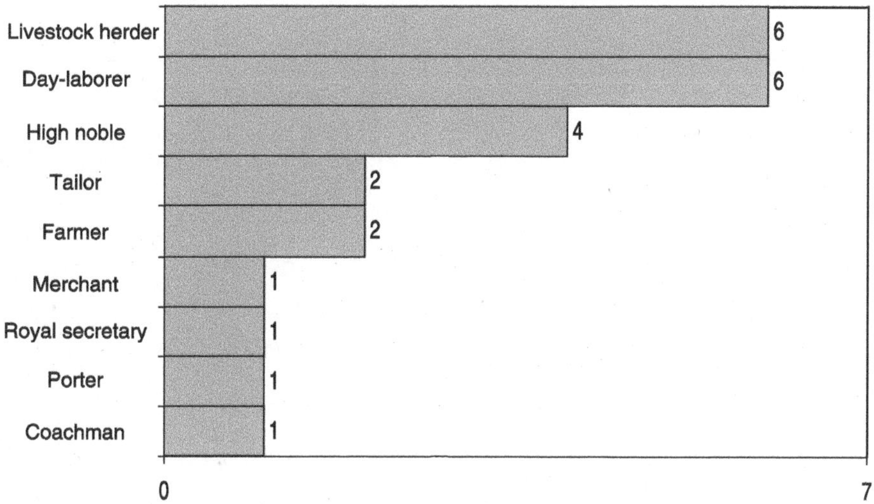

3. Occupations of allegedly impotent husbands

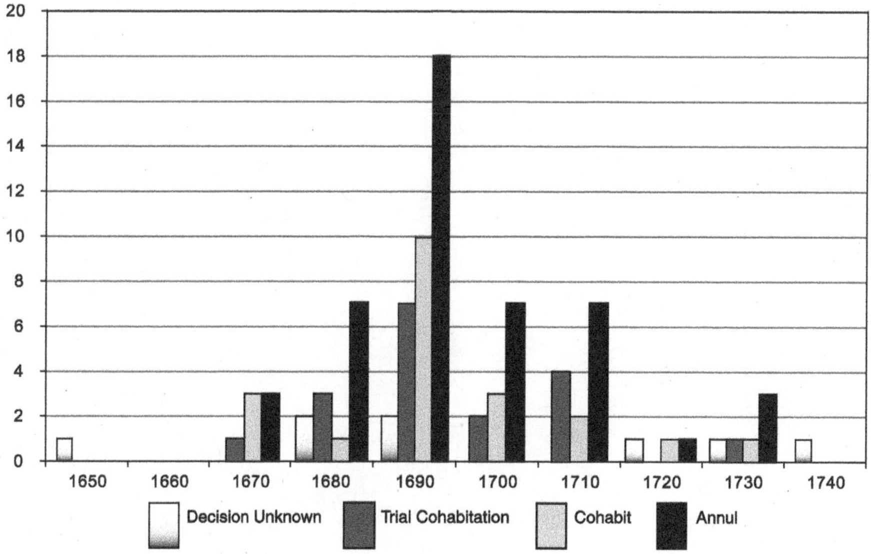

4. Changes in the decisions of the tribunal over tim

APPENDIX C. LITIGATION COSTS OF DOÑA MARÍA YGNES DE URBINA

Of the Costs Caused by Doña María Ygnes de Urbina resident of the population of the village of Lauarza in the trial that the aforementioned has litigated against Don Joseph González de Muro her husband over Divorce and it is according to the following:

First petition written by the lawyer six reales	06
Item sixty reales of copper coin for the summary testimonies taken about the abuses done to the said Doña María	60
Power of attorney two reales	02
A legal petition six reales of copper coin	06
[Drafting of] the questionnaire	12
Testimonies taken according to the questionnaire	60
[Cost of] Doña María's attorney fifty reales	50
[Cost of] of this appraisal four reales	04
To the present notary twelve reales according to his right	12
Item seven reales and a half paid to the prosecuting attorney for the review of the case dispatched to him by the Lord Provisor in which he said the causes for separation were justified	07½
Of the letter in execution of the judgment declaring it final three and a half reales	03½
	223 rs.

ACDC, Legajo 20/147/13, f. 57.

NOTES

INTRODUCTION

1. Luis Martínez Kleiser, *Refranero General Ideológico Español* (Madrid: Editorial Hernando, 1953) refrain 19,467, p. 213.

2. For instance, two lengthy complaints about the number of convenient annulments that the Catholic Church today permits are Robert H. Vasoli's *What God Has Joined Together: The Annulment Crisis in American Catholicism* (New York: Oxford University Press, 1998), and Pierre Hégy and Joseph Martos, eds., *Catholic Divorce: The Deception of Annulments* (New York: Continuum, 2000).

3. Impotence was also a popular basis for annulment in other parts of Europe. A study of the Diocese of Cambrai found that nonconsummation was by far the most common plea for annulment in the eighteenth century. See J. R. Machuelle, "Les Demandes d'annulation de mariage," chap. 6 of *La Désunion du couple sous l'Ancien Régime: l'Exemple du Nord,* ed. Alain Lottin (Villeneuve-d'Ascq: Universite de Lille III; Paris: Editions Universitaires, 1975), 139. Other important studies include Pierre Darmon, *Trial by Impotence: Virility and Marriage in Pre-Revolutionary France* (London: Hogarth Press, 1985); María del Juncal Campo Guinea, *Comportamientos matrimoniales en Navarra (siglos XVI–XVII)* (Pamplona: Gobierno de Navarra, Departamiento de Educación y Cultura: Gráficas Ona, S.A., 1998); Joanne M. Ferraro, *Marriage Wars in Late Renaissance Venice* (Oxford: Oxford University Press, 2001); Francisco Javier Lorenzo Pinar, "La mujer y el Tribunal Diocesano en Zamora durante el siglo XVI: Divorcios y nulidades matrimoniales," *Studia Zamorensia* 3 (1996): 77–88; Thomas Max Safley, *Let No Man Put Asunder: The Control of Marriage in the German Southwest: A Comparative Study, 1550–1600* (Kirksville, MO: Sixteenth Century Journal Publishers, 1984).

4. See, for instance, Allyson M. Poska, "When Love Goes Wrong: Getting Out of Marriage in Seventeenth-Century Spain," *Journal of Social History* 29 (Summer 1996): 871–82. On abandonment as a common means of de facto divorce, see Renato Barahona, *Sex Crimes, Honour, and the Law in Early Modern Spain: Vizcaya, 1528–1735* (Toronto: University of Toronto Press, 2003), 100. Joanne Ferraro also discusses the real possibility of divorce in Catholic Europe in *Marriage Wars in Late Renaissance Venice,* 22, 37. Ruth MacKay documents a woman suing for divorce from a rowdy soldier in her study *The Limits of Royal Authority: Resistance and Obedience in Seventeenth-Century Castile* (Cambridge: Cambridge University Press, 1999), 154. In Islamic Spain divorce was also permitted; see Manuela Marín, "Marriage and Sexuality in Al-Andalus," *Marriage and Sexuality in Medieval and Early Modern Iberia,* ed. Eukene Lacarra Lanz (New York: Routledge, 2002), 17. See also Isabel Testón Nuñez, *Amor, Sexo y Matrimonio en Extremadura* (Badajoz: Universitas Editorial, 1985).

5. Miguel de Cervantes, "The Divorce Court Judge," *Eight Interludes,* trans. Dawn L. Smith (London: Everyman Press, 1996), 13.

6. For example, in his study of women in colonial Peru, Luis Martín has also used "divorce" to explain the role of ecclesiastical divorces in the past. As I do, he emphasizes abuse as the main plea of Catholic divorce. See Martín, "Divorcees, Concubines, and Repentant Women," chap. 6 of *Daughters of the Conquistadores: Women of the Viceroyalty of Peru* (Albuquerque: University of New Mexico Press, 1983).

7. Joseph Martos outlines the incongruity between the Catholic Church's theology and its practice in "Catholic Marriage and Marital Dissolution in Medieval and Modern Times," in *Catholic Divorce,* ed. Hégy and Martos.

8. I realize, of course, that this annulment was not made by the Catholic Church, but by Henry's own newly founded Anglican Church. Yet the reasoning and canon law that the Archbishop of Canterbury used was, at that point of England's break with the Catholic Church, the same.

9. Roderick Phillips, *Putting Asunder: A History of Divorce in Western Society* (Cambridge: Cambridge University Press, 1988).

10. For Phillips's discussion on these points, see Phillips, *Putting Asunder,* 9–34.

11. Roderick Phillips is certainly not alone in viewing divorce primarily as a result of romance outside marriage. Isabel Testón Nuñez also begins with the search for satisfying love as the motivation for divorce in her *Amor, Sexo y Matrimonio en Extremadura.* Protestant religious reformers also began with adultery as the most legitimate reason to divorce (generally for a husband to divorce his adulterous wife).

12. Jeffrey Watt, *The Making of Modern Marriage: Matrimonial Control and the Rise of Sentiment in Neuchâtel, 1550–1800* (Ithaca, NY: Cornell University Press, 1992).

13. Phillips, *Putting Asunder,* 84–85.

14. On matriarchy among the Basques, see Charlotte Crawford, "The Position of Women in a Basque Fishing Community," in *Anglo-American Contributions to Basque Studies: Essays in Honor of Jon Bilbao,* ed. William A. Douglass et al. ([Reno, NV]: Desert Research Institute, 1977), 145–60; Andrés Ortiz-Osés and Franz-Karl Mayr, *El matriarchalismo vasco* (Bilbao: Universidad de Deusto, 1998); Renato Barahona, *Sex Crimes,* 38; A. R. Whiteway, "Customs of the Western Pyrenees," *English Historical Review* 15, no. 60 (October 1900): 627–28; Juan Javier Pescador, *The New World Inside a Basque Village: The Oiartzun Valley and Its Atlantic Emigrants, 1550–1800* (Reno: University of Nevada Press, 2004), xxii.

15. Aside from the dozens of husbands in this study who asked the church court to force their wives to return to their houses and submit to their authority, Tomás Mantecón documents an eighteenth-century case in which a husband asked the local secular authorities to force his wife to obey him in all things. See Tomás Mantecón Novellán, *La muerte de Antonia Isabel Sánchez: Tiranía y escándalo en una sociedad rural del norte español en el Antiguo Régimen* (Alcalá de Henares: Centro de Estudios Cervantinos, 1998), 98.

16. Martínez Kleiser, *Refranero General Ideológico Español,* 454–55.

17. Allyson M. Poska, *Regulating the People: The Catholic Reformation in Seventeenth-Century Spain* (Leiden: Brill, 1998).

18. An exception was the marriage of Joseph and the Virgin Mary. According to Catholic theology, *the* ideal husband and wife never had sex before or after the birth of Jesus.

19. For an in-depth study of virginity and law in northern Spain, see Barahona, *Sex Crimes.* For the importance of virginity in Hispanic culture, see Ann Twinam, "Honor, Sexuality, and Illegitimacy in Colonial Spanish America," in *Sexuality and Marriage in Colonial Latin America,* ed. Asunción Lavrin (Lincoln: University of Nebraska Press, 1992), 118–55. For a full exploration of honor in Spain, see Abigail Dyer, "Heresy and Dishonor: Sexual Crimes before the Courts of Early Modern Spain" (PhD diss., Columbia University, 2000).

20. Here I refer to the contrast between the "aristocratic" and "ecclesiastical" models of marriage described by Georges Duby in *Medieval Marriage: Two Models from Twelfth-Century France,* trans. Elborg Forster (Baltimore: Johns Hopkins University Press, 1978).

21. A marriage is not indissoluble until both steps, (a) consent—which imparts sacramentality—and (b) consummation, are taken. This two-step formulation is described in detail in Antonio Molina Melia, *La disolución del matrimonio inconsumado: Antecedentes históricos y Derecho vigente* (Salamanca: Universidad Pontifica de Salamanca, 1987), 20. See also the detailed discussion of Hincmar and impotence in Catherine Rider, *Impotence and Magic in the Middle Ages* (Oxford: Oxford University Press, 2006), 31–42.

22. There is no study that specifically illuminates the workings of Spanish church courts. Three recent studies, however, do make use of ecclesiastical court materials and thereby reveal aspects of ecclesiastical justice: María del Juncal Campo Guinea, *Comportamientos matrimoniales en Navarra;* Daniel Charles Becker, "'There Is No Harm in a Boy Talking to a Girl': The Control of Sexuality and Marriage in Early Modern Navarre and Guipúzcoa" (PhD diss., University of Maryland, 1997); and Isabel Testón Nuñez, *Amor, Sexo y Matrimonio en Extremadura.*

23. See, for instance, Helen Nader, *Liberty in Absolutist Spain: The Habsburg Sale of Towns, 1516–1700* (Baltimore: Johns Hopkins University Press, 1990), or Ruth MacKay, *Limits of Royal Authority.*

24. Examples of some of these works are Pablo Díaz Bodegas, *La diócesis de Calahorra y La Calzada en el sigo XIII* (Logroño: Diocesis de Calahorra and La Calzada-Logroño, 1995), and Milagros García Calonge, *El poder municipal de Calahorra en el siglo XVII: Aspectos institucionales* (Calahorra, La Rioja: Amigos de la Historia de Calahorra, 1998).

25. I will refer to Campo Guinea's work occasionally throughout this study for comparative purposes. See Campo Guinea, *Comportamientos matrimoniales.*

26. Philip II elevated Burgos to the seat of an archbishopric in 1572 and placed Calahorra and La Calzada under its jurisdiction. Calahorra and La Calzada had previously been under the jurisdiction of Pamplona, and before that, of Zaragoza. Henry

Kamen, *The Phoenix and the Flame: Catalonia and the Counter Reformation* (New Haven, CT: Yale University Press, 1993), 74.

27. Eliseo Sáinz Ripa, *Sedes episcopales de La Rioja,* vol. 3, *Siglos XVI–XVII* (Logroño: Obispado de Calahorra y La Calzada-Logroño, 1996), 22–25.

28. The Diocese of Calahorra and La Calzada was very jurisdictionally heterogeneous, spanning parts of the provinces of Vizcaya, Burgos, Navarra, and Alava. A description of the diocese in 1846 in the *Diccionario Geográfico-Estadístico-Histórico de España y sus Posesiones de Ultramar* gives the number of towns under its jurisdiction as 954, with 747 parishes. Though this source is rather late for the period in question, all the main towns that are described as being part of the diocese in the nineteenth century (Bilbao, Logroño, Alfaro, Nájera, etc.) litigated in its tribunal in the seventeenth century. See Pascual Madoz, *Diccionario Geográfico-Estadístico-Histórico de España y sus Posesiones de Ultramar* (Madrid: Est. Literario-Tipográfico P. Mudoz, 1846), 5:241–42.

29. For examples of this opinion, see Richard Kagan, *Lawsuits and Litigants in Castile, 1500–1700* (Chapel Hill: University of North Carolina Press, 1981), 126, in which he sees the rise in European litigiousness in the beginnings of the Italian city-states. Tomás Mantecón has also demonstrated that, in northern Spain, there were clearly more cases per capita in urban areas and that the larger the geographic jurisdiction the lower the number of cases per capita (Mantecón, *La muerte de Antonia Isabel Sánchez,* 15).

30. Richard Kagan, *Lawsuits and Litigants,* 86–89.

31. J. R. Machuelle and Alain Lottin, "Les Divorcés," chap. 5 of *La Désunion du couple sous l'Ancien Régime: l'Exemple du Nord,* ed. Alain Lottin (Villeneuve-d'Ascq: Universite de Lille III; Paris: Editions universitaires, 1975), 115.

32. For the main proponent of this view, see Henry Kamen, *Spain in the Later Seventeenth Century, 1665–1700* (London: Longman, 1980).

33. Regarding Spanish orthography, I have decided not to modernize the spelling of names and words used in the documents. The contemporary way names and words were spelled varied from case to case, page to page, and line to line. This inconsistency in orthography, I believe, was not only an aspect of the language of the day, but may reveal something of the mentality of law and rhetoric in early modern Spain.

1: GERÓNIMA MARTÍNEZ DE TEXADA V. DIEGO BELASCO, LOGROÑO, 1681

1. For a discussion of the legal position of widows in early modern Europe, see Thomas Kuehn, "Daughters, Mothers, Wives, and Widows: Women as Legal Persons," in *Time, Space, and Women's Lives in Early Modern Europe,* ed. Anne Shutte et al. (Kirksville, MO: Truman State University, 2001). Ethnographer Stanley Brandes notes that in common parlance there are many refrains and jokes made by Spaniards of the opinion that wives hope for, and subversively bring on, the deaths of their husbands. See Brandes, *Metaphors of Masculinity: Sex and Status in Andalusian Folklore* (Philadelphia: University of Pennsylvania Press, 1980), 87.

2. "La desfloro y priuo de su virginedad con el mienbro natural sin fuerza ni violenzia alguna." Archivo Catedralicio y Diocesano de Calahorra, hereafter abbreviated as ACDC, legajo 494/23, fol. 1, Feb. 8, 1681.

3. A brief discussion of the impact of the Real Pragmática of 1776, which moved some marital issues from the ecclesiastical into the secular jurisdiction, can be found in Susan M. Socolow, "Acceptable Partners: Marriage Choice in Colonial Argentina, 1778–1810," in *Sexuality and Marriage in Colonial Latin America,* ed. Lavrin, 210.

4. "En la primera segunda o tercera noche que enpezo acostarse con la suso dha la desfloro y priuo de su virginedad con el mienbro natural sin fuerza ni violenzia alguna." ACDC, legajo 27/494/23, fol. 1 back, Feb. 8, 1681.

5. ACDC, legajo 27/494/23, fol. 2, Feb. 8, 1681.

6. For a thorough discussion of the importance of virginity to social status in Hispanic societies as well as the ability of women to manipulate and construct their public reputations, see Ann Twinam, "Honor, Sexuality, and Illegitimacy," 118–55.

7. Renato Barahona has recently explored the monetary worth of the loss of virginity in seduction cases in this area of Spain. Some women claimed upwards of 100 ducats for the loss of their virginity. See Barahona, *Sex Crimes,* 28–29.

8. ACDC, legajo 27/494/23, fol. 8, Feb. 26, 1681.

9. Virginity tests were important throughout medieval and early modern European history. For a discussion of this interesting subject, see Kathleen Coyne Kelly, *Performing Virginity and Testing Chastity in the Middle Ages* (London: Routledge, 2000). For early modern Spain, see Barahona, *Sex Crimes,* 18.

10. ACDC, legajo 27/494/23, fol. 8, Feb. 26, 1681.

11. ACDC, legajo 495/6, fol. 1, 1692.

12. ACDC, legajo 80/14, fol. 1., and legajo 27/611/17, testimony by Carlos Canos, fol. 16.

13. In 1736, sixteen-year-old Marie-Catherine Chardon claimed her husband used his fingers to remove the proof of her virginity. See Monique Cuillieron, "Les causes matrimoniales des officialités de Paris au Siècle des Lumières 1726–1789," *Revue historique de droit francais et etranger* 66, no. 4 (1988): 531.

14. ACDC, legajo 27/494/23, fol. 8, Feb. 26, 1681.

15. ACDC, legajo 27/494/23, fol. 6, Feb. 14, 1681.

16. Diego's use of witchcraft as a defense for impotence is covered in detail later in this chapter.

17. ACDC, legajo 222/2, Castillo, 1681; legajo 650/2, San Roman, 1679; legajo 24/2, Alegria, 1683. Bad breath as a possible excuse for divorce had a precedent as early as the twelfth century with French King Philip Augustus's effort to divorce Ingeborg of Denmark. See Rider, *Magic and Impotence,* 73.

18. For a French description of the exorcism of impotence curses, see Pierre Darmon, *Trial by Impotence,* 33–34, in which the afflicted couple is beat with a switch while tied to a pole, back to back, and naked. Rider surveys medieval impotence cures throughout *Magic and Impotence,* but especially on pages 148–53.

19. The most recent and thorough study of impotence spells is the aforementioned

Rider, *Impotence and Magic.* Arturo Morgado García's study of witchcraft in early modern Spain cites many spells used to render men impotent or reverse such curses. See *Demonios, magos y brujas in la España moderna* (Cádiz: Servicio de Publicaciones de la Universidad de Cádiz, 1999). Darmon also gives an overview of much of the early modern literature and folklore regarding impotence spells; he believes that, on the whole, people feared and used such practical magic (Darmon, *Impotence,* 28–34). María Helena Sánchez Ortega asserts that love magic was well known to many ordinary Europeans in the early modern period. See "Women as a Source of 'Evil' in Counter-Reformation Spain," in *Culture and Control in Counter-Reformation Spain,* ed. Anne J. Cruz and Mary Elizabeth Perry (Minneapolis: University of Minnesota Press, 1992), 199. In her study of the Kingdom of Navarra, María Juncal Campo Guinea found three impotence cases out of twenty-two (1612, 1643, and 1651) allegedly caused by some type of maleficio, presumably witchcraft. See Campo Guinea, *Comportamientos matrimoniales,* 244.

20. ACDC, legajo 27/494/23, fol. 10, March 7, 1681.

21. ACDC, legajo 27/494/23, fol. 10

22. For the common assumptions equating hernia surgery with castration, see Valeria Finucci, *The Manly Masquerade: Masculinity, Paternity, and Castration in the Italian Renaissance* (Durham: Duke University Press, 2003), 239n36, as well as Michael R. McVaugh, "Treatment of Hernia in the Later Middle Ages: Surgical Correction and Social Construction," in *Medicine from the Black Death to the French Disease,* ed. Roger French et al. (Singapore: Ashgate, 1998). The most notorious cause of castration was the purposeful creation of a castrato singer. The need for castrati in the late sixteenth century had arisen as a consequence of the church's post-Tridentine efforts to enforce the cloistered life of religious women. Women were prohibited from participating in many musical productions. Castrates were used to replace high female voices. Later, new musical tastes in the sixteenth and seventeenth centuries for Italian opera increased the demand for castrati. The castrato, possessing the voice of a boy and lung capacity of an adult, was uniquely able to perform lengthy ornamentation without taking a breath, a musical quality much desired by wealthy patrons. See Richard Sherr, "Gugliemo Gonzaga and the Castrati," *Renaissance Quarterly* 33, no. 1 (Spring 1980): 33–56.

23. ACDC, legajo 27/494/23, fol. 11.

24. See Joan Cadden, *Meanings of Sex Differences in the Middle Ages: Medicine, Science, and Culture* (Cambridge: Cambridge University Press, 1993). For a description of the medical ideal of a masculine complexion—strong, stout, reddish, and hairy—see Jon Arrizabalaga, "Medical Responses to the 'French Disease' in Europe at the Turn of the Sixteenth Century," in *Sins of the Flesh: Responding to Sexual Disease in Early Modern Europe,* ed. Kevin Siena (Toronto: Centre for Reformation and Renaissance Studies, 2005), 47.

25. ACDC, legajo 27/494/23, fol. 11.

26. ACDC, legajo 27/494/23, fol. 12, March 7, 1681.

27. ACDC, legajo 27/494/23, fol. 12, March 7, 1681

28. ACDC, legajo 27/222/2, Castillo, fol. 12, Oct. 2, 1681.

29. ACDC, legajo 27/494/23, fol. 16, March 18, 1681. On Rhazes and his discussion of sex, see John T. Noonan, *Contraception: A History of Its Treatment by the Catholic Theologians and Canonists* (Cambridge: Harvard University Press, 1986), 204.

30. ACDC, legajo 27/494/23, fol. 16.

31. ACDC, legajo 27/494/23, fol. 16.

32. The couples were neighbors of the same age, and Joseph González claimed to have escorted Diego to Arbeyza to be exorcized of impotence.

33. ACDC, legajo 27/494/23, fol. 38.

34. ACDC, legajo 27/494/23, fol. 39, Aug. 27, 1681.

35. ACDC, legajo 27/494/23, fol. 41, Aug. 28, 1681.

36. Pierre Darmon, for example, argues that ecclesiastical judges took perverse pleasure in persecuting and emasculating laymen. See Pierre Darmon, *Damning the Innocent: A History of the Persecution of the Innocent in Pre-Revolutionary France,* trans. Paul Keegan (New York: Viking, 1986), 2.

37. ACDC, legajo 27/494/23, fol. 44, July 9, 1691.

38. ACDC, legajo 27/494/23, fol. 45.

39. ACDC, legajo 494/23, fol. 46.

40. Heath Dillard, *Daughters of the Reconquest: Women in Castilian Town Society, 1100–1300* (Cambridge: Cambridge University Press, 1984), 154.

41. On competition between Spanish jurisdictions, see Kagan, *Lawsuits and Litigants.* He has aptly described early modern Spanish courts as having to compete for litigants.

2: THE REFORMS OF BISHOP PEDRO DE LEPE DORANTES (1686–1700)

1. *Constituciones Sinodales del Obispado de Calahorra* (Lyón, 1555), bk. 3, 56. Quoted in Tomas Marín, "Un registro de partidas bautismales anterior al Concilio Tridentino (1499–1546)," *REDC* 3 (1948): 783–93.

2. For a thorough discussion of the debate on the relative power of the state in early modern Spain and Europe, see MacKay, *The Limits of Royal Authority.*

3. Joseph Martos provides an excellent overview of the separate traditions of European marital traditions in "Catholic Marriage and Marital Dissolution in Medieval and Modern Times," in *Catholic Divorce.*

4. For an excellent overview of the biblical examples of marriage that influenced medieval Europeans, see Christopher N. L. Brooke, *The Medieval Idea of Marriage* (Oxford: Oxford University Press, 1989), 41–54.

5. This battle between church and aristocratic marriage models and their purposes is described in Georges Duby, *Medieval Marriage.*

6. James Brundage, *Law, Sex, and Christian Society in Medieval Europe* (Chicago: University of Chicago Press, 1987), 131.

7. On Germanic sexual attitudes, see ibid., 127.

8. Thessalonians 4:3, *New King James Version* (Nashville: Thomas Nelson, 1982).

9. Gonzalo de Alba, "Libro sinodal," April 6, 1410, Salamanca, *Synodicon hispanum,* ed. Antonio García y García (Madrid: Biblioteca de Autores Cristianos, 1987), 3:274.

10. Brundage, *Law, Sex, and Christian Society,* 154–64.

11. Ibid., 229.

12. Ibid., 229–55.

13. Antonio García y García, "La Canonísta Iberica (1150–1250)," *Bulletin of Medieval Canon Law* 11 (1981): 53–54.

14. A detailed investigation of the *Siete Partidas* on marriage can be found in Marilyn Stone's *Marriage and Friendship in Medieval Spain: Social Relations According to the Fourth Partida of Alfonso X* (New York: P. Lang, 1990).

15. Dillard, *Daughters,* 38.

16. Federico R. Aznar Gil, *La institución matrimonial en la Hispania Cristiana bajomedieval (1215–1563)* (Salamanca: Publicaciones Universidad Pontífica, 1989), 43–44.

17. Aznar Gil, *La institución matrimonial,* 347.

18. Ibid., 40.

19. Renato Barahona, "Courtship, Seduction and Abandonment in Early Modern Spain," in *Sex and Love in Golden Age Spain,* ed. Alain Saint-Saëns, 43–55 (New Orleans: University Press of the South, 1996).

20. Gonzalo de Alba, "Libro sinodal," Salamanca, April 6, 1410, *Synodicon hispanum,* ed. García, 3:275.

21. *Constituciones Sinodales del Obispado de Calahorra* (Lyón, 1555), bk. 3, 56. Quoted in Tomás Marín, "Un registro."

22. "Sínodo de Antonio de Guevara," Mondoñedo, Nov. 13, 1541, *Synodicon hispanum,* ed. García, 3:73.

23. "Sínodo de Cristóbal de Rojas y Sandoval," Oviedo, May 4–23, 1553, *Synodicon hispanum,* ed. García, 2:550.

24. "Sínodo de Rodrigo de León," Santiago de Compostela, Aug. 17, 1289, *Synodicon hispanum,* ed. García, 1:276.

25. "Constituciones antiguas del obispado de Orense," Orense, 15th cent., *Synodicon hispanum,* ed. García, 1:113.

26. Ibid., 1:113.

27. Campo Guinea, *Comportamientos matrimoniales.*

28. "Sínodo de Diego Avellaneda," Tuy, June 26–28, 1528, *Synodicon hispanum,* ed. García, 1:508.

29. Ibid., 1:507.

30. "Constituciones antiguas del obispado de Orense," Orense, 15th cent., *Synodicon hispanum,* ed. García, 1:126.

31. Francisco Cantera, "La Juderia de Calahorra," *Sepharad* 15, fasc. 2, n.d.

32. ACDC, legajo 27/187/12.

33. Brundage, *Law, Sex, and Christian Society,* 379–80.

34. "Constituciones antiguas del obispado de Orense," Orense, 15th cent., *Synodicon hispanum,* ed. García, 1:126.

35. Quoted in Aznar Gil, *La institución matrimonial,* 344.

36. Quoted in ibid., 345.

37. Gonzalo de Alba, "Libro sinodal," Salamanca, April 6, 1410, *Synodicon hispanum,* ed. García, 3:278–79. Acting like a "prostitute" would have generally implied taking pleasure in sex, which would include any sex act other than coitus and any sexual position other than the missionary position.

38. Ibid.

39. "Sínodo de Pedro de Acuña y Avellaneda," Astorga, July 16–20, 1553, *Synodicon hispanum,* ed. García, 2:160.

40. Jacqueline Murry, "On the Origins and Role of 'Wise Women' in Causes for Annulment on the Grounds of Male Impotence," *Journal of Medieval History* 16 (1990): 235–49.

41. On impotence as grounds for annulment, see Brundage, *Law, Sex, and Christian Society,* 376–78, and Darmon, *Trial by Impotence.*

42. "Sínodo de Gonzalo Osorio," León, April 22, 1303, *Synodicon hispanum,* ed. García, 2:275.

43. Gonzalo de Alba, "Libro sinodal," Salamanca, April 6, 1410, *Synodicon hispanum,* ed. García, 3:278–79.

44. "Sínodo de Pedro Arias de Baamonde," Mondoñedo, Aug. 19, 1447, *Synodicon hispanum,* ed. García, 1:33.

45. "Sínodo de Diego de Deza, 9–18 Julio 1497," Salamanca, *Synodicon hispanum,* ed. García, 3:419.

46. "Sínodo de Pedro Pacheco," Mondoñedo, Nov. 13, 1534, *Synodicon hispanum,* ed. García, 1:58.

47. The three studies I mention here are Campo Guinea's *Comportamientos matrimoniales,* Barahona's "Courtship, Seduction and Abandonment in Early Modern Spain," and Poska's "When Love Goes Wrong."

48. For Burgundian marital dilemmas, see James R. Farr, "Marriage and the Uses of the Law: Legislation, Abduction, and Litigation," chap. 4 in *Authority and Sexuality in Early Modern Burgundy (1550–1730)* (New York: Oxford University Press, 1995), 90–123; and for England, see John R. Gillis, "Courtship and Marriage in the Sixteenth and Seventeenth Centuries," pt. 1 of *For Better, For Worse: British Marriages, 1600 to Present,* 11–105 (New York: Oxford University Press, 1985).

49. See, for example, Campo Guinea, *Comportamientos matrimoniales.*

50. Poska, *Regulating the People,* and Kamen, *Phoenix and the Flame.*

51. José Manuel Cifuentes Pazos, *La economia de las iglesias vizcainos en el siglo XVII* (Bilbao: Ediciones Beta III mileno, S.L., 2000), 28–29.

52. Sáinz Ripa, *Sedes episcopales de La Rioja,* 3:485. Cifuentes Pazos also notes the synods of the seventeenth century were evidence of efforts to reform the diocese, though he also gives credit to the earlier synods of 1601 and 1620. See Cifuentes Pazos, *La economía de las iglesias vizcaínas,* 19.

53. Sáinz Ripa, *Sedes episcopales de La Rioja,* 3:485.

54. Pedro de Lepe Dorantes, Constituciones synodales antiguas, y modernas del obispado de Calahorra y La Calzada (Madrid: Antonio González de Reyes, 1700), 655–56.

55. Sáinz Ripa, *Sedes episcopales de La Rioja,* 3:500.

56. Pedro Gutierrez Achutegui, *Historia de la muy noble antigua y leal ciudad de Calahorra* (Logroño: Talleres Gráficas de Editorial Ochoa, 1981), 71. Calahorra's twelfth-century codices are still used as important sources for understanding medieval Spanish daily life.

57. Sáinz Ripa, *Sedes episcopales de La Rioja,* 3:493.

58. ACDC, legajo 27/323/32.

59. ACDC, legajo 27/325/21.

60. ACDC, legajo 27/520/19.

61. Unfortunately, a complete count of the cases in the ACDC is beyond the scope of this study, and would have been enormously time consuming. My conclusions, however, are based on my thorough perusal of the archive's catalogs, which are divided into four categories: *beneficios, capillas, matrimonial,* and *criminal.* The criminal sections are by far the smallest.

62. ACDC, legajo 27/288/28.

63. Kagan, *Lawsuits and Litigants,* 33.

64. Three of these studies are the previously mentioned Campo Guinea, *Comportamientos matrimoniales,* Testón Nuñez, *Amor, Sexo y Matrimonio,* and Becker, "There Is No Harm in a Boy Talking to a Girl."

65. Here I make reference to priests inheriting benefices from their fathers. This occurred at the local parish level but was likely rare within the court itself.

66. Kamen, however, attributes this spending to the fervor of the Counter-Reformation, not idle extravagance as I do.

67. Sáinz Ripa, *Sedes episcopales de La Rioja,* 3:49.

68. Ibid., 45.

69. Ibid., 54.

70. See Cifuentes Pazos, *La economia de las iglesias vizcainos,* 51–52.

71. Ibid., 71.

72. Kagan explores the links between litigation and bribes in early modern Spain. He concludes that gift giving and bribery were important factors in winning many cases and were often a calculated expense of litigation. Yet this study deals with a very different court than the Royal Chancery Court in Valladolid, the court Kagan was mainly concerned with. There is no evidence in this study that could lead to the assumption that bribery was an important aspect of these cases. See Kagan, *Lawsuits and Litigants,* 39.

73. Watt, *Modern Marriage.*

74. Annulments that the court allowed hovered around 50 percent over the century of this study.

75. Antonio Domínguez Ortiz, *La sociedad española en el siglo XVII,* 2 vols. (Granada: Universidad de Granada, 1992).

76. Lepe, *Constituciones,* 293.

77. An interesting recent survey of Inquisition cases of bigamy is Richard Boyer's *Lives of the Bigamists: Marriage, Family, and Community in Colonial Mexico* (Albuquerque: University of New Mexico Press, 1995).

78. Antonio Bombín Pérez, *La Inquisición en el País Vasco: El tribunal de Logroño (1570–1610)* (Bilbao: Servicio Editorial, Universidad del País Vasco, 1997), 162.

79. William Monter, *Frontiers of Heresy: The Spanish Inquisition from the Basque Lands to Sicily* (Cambridge: Cambridge University Press, 1990), 144.

80. ACDC, legajo 20/168/05.

81. An example of how closely the Inquisition's fiscal worked with inquisitors can be found in Antonio Bombín Pérez, *La Inquisición en el País Vasco,* 30.

82. Lepe, *Constítuciones,* 290.

83. Kagan, *Lawsuits and Litigants,* 58. On positions in the Inquisition also being inherited, see Joseph Perez, *The Spanish Inquisition,* trans. Janet Lloyd (New Haven: Yale University Press, 2005), 118.

84. On lawyers and attorneys in early modern Spain, see Kagan, *Lawsuits and Litigants,* 52–78.

85. ACDC, legajos 27/566/40 and 27/288/28.

86. Lepe, *Constituciones,* 287.

87. "Habia negado a una mujer la bendicion post partum hasta que le diese una gallina," 1674, ACDC, legajo 27/109/33.

88. Machuelle and Lottin, "Les Divorcés," 113. For Vizcaya, Cifuentes Pazos notes that vicars were prohibited from hearing matrimonial cases beginning in 1530. See Cifuentes Pazos, *La economía de las iglesias vizcaínas,* 13.

89. Lepe, *Constituciones,* 224.

90. Archivo Historico Provincial de Logroño (hereafter abbreviated as AHPL), legajo J 965/3.

91. ACDC, legajo 27/288/28.

92. Lepe, *Constituciones,* 296.

93. Ibid., 294.

94. ACDC, legajo 17/742-15.

95. Lepe, *Constituciones,* 303.

96. ACDC, legajo 27/649/21, fol. 9.

97. ACDC, legajo 27/222/2, declaration of Dr. D. Juan Muñoz, fols. 28–35.

98. "Lo Que Toca Al Oficio de Provisor deste Obispado," Lepe, *Constituciones,* 279.

99. ACDC, legajo 27/345/31.

100. This is, for instance, Kagan's conclusion in *Lawsuits and Litigants,* 248.

101. Becker, "There Is No Harm in a Boy Talking to a Girl."

3: IMPOTENT WOMEN, DISCARDED WIVES

Portions of this chapter have appeared in Edward Behrend-Martínez, "Female Sexual Potency in a Spanish Church Court 1673–1735," *Law and History Review* 24, no. 2 (Summer 2006): 297–330.

1. Martínez Kleiser, *Refranero General Ideológico Español*, refrain 43,963, p. 501.

2. "Impotencia. Privativamente se dice de la incapacidad de engendrar ò concebir. Lat. *Impotentia.* Nebrix. Chron. part. 1. cap. I. Porque segun la *impoténtia* del Rey. . . . creían que lo concebido por la Réina era de otro y no del Rey." *Diccionario de Autoridades: Diccionario de la lengua castellana, en que se explica el verdadero sentido de las voces, su naturaleza y calidad, con las phrases o modos de hablar, los proverbios o refranes, y otras cosas convenientes al uso de la lengua [. . .]. Compuesto por la Real Academia Española. Tomo quarto. Que contiene las letras G.H.I.J.K.L.M.N.* (Madrid: Real Academia Española, 1734), 230.

3. On questions linking sex and capitalism, see Bryan S. Turner, *The Body and Society: Explorations in Social Theory* (Oxford: Basil Blackwell, 1984), esp. 13–15.

4. I follow here in the vein of Thomas Laqueur's interest in the construction of sex rather than gender. I use the term *sex* here to refer to how early modern people perceived and defined the female genitalia: the vagina, uterus, ovaries, and so on. See Laqueur, *Making Sex: Body and Gender from the Greeks to Freud* (Cambridge: Harvard University Press, 1990).

5. Anal sex was clearly thought to be "against nature."

6. Laqueur, *Making Sex*, 64. On the commonly held belief that women's "seed," and therefore the female orgasm, was required for conception, see Joseph Bajada, *Sexual Impotence: The Contribution of Paolo Zacchia, 1584–1659* (Roma: Editrice Pontifica Università Gregoriana, 1988), 52–53.

7. On Galenic and Aristotelian views of the female sex, see Laqueur, *Making Sex*, 26–32.

8. Nicolas Abercrombie and Bryan Turner, "The Dominant Ideology Thesis," *British Journal of Sociology* 29, no. 2 (June 1978): 153.

9. Ibid., 154.

10. Transmission of the baserri from one generation to the next was decided by elders: it could often be a woman, but always was the person seen as best fit to govern the baserri. See Pescador, *The New World Inside a Basque Village*, xxii. On matriarchy in the Basque country, see Ortiz-Osés and Mayr, *El matriarchalismo vasco.*

11. Other types of intimate contact were either not sex (anything not penetrative) or not natural (such as anal intercourse). For an excellent introduction to premodern concepts of sex, see Ruth Mazo Karras, *Sexuality in Medieval Europe: Doing unto Others* (New York: Routledge Press, 2005).

12. Darmon, *Trial by Impotence*, 36.

13. Ibid.

14. Ibid., 56–57.

15. Ibid.

16. Natalie Z. Davis, *The Return of Martin Guerre* (Cambridge: Harvard University Press, 1983), 28.

17. Darmon, *Trial by Impotence*, 36.

18. According to John McCarthy, today all that is required for female potency in Catholic doctrine "is a penetrable vagina capable of receiving the penis and the semen." See McCarthy, "The Marriage Capacity of the 'Mulier Excisa,'" *Ephemerides iuris canonici* 2, no. 2 (1947): 261–85.

19. Ferraro, *Marriage Wars*.

20. Thomas Max Safley, "Marital Litigation in the Diocese of Constance, 1551–1620," *Sixteenth Century Journal* 12 (1981): 72.

21. Cuillieron, "Les Causes matrimoniales," 530.

22. Campo Guinea, *Comportamientos matrimoniales*, 237.

23. See, for instance, studies on the Diocese of Zamora and the Diocese of Barcelona: Lorenzo Pinar, "La mujer y el Tribunal Diocesano," and A. Gil Ambrona, "Las mujeres bajo la jurisdicción eclesiástica: Pleitos matrimoniales in la Barcelona de los siglos XVI y XVII," *Nuevas preguntas, nuevas miradas. Fuentes y documentación para la historia de las mujeres (siglos XIII–XVIII)* (Granada, 1992).

24. For examples of the connection between witchcraft and impotence, see Walter Stephens, "Witches Who Steal Penises: Impotence and Illusion in *Malleus Maleficarum*," *Journal of Medieval and Early Modern Studies* 28 (1998): 495–29; Nancy Cotton, "Castrating (W)itches: Impotence and Magic in *The Merry Wives of Windsor*," *Shakespeare Quarterly* 38 (Autumn 1987): 320–26; and on Mexico, Ruth Behar, "Sexual Witchcraft, Colonialism, and Women's Powers," in *Sexuality and Marriage in Colonial Latin America*, ed. Lavrin.

25. ACDC, legajo 20/164/05, fol. 51, testimony of Juachina Cordón, June 20, 1736.

26. ACDC, legajo 20/164/05, fol. 27, testimony of Franzisco Rodríguez, July 31, 1735.

27. ACDC, legajo 27/222/2, Castillo, 1681, fol. 1.

28. ACDC, legajo 27/309/3, fol. 1.

29. ACDC, legajo 27/309/3, fol. 16.

30. Michael J. O'Dowd and Elliot E. Philipp, *The History of Obstetrics and Gynaecology* (New York: Parthenon, 1994), 309–10. According to Kathleen Coyne Kelly, an imperforate hymen was considered a danger to a woman's health in the Middle Ages. See Kelly, *Performing Virginity*, 10.

31. This section of the declaration was underlined and bracketed in the documentation. Though the judge or his secretary were the likely highlighters of the passage, we cannot be sure who actually underlined it. ACDC, legajo 27/309/3, fol. 47.

32. ACDC, legajo 27/309/3, fol. 14.

33. A succinct overview of the position of Saints Augustine, Jerome, and the Catholic Church on women and sex in marriage can be found in Merry Wiesner-Hanks, *Christianity and Sexuality in the Early Modern World: Regulating Desire, Reforming Practice* (London: Routledge, 2000), 31–32.

34. Quoted in N. H. Keeble, ed., *The Cultural Identity of Seventeenth-Century*

Woman: A Reader (London: Routledge, 1994), 126. I recognize that the English church at this time (1622), of course, was not part of the Roman Catholic Church. Yet, regarding marriage, the English church during the early modern period changed little of the Catholic canon law on marriage that it had inherited. Its conditions for separation and annulment were not appreciably different from Catholic legal practice. See Martin Ingram, *Church Courts, Sex, and Marriage in England, 1570–1640* (Cambridge: Cambridge University Press, 1987), 146.

35. Brandes, *Metaphors of Masculinity*, 76.

36. Again, the latest word and most thorough study of this topic is Rider, *Impotence and Magic*. Arturo Morgado García's study of witchcraft in early modern Spain cites many spells used to render men impotent or reverse such curses (Morgado García, *Demonios, magos y brujas*, 99–103). Darmon also gives an overview of much of the early modern literature and folklore regarding impotence spells, and he believes that, on the whole, people feared and used such practical magic (Darmon, *Trial by Impotence*, 28–34). María Helena Sánchez Ortega asserts that love magic was well known to many ordinary Europeans in the early modern period. See Sánchez Ortega, "Women as a Source of 'Evil,'" 199. In her study of the Kingdom of Navarra, María Juncal Campos Guinea found three impotence cases out of twenty-two (1612, 1643, and 1651) allegedly caused by some type of maleficio, presumably witchcraft. Campo Guinea, *Comportamientos matrimoniales*, 244. See also Thomas Kranmer's *Malleus maleficarum* (1486; New York: Dover, 1971).

37. See, for instance, "Concerning Witches Who Copulate with Devils," in Thomas Kranmer's influential and infamous *Malleus maleficarum*, 41.

38. María Helena Sánchez Ortega details the use of many of these ingredients in early modern spells in "Sorcery and Eroticism in Love Magic," *Cultural Encounters: The Impact of the Inquisition in Spain and the New World*, ed. Anne Cruz and Mary Elizabeth Perry (Berkeley and Los Angeles: University of California Press, 1991).

39. Sánchez Ortega, "Women as a Source of 'Evil.'"

40. See Leviticus 15, especially verses 19–20.

41. Fernando Salmón and Montserrat Cabré, "Fascinating Women: The Evil Eye in Medical Scholasticism," in *Medicine from the Black Death to the French Disease*, ed. Roger French et al., 53–84 (Aldershot: Ashgate, 1998).

42. ACDC, legajo 27/187/38, fol. 1. On spells to make women impotent, see Rider, *Impotence and Magic*, 82.

43. ACDC, legajo 27/187/38, fol. 9.

44. Ibid.

45. For many of the descriptions of various spells, see the fifteenth-century *Malleus maleficarum* of Thomas Kranmer.

46. ACDC, legajo 27/187/38.

47. Pseudo-Albertus Magnus, *Women's Secrets: A Translation of Pseudo-Albertus Magnus's De Secretis Mulierum with Commentaries*, trans. Helen Rodnite Lemay (New York: State University of New York Press, 1992), 66–67.

48. Ibid., 121.

49. Helen Rodnite Lemay, introduction to Pseudo-Albertus Magnus, *Women's Secrets,* 1. However, Paolo Zacchia, Rome's expert on canon law and medicine who was often cited by doctors in these cases, asserted that sperm could not survive outside the uterus, and therefore women could not conceive in this manner. See Bajada, *Sexual Impotence,* 37.

50. ACDC, legajo 27/650/4, fol. 22.

51. On the language of seduction in this area of early modern Spain, see Renato Barahona's recent book *Sex Crimes, Honour, and the Law in Early Modern Spain,* 41–59.

52. ACDC, legajo 27/650/4, fol. 17.

53. ACDC, legajo 27/650/4, fol. 22.

54. "Seminationem autem femineam habere potest mulier eunuchissa, quemadmodum et sana acintegra," from the *Synopsis rerum moralium et juris pontificii,* ed. Benedetto Ojetti, n1399. Quoted in McCarthy, "The Marriage Capacity," 266.

55. Bajada, *Sexual Impotence,* 15.

56. Louise Vasvári, "Intimate Violence: Shrew Taming as Wedding Ritual in the *Conde Lucanor,*" in *Marriage and Sexuality,* ed. Lacarra Lanz.

57. Brandes, *Metaphors of Masculinity,* 92.

58. The vocabulary of the female castrate changed considerably, however, once it was appropriated by Freud to describe an inherent absence in the female sex. He was fixated, of course, on the phallus rather than the testicles.

59. ACDC, legajo 27/370/71, fol. 1. The petition here uses the word *potrero,* which usually refers to the individual whose job it is to castrate, or geld, livestock. However, *potrero* can also apply to a hernia surgeon. In this passage I leave the ambiguity because the more specific word *hernista,* hernia surgeon, is not used here as it is later in the trial and in other cases.

60. McVaugh, "Treatment of Hernia."

61. Bajada, *Sexual Impotence,* 77.

62. ACDC legajo 27/370/71, fol. 2.

63. See Laqueur, *Making Sex,* 28–29.

64. See ibid., 140–41.

65. See ACDC, legajo 27/566/40.

66. ACDC, legajo 20/164/5, fol. 31 back.

67. For many Spanish *arbitristas,* the political and economic pundits who attempted to solve Spain's vast problems through published opinions, depopulation was a key factor that caused Spain's perceived decline in the seventeenth century. See David Sven Reher, *Town and Country in Pre-Industrial Spain: Cuenca, 1550–1870* (Cambridge: Cambridge University Press, 1990), 18n.

68. Don Diego de Saavedra Fajardo, *Obras de Don Diego de Saavedra Fajardo y del licenciado Pedro Fernández Navarrete, Biblioteca Autores Españoles desde la formación del lenguaje hasta nuestros dias* (Madrid: Ediciones Atlas, 1945), 25:426.

69. Brundage, *Law, Sex, and Christian Society,* 83–86.

70. Spanish refrain quoted in Brandes, *Metaphors of Masculinity,* 86

71. On the early modern view that women were sexually insatiable, see Merry Wiesner-Hanks, *Women and Gender in Early Modern Europe,* 2nd ed. (Cambridge: Cambridge University Press, 2000), 57–58. Regarding the idea that male lust was also a concern during the early modern period, see Wiesner-Hanks, "Lustful Luther: Male Libido in Luther's Lectures on Genesis," *Festschrift Honoring James Brundage,* ed. M. H. Hoeflich (Washington, DC: Catholic University of America Press, 2004).

72. Ornella Moscucci, "Men-Midwives and Medicine: The Origins of a Profession," in *The Science of Woman: Gynaecology and Gender in England 1800–1929* (Cambridge: Cambridge University Press, 1990), 43–74.

73. A general discussion and refutation of Freud's concept of women's "castration complex" appears in Luce Irigaray's 1974 essay, "Another 'Cause'—Castration," reprinted in *Feminisms: An Anthology of Literary Theory and Criticism,* ed. Robyn R. Warhol and Diane Price Herndl, 430–37 (New Brunswick, NJ: Rutgers University Press, 1997). See also Elisabeth Young-Bruehl, ed., *Freud on Women: A Reader* (New York: W. W. Norton, 1990). For a more contentious refutation of Freud's views, see Germaine Greer's *The Female Eunuch* (New York: McGraw-Hill, 1971).

4: THE PROSECUTION AND SEXUAL PERSECUTION OF IMPOTENT MEN

1. Martínez Kleiser, *Refranero General Ideológico Español,* refrain 32,505, p. 369.

2. Darmon, *Damning the Innocent,* 131.

3. Davis, *Return of Martin Guerre,* 20–21.

4. Brundage, *Law, Sex, and Christian Society,* 115.

5. Catherine Rider, *Magic and Impotence in the Middle Ages* (Oxford: Oxford University Press, 2006), 72.

6. Ibid., appendix 2, 229–32.

7. Safley, "Marital Litigation," 72.

8. See Guido Ruggiero, *Binding Passions: Tales of Magic, Marriage, and Power at the End of the Renaissance* (New York: Oxford University Press, 1993), and Joanne Ferraro, *Marriage Wars.*

9. Campo Guinea, *Comportamientos matrimoniales,* 241.

10. Darmon, *Trial by Impotence,* 118.

11. Foucault does not examine impotence trials in particular, but he sees the church's investigation of sex and sexuality as a means to control and as conduit for institutional power. He argues that the seventeenth-century church's obsessive probes into people's sexual lives proves that institutionalized religion used sexual discourse to control the laity. The church's attempt to contain and monopolize sexual discourse, according to Foucault, was one characteristic of the ideological power that it wielded over the laity. Foucault makes his argument about the church's sexual discourse as part of his explanation of the development of how people "discussed" sex in the seventeenth century. It should be noted that Foucault relies solely on what was written; therefore all his conclusions about the development of discourse are dependent on simultaneous growth in the production of the written and printed word. He

makes no mention of this connection between alleged changes in discourse and the expansion of printed materials. See Foucault, *An Introduction,* vol. 1 of *The History of Sexuality,* 2nd ed., trans. Robert Hurley (New York: Vintage Books, 1990).

12. See, for instance, the links between the impotence of Henry IV, "the Impotent," of Castile and the weakness of his royal authority in Barbara Weissberger, "'A tierra, puto!': Alfonso de Palencia's Discourse of Effeminacy," in *Queer Iberia: Sexualities, Cultures, and Crossings from the Middle Ages to the Renaissance,* ed. Josiah Blackmore and Gregory S. Hutcheson, 291–324 (Durham, NC: Duke University Press, 1999).

13. On the Inquisition's persecution of sodomy, see Federico Garza Carvajal, *Butterflies Will Burn: Prosecuting Sodomites in Early Modern Spain and Mexico* (Austin: University of Texas Press, 2003).

14. In Spain and all other Catholic nations, canon law on matrimony remains active and continues to dispense annulments, some of which are based on impotence. For the most current application of such law, see Santiago Panizo Orallo, *Temas procesales y nulidad matrimonial* (Madrid: Edigrafos, S.A., 1999), as well as his earlier *Nulidades de matrimonio por incapacidad* (Salamanca: Universidad Pontifica de Salamanca, 1982).

15. Today, disaffection or incompatibility suffice as grounds for annulments as well as divorces.

16. I believe that the role of local clerics in controlling the sexual behavior of the laity has often been overstated by historians; yet it is clear that their daily presence in communities as confessors and parish priests often embroiled clerics in couples' personal lives. A contrary opinion comes from Richard Boyer in his study of marriage in colonial Mexico. He does not see clerical intervention in marriages as significant after they performed the nuptial blessing (Boyer, *Bigamists,* 102). Perhaps these conflicting conclusions are the result of the differences between colonial and European contexts.

17. ACDC, legajo 27/566/40, fol. 7.

18. ACDC, legajo 27/188/26, fol. 1.

19. Darmon argues that this papal order first allowed impotence trials to be prosecuted ex officio. Quoted in Darmon, *Trial by Impotence,* 19. For more detail on the context of Sixtus V's order, see Merry E. Wiesner-Hanks, *Christianity and Sexuality in the Early Modern World,* 109.

20. ACDC, legajo 27/476/35.

21. ACDC, legajo 27/476/35.

22. Darmon, *Trial by Impotence,* 107.

23. ACDC, legajo 27/656/57.

24. Linda Guzzetti, "Separations and Separated Couples in Fourteenth-Century Venice," in *Marriage in Italy, 1300–1650,* ed. Trevor Dean and K. J. P. Lowe, 249–74 (Cambridge: Cambridge University Press, 1998).

25. ACDC, legajo 27/492/26.

26. Susan M. Socolow, "Acceptable Partners," 210.

27. ACDC, legajo 345/31.

28. Darmon, *Trial by Impotence,* 118–19.

29. Vagabonds who wanted to marry in the diocese of Calahorra and La Calzada petitioned the court for licenses to marry. See ACDC, legajo 27/652/2.

30. For a general ethnographic treatment of a Spanish hamlet and its communal, municipal character, see Susan Freeman, *Neighbors: The Social Contract in a Castilian Hamlet* (Chicago: University of Chicago Press, 1970).

31. It is interesting to note Susan Freeman's quotation from an ethnographic informant, albeit from a twentieth-century Spanish villager: "Nobody wants to be a shepherd. The shepherd isn't a complete man." Quoted in Freeman's *Neighbors,* 175.

32. ACDC, legajo 27/658/46.

33. ACDC, legajo 27/21/14, fol. 14, declaration before the court, Sept. 16, 1693.

34. ACDC, legajo 27/495/6, fol. 37.

35. ACDC, legajo 27/495/6, fol. 15.

36. See Keith Thomas, *Religion and the Decline of Magic* (New York: Scribner's, 1971).

37. Darmon asserts that annulments due to maleficio allowed both partners to remarry (Darmon, *Trial by Impotence,* 29). As further evidence that witchcraft was rarely recognized as a cause for annulment in the present study, the church court gave only one couple permission to annul their marriage and permission to both freely remarry; and this decision was defined as impotencia respectiva and not maleficio.

38. ACDC, legajo 27/345/31, fols. 231–33. This reference is to the *Fustis dæmonum* of Hieronymous Mengus, first published as part of an anthology on exorcism in Cologne, 1616. See Richard Holbrook, "Exorcism with a Stole," *Modern Language Notes* 20, no. 4 (April 1905): 111–15.

39. ACDC, legajo 27/345/31, fols. 231–33.

40. ACDC, legajo 27/345/31, testimony of Pedro Ignacio Vélez de Idiáquez y Guevarra, fols. 253–55.

41. Gustav Henningsen, *The Witches Advocate: Basque Witchcraft and the Spanish Inquisition, 1609–1614* (Reno: University of Nevada Press, 1980).

42. ACDC, legajo 27/710/15, testimony of Pedro Zorzano in affidavit fols. 48–57.

43. Rider also makes a very strong case that impotence magic was prevalent among the peasantry throughout the medieval period. See Rider, *Impotence and Magic,* 58. On impotence spells, see note 19, chap. 1.

44. Darmon, *Trial by Impotence,* 27–28. On the prevalence of impotence because of tying the Aiguillette, see Emmanuel LeRoy Ladurie, "The Aiguillette: Castration by Magic," in *The Mind and Method of the Historian,* trans. Siân Reynolds and Ben Reynolds (Chicago: University of Chicago Press, 1981), 84–96.

45. ACDC, legajo 20/164/6, fol. 7.

46. See Joan Cadden, "Western Medicine and Natural Philosophy," in *Handbook of Medieval Sexuality,* ed. Vern L. Bullough and James A. Brundage (New York: Garland, 1996), 59.

47. See Joyce Salisbury, "Gendered Sexuality," in *Handbook of Medieval Sexuality,* ed. Bullough and Brundage (New York: Garland, 1996), 91.

48. ACDC, legajo 27/214/2, fol. 14.

49. ACDC, legajo 27/214/2, fol. 14.

50. ACDC, legajo 27/222/2, fols. 26–33.

51. Impotencia respectiva referred to two distinct individuals who were incapable of having sex, usually owing to disparities in the sizes of their genitalia. Impotencia relativa was often confused in court documents with impotencia respectiva, but actually concerned impotent individuals who were only capable of having sex with certain types of people, as in the cases of men deemed impotent with virgins but potent with nonvirginal women. Darmon reviews the different classes of impotence according to canon law in *Trial by Impotence,* 15.

52. ACDC, legajo 27/222/2, fol. 17.

53. Murry, "On the Origins and Role of 'Wise Women.'"

54. ACDC, legajo 27/495/6, fols. 44–45.

55. Ibid.

56. Darmon explains that septima manus was a procedure in canon law more closely associated with the Roman Catholic Church, rather than the Gallican Church, and emerged in the twelfth and thirteenth centuries with the elaboration of canon law in the High Middle Ages (*Trial by Impotence,* 74). See also Rider's discussion of seven witnesses, *Impotence and Magic,* 61.

57. ACDC, legajo 27/457/25, fol. 16.

58. ACDC, legajo 20/164/9, Garazo, 1727.

59. ACDC, legajo 27/494/23, fol. 16.

60. ACDC, legajo 27/650/4, declaration by Francisco Saenz, July 15, 1688.

61. ACDC, legajo 27/710/16.

62. See Darmon's example of the De Langley case in which the man, found impotent, remarries (*Trial by Impotence,* 87).

5: RHETORICS OF DIVORCE, REPUTATION, AND THE MALE BODY

1. Cervantes, "The Divorce Judge," 13.

2. Phillips, *Putting Asunder,* 12.

3. Darmon, *Trial by Impotence,* 2.

4. This impression of clerical sexual incontinence is from my reading of nearly three hundred ecclesiastical court cases. I found several casual instances of clerics who had had sexual relations with women and fathered children.

5. ACDC, legajo 27/439/7, fols. 2, 15.

6. ACDC, legajo 27/649/21, fol. 1.

7. ACDC, legajo 27/628/1, fol. 1.

8. ACDC, legajo 27/538/54.

9. ACDC, legajo 20/146/11, fol. 101.

10. Kagan, *Lawsuits and Litigants,* 34. I was unable to find any case titled divorce or separation in the catalogs of the Archive of the Real Chancillería in Valladolid (Archivo de la Real Chancillería de Valladolid) as well as the provincial archive in Logroño (Archivo Historico Provincial Logroño).

11. ACDC, legajo 27/334/7, Petition by the Fiscal General, Feb. 18, 1679.

12. ACDC, legajo 27/334/7, fol. 1.

13. ACDC, legajo 27/29/5, fol. 1.

14. ACDC, legajo 27/29/5, fol. 2.

15. ACDC, legajo 27/29/5, fol. 7.

16. ACDC, legajo 27/29/5, fol. 7.

17. Darmon, *Trial by Impotence,* 72.

18. Ibid., 102.

19. For the European attitude that considered homosexuality a perversion of nature, see Joan Cadden, *Sex Differences,* 64.

20. See ibid., 59.

21. Molina, *Disolución,* 33.

22. ACDC, legajo 27/389/14, fol. 36.

23. ACDC, legajo 27/520/19, fol. 3.

24. ACDC, legajo 27/520/19, fol. 3.

25. ACDC, legajo 27/520/19, fol. 9.

26. Lepe, *Constituciones,* 306.

27. Twinam, "Honor, Sexuality, and Illegitimacy."

28. ACDC, legajo 27/631/11, fol. 2.

29. ACDC, legajo 27/631/11, fol. 3.

30. See Finucci, *Manly Masquerade,* 256. The Council of Nicaea found the self-castration of certain aesthetic monks disturbing and worked to prevent them from entering the church hierarchy.

31. There has been a great deal of work on hermaphrodites over the past two decades. Several famous cases have been unearthed and explored by historians of gender. Two important overviews will provide interested readers with a point of departure: Patrick Graille, *Les Hermaphrodites: Aux XVIIe et XVIIIe siècles* (Paris: Les Belles Lettres, 2001), and Alice Domurat Dreger's *Hermaphrodites and the Medical Invention of Sex* (Cambridge: Harvard University Press, 1998). Darmon relates two similar cases of French hermaphrodites: Marin Le Marcis in 1601 and that of Grandjean in 1777 (*Trial by Impotence,* 41–48).

32. Take, for instance, the importance of the coif that denoted the difference between girl and married woman. Synodal decrees in early modern Spain chastised women who took the *toca de mujer* without being legitimately married or after sexual relations: "que, de aqui adelante, ninguna muger, despues que hiziere vida maridable con su marido, sea osada de andar sino con toca de casada" ("Sínodo de Antonio de Guevara," Mondoñedo, Nov. 13, 1541, *Synodicon hispanum,* ed. García, 3:73). This change in women was particularly marked by a change in hairstyle and headdress. As for men, passage into adulthood was accomplished by marriage or entrance into religion. See Barahona, *Sex Crimes,* 33, and Farr "Pure and Disciplined Body," 406.

33. This idealization of the hermaphrodite is contained in the origin of the word in Greek mythology: Hermaphrodite was the offspring of Hermes and Aphrodite.

Thus the original hermaphrodite was not a monster but a product of Hermes, clever messenger of the gods, and Aphrodite, goddess of beauty and love (Graille, *Les Hermaphrodites,* 18–19). An early modern example of the hermaphrodite as a utopian sexual being, containing in itself the best of both sexes, is Thomas Artus sieur d'Embry's *Les Hermaphrodites,* 1605. Aside from a select literature and fables that idealized the hermaphrodite, there was a pervasive sentiment that regarded her/him as a monster, not only among the populace, but also increasingly among the educated of the Enlightenment who, newly wed to the idea of a binary sexual system, saw no natural place in creation for anything in between the sexes (Graille, *Les Hermaphrodites,* 60).

34. Anton Blok, "Rams and Billy-Goats: A Key to the Mediterranean Code of Honour," *Man,* n.s., 16, no. 3 (September 1981): 432. See also Julian Pitt-Rivers, *The People of the Sierra* (1945; Chicago: University of Chicago Press, 1971), 90.

35. Spain, once a part of and greatly affected by the Islamic world, had witnessed the production of eunuchs over the centuries. Various historians have assumed that the creation of castrati in Spain was a Christian Mediterranean version of the Islamic Mediterranean production of and trade in eunuchs. Sherr argues that the Mediterranean or Muslim worlds cannot be blamed for beginning the practice of castration in early modern Europe. He points out that many of the early castrati came from northern France and the Low Countries long before Italy and Spain would dominate the castrati production and profession. See Richard Sherr, "Gugliemo Gonzaga," 37. On the prevalence of castration in the eastern Mediterranean, see Kathryn M. Ringrose, *The Perfect Servant: Eunuchs and the Social Construction of Gender in Byzantium* (Chicago: University of Chicago Press, 2003).

36. Contemporaries, social commentators, and later historians have mainly settled on two possible reasons for early modern castration: one medical and the other musical. Clearly there were medical reasons that justified castration in the seventeenth and eighteenth centuries. Childhood illnesses and accidents occasionally resulted in the removal of testicles. Before 1772, childhood inguinal hernias frequently required surgery. In 1772 a protective belt called the *manezuela* was invented to prevent inguinal hernias. See Nicolás Morales, "El real colegio de niños cantors y una práctica discutida a finales del siglo XVIII: La castración," *Revista de Musicología* 20, no. 1 (Enero–Diciembre 1997): 7. Inguinal hernias occasionally occur in young boys when the inguinal canal that separates the intestinal cavity from the groin fails to close before the birth of the male infant. If open, part of the intestines can descend out of the inguinal canal, producing a hernia. This condition required an operation to prevent the hernia from growing and endangering the life of the child. Such surgery usually involved the removal of at least one testicle; perhaps both were removed. In fact, most court cases about castration focused on the question of what the hernia surgeon actually did. According to the oft repeated testimony in these court cases, a surgeon specialized in hernias called a *hernista* (hernia surgeon) or sometimes *potrero* (gelder) would perform the operation. He would open the scrotum, remedy the intestinal hernia, and then remove one testicle completely.

37. Finucci, *Manly Masquerade,* 248.

38. "¡Linda cosa, la voz sutil y melosa, en un hombre muy barbado!" Act 1 of *El Examen de Maridos,* Juan Ruíz de Alarcón, 1633.

39. ACDC, legajo 27/566/40, fol. 7.

40. ACDC, legajo 566/40, fol. 1 back.

41. Bajada, *Sexual Impotence,* 16.

42. Interest in the castrati singers has been the main reason for historical investigations of castration in Europe. Music historians and musicologists have provided the social background of castration. Understandably, but unfortunately, their focus has almost exclusively been the production of castrati. This leads to the assumption that the production of castrati was the exclusive reason for castration of young boys. Patrick Barbier's *Histoire des castrats,* for instance, emphasizes the prevalence of castration in early modern Italy, and then takes for granted that all these boys had been castrated because of the popularity of castrati. He simply does not deal with castration as a European phenomenon outside of music. See Barbier, *Histoire des castrats* (Paris: Bernard Grasset, 1989), 29.

43. Barbier, *Histoire des castrats,* 16.

44. McVaugh, "Treatment of Hernia," 134.

45. See note 22 of chapter 1.

46. A. Agüello Castrillo, *Disertacion chirurgica,* ed. Pantaleon Aznar (Madrid 1775), 15. Quoted in Morales, "El real colegio de niños," 9.

47. Ibid.

48. ACDC, legajo 27/566/40, fol. 16.

49. AHPL, legajo J 965/3, from an impotence case before the local abbot's court of the Abbey of Nájera, part of the Diocese of Calahorra and La Calzada, fol. 4.

50. ACDC, legajo 27/571/50, fol. 2.

51. ACDC, legajo 27/571/50, fol. 6.

52. Ibid.

53. Patrick Barbier, *The World of the Castrati: A History of an Extraordinary Operatic Phenomenon,* trans. Margaret Crosland (London: Souvenir Press, 1996), 20.

54. ACDC, legajo 27/714/65.

55. Ibid.

56. ACDC, legajo 27/495/6, followed by fol. 1.

57. Several of my conclusions on virginity here have benefited from and, I hope, dovetail with those of Ann Twinam's in "Honor, Sexuality, and Illegitimacy in Colonial Spanish America," 120. The cult of the hymen continues, of course, in our own day: it is a popular belief in South Africa that sex with a virgin will rid one of HIV and AIDS.

58. Wiesner-Hanks, *Christianity and Sexuality,* 30.

59. ACDC, legajo 27/495/29, fol. 152.

60. For centuries canonists debated what was actually the basis of matrimony. Though several canonists, especially Peter Lombard and those in the Parisian School, emphasized the importance of consent over sexual consummation, the fundamental

importance and centrality of *commixtio carnis* could never be denied. Gratian and later canonists settled on a two-step matrimonial process initiated by consent, but solidified and perfected by sexual consummation. An excellent overview of this problem can be found in Molina, *Disolución.*

61. ACDC, legajo 27/575/55, fol. 1.

62. ACDC, legajo 27/115/24, responda by the Fiscal General, Nov. 29, 1680, fol. 5.

63. ACDC, legajo 20/164/5, fol. 16.

64. Darmon, *Trial by Impotence,* 17.

65. ACDC, legajo 27/345/31, fol. 172.

66. AHPL, legajo J 965/3, fol. 11.

67. ACDC, legajo 23/96–131, demanda of April 30, 1751.

68. Darmon, *Trial by Impotence,* 149.

69. ACDC, legajo 27/345/31, questions submitted by the prosecution, question #4, fols. 164–67.

70. ACDC, legajo 27/723/74, fol. 1.

71. ACDC, legajo 27/450/1, fol. 1

72. ACDC, legajo 27/468/55.

73. ACDC, legajo 27/345/31, fol. 229.

74. Darmon, *Trial by Impotence,* 22.

CONCLUSION

1. Martínez Kleiser, *Refranero General Ideológico Español,* refrain 19,473, p. 213.

2. For an excellent explanation of how the censo de quitar functioned, see Asunción Lavrin, "The Role of the Nunneries in the Economy of New Spain in the Eighteenth Century," *Hispanic American Historical Review* 46, no. 4 (November 1966): 371–93. See also John Huxtable Elliott, *Imperial Spain, 1469–1716* (New York: St. Martin's Press, 1964), 189, and Henry Arthur Francis Kamen, *Spain, 1469–1714: A Society of Conflict* (London: 1983), 108.

3. Lawrence Stone, *Road to Divorce: England 1530–1987* (Oxford: Oxford University Press, 1990), 1–2.

4. An influential proponent of the view that the eighteenth century witnessed a crucial new role for affection in marriage is Lawrence Stone, who has carried out studies of divorces in early modern England.

5. Beatrice Gottlieb, *The Family in the Western World: From the Black Death to the Industrial Age* (New York: Oxford University Press, 1993), 105.

6. Robert Kingdon has demonstrated that adultery by wives was the main legitimate grounds for divorce in Calvin's Geneva. See Kingdon, *Adultery and Divorce in Calvin's Geneva* (Cambridge: Harvard University Press, 1995).

7. This incident is related by Watt, *Modern Marriage,* 147.

8. On wife battery in contemporary Spain, for instance, see Miguel Lorente Acosta, *Mi marido me pega lo normal: Agresión a la mujer: Realidades y mitos* (Barcelona: Ares y Mares, 2001).

9. Watt, *Modern Marriage,* 147.

10. Elizabeth A. Foyster, *Manhood in Early Modern England: Honour, Sex, and Marriage* (London: Longman, 1999), 9.

11. "La murmuración podía llegar a ser a una condena." Mantecón Novellán, *La muerte de Antonia Isabel Sánchez,* 80.

12. Foyster, *Manhood,* 60.

13. ACDC, legajo 27/611/17, testimony of Christobal Garzes de los Hayo, fol. 13.

14. Kagan, *Lawsuits and Litigants,* 10.

15. Ferraro, *Marriage Wars.*

BIBLIOGRAPHY

PRIMARY SOURCES

Alba, Gonzalo de. "Libro sinodal." Salamanca, April 6, 1410. *Synodicon Hispanum.* Edited by Antonio García y García. Vol. 3. Madrid: Biblioteca de Autores Cristianos, 1987.

Archivo Catedralicio y Diocesano de Calahorra, Calahorra (La Rioja), Spain.

Archivo de la Real Chancillería de Valladolid, Valladolid (Castile and Leon), Spain.

Archivo Diocesano de Pamplona (Navarra), Spain.

Archivo Historico Provincial Logroño, Logroño (La Rioja), Spain.

Artus sieur d' Embry, Thomas. *Les Hermaphrodites,* 1605.

Cervantes, Miguel de. "The Divorce Judge." *Eight Interludes.* Translated and edited by Dawn L. Smith. London: Everyman Press, 1996.

———. "El juez de los divorcios." *Entremeses.* Edited by Celsa Carmen García Valdés. Madrid: Santillana, S.A., 1997.

Diccionario de Autoridades: Diccionario de la lengua castellana, en que se explica el verdadero sentido de las voces, su naturaleza y calidad, con las phrases o modos de hablar, los proverbios o refranes, y otras cosas convenientes al uso de la lengua [. . .]. Compuesto por la Real Academia Española. Tomo quarto. Que contiene las letras G.H.I.J.K.L.M.N. Madrid: Real Academia Española, 1734.

Erauso, Catalina de. *Memoir of a Basque Transvestite in the New World.* Translated by Michele Stepto and Gabriel Stepto. Boston: Beacon Press, 1996.

Kranmer, Thomas. 1486. *Malleus maleficarum.* New York: Dover, 1971.

León, Fray Luis de. 1583. *La perfecta casada. Escritores misticos españoles.* Barcelona: Ediciones Océano, S.A., 1982.

Lepe Dorantes, Pedro de. *Constituciones synodales antiguas, y modernas del obispado de Calahorra y La Calzada.* Madrid: Antonio Gonzalez de Reyes, 1700.

Pseudo-Albertus Magnus. Women's Secrets: A Translation of Pseudo-Albertus Magnus's De Secretis Mulierum with Commentaries. Translated by Helen Rodnite Lemay. Albany: State University of New York Press, 1992.

Ruíz de Alarcón, Juan. 1633. El Examen de Maridos. Edited by Agustín Millares Carlo. Madrid: Espasa-Calpe 1960.

Saavedra Fajardo, Don Diego de. *Obras de Don Diego de Saavedra Fajardo y del licenciado Pedro Fernández Navarrete, Biblioteca Autores Españoles desde la formación del lenguaje hasta nuestors dias.* Vol. 25. Madrid: Ediciones Atlas, 1945.

SECONDARY LITERATURE

Abercrombie, Nicolas, and Bryan Turner. "The Dominant Ideology Thesis." *British Journal of Sociology* 29, no. 2 (June 1978): 149–70.

Arrizabalaga, Jon. "Medical Responses to the 'French Disease' in Europe at the Turn of the Sixteenth Century." In *Sins of the Flesh: Responding to Sexual Disease in Early Modern Europe,* edited by Kevin Sienna, 33–55. Toronto: Centre for Reformation and Renaissance Studies, 2005.

Aznar Gil, Federico R. *La institución matrimonial en la Hispania Cristiana bajomedieval (1215–1563).* Salamanca: Publicaciones Universidad Pontifica Salamanca, 1989.

Bajada, Joseph. *Sexual Impotence: The Contribution of Paolo Zacchia, 1584–1659.* Roma: Editrice Pontifica Università Gregoriana, 1988.

Barahona, Renato. "Courtship, Seduction, and Abandonment in Early Modern Spain." In *Sex and Love in Golden Age Spain,* edited by Alain Saint-Saëns, 43–55. New Orleans: University Press of the South, 1996.

———. *Sex Crimes, Honour, and the Law in Early Modern Spain: Vizcaya, 1528–1735.* Toronto: University of Toronto Press, 2003.

Barbier, Patrick. *Histoire des castrats.* Bernard Grasset: Paris, 1989.

———. *The World of the Castrati: A History of an Extraordinary Operatic Phenomenon.* Translated by Margaret Crosland. London: Souvenir Press, 1996.

Becker, Daniel Charles. "'There Is No Harm in a Boy Talking to a Girl': The Control of Sexuality and Marriage in Early Modern Navarre and Guipúzcoa." PhD diss., University of Maryland, 1997.

Behar, Ruth. "Sexual Witchcraft, Colonialism, and Women's Powers." In *Sexuality and Marriage in Colonial Latin America,* edited by Asunción Lavrin, 178–206. Lincoln: University of Nebraska Press, 1992.

Behrend-Martínez, Edward. "An Early Modern Spanish 'Divorce Court' and the Rhetoric of Matrimony (1654–1715)." In *Disciplines on the Line: Feminist Research on Spanish, Latin American, and U.S. Latina Women,* edited by Anne J. Cruz, 145–166. New York: Juan de la Cuesta Press, 2003.

———. "Female Sexual Potency in a Spanish Church Court 1673–1735." *Law and History Review* 24, no. 2 (Summer 2006): 297–330.

———. "Manhood and the Neutered Body in Early Modern Spain." *Journal of Social History* 38, no. 4 (Summer 2005): 1073–93.

Blok, Anton. "Rams and Billy-Goats: A Key to the Mediterranean Code of Honour." *Man,* n.s., 16, no. 3 (September 1981): 427–40.

Bombín Pérez, Antonio. *La Inquisición en el País Vasco: El tribunal de Logroño (1570–1610).* Bilbao: Servicio Editorial, Universidad del País Vasco, 1997.

Bonfield, Lloyd. *Marriage, Property, and Succession.* Berlin: Duncker & Humbolt, 1992.

Boyer, Richard. *Lives of the Bigamists: Marriage, Family, and Community in Colonial Mexico.* Albuquerque: University of New Mexico Press, 1995.

———. "Women, *La Mala Vida,* and the Politics of Marriage." In *Sexuality and Marriage in Colonial Latin America,* edited by Asunción Lavrin, 252–86. Lincoln: University of Nebraska Press, 1992.

Brandes, Stanley. *Metaphors of Masculinity: Sex and Status in Andalusian Folklore.* Philadelphia: University of Pennsylvania Press, 1980.

Brooke, Christopher N. L. *The Medieval Idea of Marriage.* Oxford: Oxford University Press, 1989.

Brucker, Gene. *Giovanni and Lusanna: Love and Marriage in Renaissance Florence.* Berkeley and Los Angeles: University of California Press, 1986.

Brundage, James A. *Law, Sex, and Christian Society in Medieval Europe.* Chicago: University of Chicago Press, 1987.

———. *Medieval Canon Law.* London: Longman, 1995.

———. "The Problem of Impotence." In *Sexual Practices and the Medieval Church,* edited by Vern L. Bullough and James Brundage, 135–40. Buffalo, NY: Prometheus Books, 1982.

Bullough, Vern L. "On Being Male in the Middle Ages. In *Medieval Masculinities: Regarding Men in the Middle Ages,* edited by Claire A. Lees, 31–46. Minneapolis: University of Minnesota Press, 1994.

Cadden, Joan. *Meanings of Sex Differences in the Middle Ages: Medicine, Science, and Culture.* Cambridge: Cambridge University Press, 1993.

———. "Western Medicine and Natural Philosophy." In *Handbook of Medieval Sexuality,* edited by Vern L. Bullough and James A. Brundage, 51–80. New York: Garland, 1996.

Campo Guinea, María del Juncal. *Comportamientos matrimoniales en Navarra (Siglos XVI–XVII).* Pamplona: Gobierno de Navarra, Departamiento de Educación y Cultura: Gráficas Ona, S.A., 1998.

Cantera, Francisco. "La Juderia de Calahorra." *Sepharad* 15, fasc. 2, n.d.

Casey, James. *Early Modern Spain: A Social History.* London: Routledge, 1999.

Cifuentes Pazos, José Manuel. *La economia de las iglesias vizcainos en el siglo XVII.* Bilbao: Ediciones Beta III mileno, S.L., 2000.

Cook, Alexandra Parma, and Noble David Cook. *Good Faith and Truthful Ignorance: A Case of Transatlantic Bigamy.* Durham, NC: Duke University Press, 1991.

Corteguera, Luis R. "The Painter Who Lost His Hat: Artisans and Justice in Early Modern Barcelona." *The Sixteenth Century Journal* 29, no. 4 (1998): 1023–42.

Cotton, Nancy. "Castrating (W)itches: Impotence and Magic in *The Merry Wives of Windsor.*" *Shakespeare Quarterly* 38 (Autumn 1987): 320–26.

Crawford, Charlotte. "The Position of Women in a Basque Fishing Community." In *Anglo-American Contributions to Basque Studies: Essays in Honor of Jon Bilbao,* edited by William A. Douglass et al., 145–60. Grand Junction: Desert Research Institute Publications on the Social Sciences, 1977.

Cruz, Anne. "La Bella Malmaridada: Lessons for the Good Wife." In *Culture and Control in Counter-Reformation Spain,* edited by Anne J. Cruz and Mary Elizabeth Perry, 145–70. Minneapolis: University of Minnesota Press, 1992.

———. "The Princess and the Page: Social Transgression and Marriage in the Spanish Ballad *Gerineldos.*" In *Religion, Body, and Gender in Early Modern Spain,* edited and introduced by Alain Saint-Saëns, 145–70. San Francisco: Mellen Research University Press, 1991.

Cuillieron, Monique. "Les Causes matrimoniales des officialités de Paris au Siècle des

Lumières 1726–1789." *Revue historique de droit francais et etranger* 66, no. 4 (1988): 527–59.

Darmon, Pierre. *Damning the Innocent: A History of the Persecution of the Innocent in Pre-Revolutionary France.* Translated by Paul Keegan. New York: Viking, 1986.

———. *Trial by Impotence: Virility and Marriage in Pre-Revolutionary France.* London: Hogarth Press, 1985.

Davis, Natalie Z. *The Return of Martin Guerre.* Cambridge: Harvard University Press, 1983.

Dean, Trevor, and K. J. P. Lowe, eds. *Marriage in Italy, 1300–1650.* Cambridge: Cambridge University Press, 1998.

Díaz Bodegas, Pablo. *La diócesis de Calahorra y La Calzada en el siglo XIII.* Logroño: Diocesis de Calahorra and La Calzada-Logroño, 1995.

Dillard, Heath. *Daughters of the Reconquest: Women in Castilian Town Society, 1100–1300.* Cambridge: Cambridge University Press, 1984.

Domínguez Ortiz, Antonio. *La sociedad española en el siglo XVII.* 2 vols. Granada: Universidad de Granada, 1992.

Donnell, Sidney. *Feminizing the Enemy: Imperial Spain, Transvestite Drama, and the Crisis of Masculinity.* Lewisburg, PA: Bucknell University Press, 2003.

Dreger, Alice Domurat. *Hermaphrodites and the Medical Invention of Sex.* Cambridge: Harvard University Press, 1998.

Duby, Georges. *Medieval Marriage: Two Models from Twelfth-Century France.* Translated by Elborg Forster. Baltimore: Johns Hopkins University Press, 1978.

Dyer, Abigail. "Heresy and Dishonor: Sexual Crimes Before the Courts of Early Modern Spain." PhD diss., Columbia University, 2000.

Elliott, John Huxtable. *Imperial Spain, 1469–1716.* New York: St. Martin's Press, 1964.

Farr, James R. "Marriage and the Uses of the Law: Legislation, Abduction, and Litigation." Chap. 4 in *Authority and Sexuality in Early Modern Burgundy (1550–1730).* New York: Oxford University Press, 1995.

Ferraro, Joanne M. *Marriage Wars in Late Renaissance Venice.* Oxford: Oxford University Press, 2001.

Finucci, Valeria. *The Manly Masquerade: Masculinity, Paternity, and Castration in the Italian Renaissance.* Durham, NC: Duke University Press, 2003.

Foucault, Michel. *An Introduction.* Vol. 1, *The History of Sexuality.* 2nd ed. Translated by Robert Hurley. New York: Vintage Books, 1990.

———. *Madness and Civilization: A History of Insanity in the Age of Reason.* Translated by Richard Howard. New York: Pantheon Books, 1965.

Foyster, Elizabeth A. *Manhood in Early Modern England: Honour, Sex, and Marriage.* London: Longman, 1999.

Freeman, Susan. *Neighbors: The Social Contract in a Castilian Hamlet.* Chicago: University of Chicago Press, 1970.

García Calonge, Milagros. *El poder municipal de Calahorra en el siglo XVII.* Calahorra, La Rioja: Amigos de la Historia de Calahorra, 1998.

García y García, Antonio. "La Canonísta Iberica (1150–1250)." *Bulletin of Medieval Canon Law* 11 (1981): 41–75.

———, comp. and ed. *Synodicon Hispanum.* 4 vols. Madrid: Biblioteca de Autores Cristianos, 1987.

Garza Carvajal, Federico. *Butterflies Will Burn: Prosecuting Sodomites in Early Modern Spain and Mexico.* Austin: University of Texas Press, 2003.

Gies, Frances, and Joseph Gies. *Marriage and the Family in the Middle Ages.* New York: Harper & Row, 1987.

Gil Ambrona, A. "Las mujeres bajo la jurisdicción eclesiástica: Pleitos matrimoniales in la Barcelona de los siglos XVI y XVII." *Nuevas preguntas, nuevas miradas. Fuentes y documentación para la historia de las mujeres (siglos XIII–XVIII).* Granada, 1992.

Gillis, John R. "Courtship and Marriage in the Sixteenth and Seventeenth Centuries." Pt. 1 of *For Better, For Worse: British Marriages, 1600 to Present.* New York: Oxford University Press, 1985.

Gilmore, David. *Aggression and Community: Paradoxes of Andalusian Culture.* New Haven, CT: Yale University Press, 1987.

———. *Manhood in the Making: Cultural Concepts of Masculinity.* New Haven, CT: Yale University Press, 1990.

Gottlieb, Beatrice. *The Family in the Western World: From the Black Death to the Industrial Age.* New York: Oxford University Press, 1993.

Graille, Patrick. *Les Hermaphrodites: Aux XVIIe et XVIIIe siècles.* Paris: Les Belles Lettres, 2001.

Greer, Germaine. *The Female Eunuch.* New York: McGraw-Hill, 1971.

Gutierrez Achutegui, Pedro. *Historia de la muy noble antigua y leal ciudad de Calahorra.* Logroño: Talleres Gráficas de Editorial Ochoa, 1981.

Guzzetti, Linda. "Separations and Separated Couples in Fourteenth-Century Venice." In *Marriage in Italy, 1300–1650,* edited by Trevor Dean and K. J. P. Lowe, 249–74. Cambridge: Cambridge University Press, 1998.

Haidt, Rebecca. *Embodying Enlightenment: Knowing the Body in Eighteenth-Century Spanish Literature and Culture.* New York: St. Martin's Press, 1998.

Harrington, Joel. *Reordering Marriage and Society in Reformation Germany.* Cambridge: Cambridge University Press, 1995.

Hart, Angie. "Missing Masculinity? Prostitutes' Clients in Alicante, Spain." In *Dislocating Masculinity: Comparative Ethnographies,* edited by Andrea Cornwall and Nancy Lindisfarne, 48–65. London: Routledge, 1994.

Hégy, Pierre, and Joseph Martos. *Catholic Divorce: The Deception of Annulments.* New York: Continuum, 2000.

Helmholz, R. H. *Marriage Litigation in Medieval England.* London: Cambridge University Press, 1974.

Henningsen, Gustav. *The Witches' Advocate: Basque Witchcraft and the Spanish Inquisition, 1609–1614.* Reno: University of Nevada Press, 1980.

Heras Santos, José Luis de las. *La justicia penal de los Austrias en la Corona de Castilla.* Salamanca: Universidad de Salamanca, 1991.

Holbrook, Richard. "Exorcism with a Stole." *Modern Language Notes* 20, no. 4 (April 1905): 111–15.

Houlbrooke, Ralph. *Church Courts and the People during the English Reformation 1520–1570.* Oxford: Oxford University Press, 1979.

Ingram, Martin. *Church Courts, Sex, and Marriage in England, 1570–1640.* Cambridge: Cambridge University Press, 1987.

Irigaray, Luce. "Another 'Cause'—Castration." In *Feminisms: An Anthology of Literary Theory and Criticism,* edited by Robyn R. Warhol and Diane Price Herndl, 430–37. New Brunswick, NJ: Rutgers University Press, 1997.

Kagan, Richard. *Lawsuits and Litigants in Castile, 1500–1700.* Chapel Hill: University of North Carolina Press, 1981.

Kamen, Henry. *The Phoenix and the Flame: Catalonia and the Counter Reformation.* New Haven, CT: Yale University Press, 1993.

———. *Spain, 1469–1714: A Society of Conflict.* London: Longman 1983.

———. *Spain in the Later Seventeenth Century, 1665–1700.* London: Longman, 1980.

———. *The Spanish Inquisition: An Historical Revision.* London: Weidenfeld & Nicolson, 1997.

Karras, Ruth Mazzo. *From Boys to Men: Formations of Masculinity in Late Medieval Europe.* Philadelphia: University of Pennsylvania Press, 2003.

———. *Sexuality in Medieval Europe: Doing unto Others.* New York: Routledge Press, 2005.

Keeble, N. H., ed. *The Cultural Identity of Seventeenth-Century Woman: A Reader.* London: Routledge, 1994.

Kelly, Henry Ansgar. *The Matrimonial Trials of Henry VIII.* Stanford, CA: Stanford University Press, 1976.

Kelly, Kathleen Coyne. *Performing Virginity and Testing Chastity in the Middle Ages.* London: Routledge, 2000.

Kingdon, Robert M. *Adultery and Divorce in Calvin's Geneva.* Cambridge: Harvard University Press, 1995.

Kuehn, Thomas. "Daughters, Mothers, Wives, and Widows: Women as Legal Persons." In *Time, Space, and Women's Lives in Early Modern Europe,* edited by Anne Shutte et al., 97–115. Kirksville, MO: Truman State University, 2001.

Kuttner, Stephen. "Raymond of Peñafort as Editor: The 'Decretales' and 'Constituciones' of Gregory IX." *Bulletin of Medieval Canon Law* 12 (1982): 65–80.

Ladurie, Emmanuel LeRoy. "The Aiguillette: Castration by Magic." In *The Mind and Method of the Historian,* translated by Siân Reynolds and Ben Reynolds, 84–96. Chicago: University of Chicago Press, 1981.

Laeuchli, Samuel. *Power and Sexuality; The Emergence of Canon Law at the Synod of Elvira.* Philadelphia: Temple University Press, 1972.

Laqueur, Thomas. *Making Sex: Body and Gender from the Greeks to Freud.* Cambridge: Harvard University Press, 1990.

Lavrin, Asunción. "The Role of the Nunneries in the Economy of New Spain in the

Eighteenth Century." *Hispanic American Historical Review* 46, no. 4 (November 1966): 371–93.

Lees, Claire A. *Medieval Masculinities: Regarding Men in the Middle Ages.* Minneapolis: University of Minnesota Press, 1994.

Lemay, Helen Rodnite. Introduction to *De Secretis Mulierum.* Albany: State University of New York Press, 1992.

Leneman, Leah. *Alienated Affections: The Scottish Experience of Divorce and Separation, 1684–1830.* Edinburgh: Edinburgh University Press, 1998.

Lorente Acosta, Miguel. *Mi marido me pega lo normal: Agresión a la mujer: Realidades y mitos.* Barcelona: Ares y Mares, 2001.

Lorenzo Pinar, Francisco Javier. "La mujer y el Tribunal Diocesano en Zamora durante el siglo XVI: Divorcios y nulidades matrimonials." *Studia Zamorensia* 3 (1996): 77–88.

Machuelle, J. R. "Les Demandes d'annulation de Maríage." In *La Désunion du couple sous l'Ancien Régime: l'Exemple du Nord,* edited by Alain Lottin, 137–48. Villeneuve-d'Ascq: Universite de Lille III; Paris: Editions Universitaires, 1975.

Machuelle, J. R., and Alain Lottin. "Les Divorcés." In *La Désunion du couple sous l'Ancien Régime: l'exemple du Nord,* edited by Alain Lottin, 113–35. Villeneuve-d'Ascq: Universite de Lille III; Paris: Editions Universitaires, 1975.

MacKay, Ruth. *The Limits of Royal Authority: Resistance and Obedience in Seventeenth-Century Castile.* Cambridge: Cambridge University Press, 1999.

Madoz, Pascual. *Diccionario Geográfico-Estadístico-Histórico de España y sus Posesiones de Ultramar.* Vol. 5. Madrid: Est. Literario-Tipográfico P. Mudoz, 1846.

Mantecón Novellán, Tomás. *La muerte de Antonia Isabel Sánchez: Tiranía y escándalo en una sociedad rural del norte español en el Antiguo Régimen.* Alcalá de Henares, Madrid: Centro de Estudios Cervantinos, 1998.

Marín, Manuela. "Marriage and Sexuality in Al-Andalus." In *Marriage and Sexuality in Medieval and Early Modern Iberia,* edited by Eukene Lacarra Lanz, 3–20. New York: Routledge, 2002.

Marín, Tomás. "Un registro de partidas bautismales anterior al Concilio Tridentino (1499–1546)." *REDC* 3 (1948): 783–93.

Martin, Luis. "Divorcees, Concubines, and Repentant Women." Chap. 6 of *Daughters of the Conquistadores: Women of the Viceroyalty of Peru.* Albuquerque: University of New Mexico Press, 1983.

Martín Gaite, Carmen. "Crisis in the Institution of Matrimony." In *Love Customs in Eighteenth-Century Spain,* translated by Maria G. Tomsich. Berkeley and Los Angeles: University of California Press, 1991.

Martínez Kleiser, Luis. *Refranero General Ideológico Español.* Madrid: Editorial Hernando, 1953.

Martos, Joseph. "Catholic Marriage and Marital Dissolution in Medieval and Modern Times." In *Catholic Divorce: The Deception of Annulments,* edited by Pierre Hégy and Joseph Martos, 127–53. New York: Continuum, 2000.

McCarthy, John. "The Marriage Capacity of the 'Mulier Excisa.'" *Ephemerides iuris canonici* 2, no. 2 (1947): 261–85.

McLaren, Angus. *The Trials of Manhood: Policing Sexual Boundaries, 1870–1930*. Chicago: University of Chicago Press, 1997.

McVaugh, Michael R. "Treatment of Hernia in the Later Middle Ages: Surgical Correction and Social Construction." In *Medicine from the Black Death to the French Disease,* edited by Roger French et al., 131–55. Aldershot: Ashgate, 1998.

Menefee, Samuel Pyeatt. *Wives for Sale: An Ethnographic Study of British Popular Divorce.* New York: St. Martin's Press, 1981.

Merrick, Jeffrey. "Impotence in Court and at Court." *Studies in Eighteenth-Century Culture* 25 (1996): 187–202.

Merryman, John Henry. *The Civil Law Tradition: An Introduction to the Legal Systems of Western Europe and Latin America.* 2nd ed. Stanford, CA: Stanford University Press, 1985.

Molina Melia, Antonio. *La disolución del matrimonio inconsumado: Antecedentes históricos y Derecho vigente.* Salamanca: Universidad Pontifica de Salamanca, 1987.

Monter, William. *Frontiers of Heresy: The Spanish Inquisition from the Basque Lands to Sicily.* Cambridge: Cambridge University Press, 1990.

Morales, Nicolás. "El real colegio de niños cantors y una práctica discutida a finales del siglo XVIII: La castración." *Revista de Musicología* 20, no. 1 (Enero–Diciembre 1997): 417–32.

Morgado García, Arturo. *Demonios, magos y brujas in la España moderna.* Cádiz: Servicio de Publicaciones de la Universidad de Cádiz, 1999.

Moscucci, Ornella. "Men-Midwives and Medicine: The Origins of a Profession." In *The Science of Woman: Gynaecology and Gender in England 1800–1929,* 43–74. Cambridge: Cambridge University Press, 1990.

Murry, Jacqueline. "On the Origins and Role of 'Wise Women' in Causes for Annulment on the Grounds of Male Impotence." *Journal of Medieval History* 16 (1990): 235–49.

Nader, Helen. *Liberty in Absolutist Spain: The Habsburg Sale of Towns, 1516–1700.* Baltimore: Johns Hopkins University Press, 1990.

Niccoli, Ottavia. "Menstruum Quasi Monstruum: Monstrous Births and Menstrual Taboo in the Sixteenth Century." In *Sex and Gender in Historical Perspective,* edited by Edward Muir and Guido Ruggiero, 1–25. Baltimore: Johns Hopkins University Press, 1990.

Nizza da Silva, María Beatríz. "Divorce in Colonial Brazil: The Case of São Paulo." In *Sexuality and Marriage in Colonial Latin America,* edited by Asunción Lavrin, 313–40. Lincoln: University of Nebraska Press, 1992.

Noonan, John Thomas. *Contraception: A History of Its Treatment by the Catholic Theologians and Canonists.* Cambridge: Harvard University Press, 1986.

O'Dowd, Michael J., and Elliot E. Philipp. *The History of Obstetrics and Gynaecology.* New York: Parthenon, 1994.

Ortiz-Osés, Andrés, and Franz-Karl Mayr. *El matriarchalismo vasco.* Bilbao: Universidad de Deusto, 1998.

Panizo Orallo, Santiago. *Nulidades de matrimonio por incapacidad.* Salamanca: Universidad Pontifica de Salamanca, 1982.

———. *Temas procesales y nulidad matrimonial.* Madrid: Edigrafos, S.A., 1999.

Paris, Charles B. *Marriage in XVIIth Century Catholicism; The Origins of a Religious Mentality: The Teaching of "L'École française" (1600–1660).* Tournai, Belgium: Desclée, 1975.

Pérez, Joseph. *The Spanish Inquisition.* Translated by Janet Lloyd. New Haven, CT: Yale University Press, 2005.

Pescador, Juan Javier. *The New World Inside a Basque Village: The Oiartzun Valley and Its Atlantic Emigrants, 1550–1800.* Reno: University of Nevada Press, 2004.

Phillips, Roderick. *Putting Asunder: A History of Divorce in Western Society.* Cambridge: Cambridge University Press, 1988.

———. *Untying the Knot: A Short History of Divorce.* Cambridge: Cambridge University Press, 1991.

Pitt-Rivers, Julian. *The People of the Sierra.* Chicago: University of Chicago Press, 1971. First published in 1945 by Critterion.

Poska, Allyson M. *Regulating the People: The Catholic Reformation in Seventeenth-Century Spain.* Leiden: Brill, 1998.

———. "When Love Goes Wrong: Getting Out of Marriage in Seventeenth Century Spain." *Journal of Social History* 29 (Summer 1996): 871–82.

Redondo, Augustin. *Le corps dans la société espagnole des XVIe et XVIIe siècles.* Paris: Publications de la Sorbonne, 1990.

Reher, David Sven. *Town and Country in Pre-Industrial Spain: Cuenca, 1550–1870.* Cambridge: Cambridge University Press, 1990.

Rider, Catherine. *Impotence and Magic in the Middle Ages.* Oxford: Oxford University Press, 2006.

Ringrose, Kathryn M. *The Perfect Servant: Eunuchs and the Social Construction of Gender in Byzantium.* Chicago: University of Chicago Press, 2003.

Roper, Lyndal. *Oedipus and the Devil: Witchcraft, Sexuality, and Religion in Early Modern Europe.* London: Rutledge, 1994.

Safley, Thomas Max. *Let No Man Put Asunder: The Control of Marriage in the German Southwest: A Comparative Study 1550–1600.* Kirksville, MO: Sixteenth Century Journal Publishers, 1984.

———. "Marital Litigation in the Diocese of Constance, 1551–1620." *Sixteenth Century Journal* 12 (1981): 61–77.

Sáinz Ripa, Eliseo. *Siglos XVI–XVII.* Vol. 3, *Sedes episcopales de La Rioja.* Logroño: Obispado de Calahorra y La Calzada-Logroño, 1996.

———. *Siglos XVIII–XIX.* Vol. 3, *Sedes episcopales de La Rioja.* Logroño: Obispado de Calahorra y La Calzada-Logroño, 1996.

Salisbury, Joyce. "Gendered Sexuality." In *Handbook of Medieval Sexuality,* edited by Vern L. Bullough and James A. Brundage, 81–102. New York: Garland, 1996.

Salmón, Fernando, and Montserrat Cabré. "Fascinating Women: The Evil Eye in Medical Scholasticism." In *Medicine from the Black Death to the French Disease,* edited by Roger French et al., 53–84. Aldershot: Ashgate, 1998.

Sánchez Ortega, María Helena. "Sorcery and Eroticism in Love Magic." In *Cultural Encounters: The Impact of the Inquisition in Spain and the New World,* edited by Anne Cruz and Mary Elizabeth Perry, 58–92. Berkeley and Los Angeles: University of California Press, 1991.

———. "Women as a Source of 'Evil' in Counter-Reformation Spain." In *Culture and Control in Counter-Reformation Spain,* edited by Anne J. Cruz and Mary Elizabeth Perry, 196–215. Minneapolis: University of Minnesota Press, 1992.

Schiebinger, Londa. *The Mind Has No Sex?: Women in the Origins of Modern Science.* Cambridge: Harvard University Press, 1989.

Sheehan, Michael M. "*Maritalis Affectio* Revisited." In *The Olde Daunce: Love, Friendship, Sex and Marriage in the Medieval World,* edited by Robert R. Edwards and Stephen Spector, 32–56. Albany: State University of New York Press, 1991.

Sherr, Richard. "Gugliemo Gonzaga and the Castrati." *Renaissance Quarterly* 33, no. 1 (Spring 1980): 33–56.

Socolow, Susan M. "Acceptable Partners: Marriage Choice in Colonial Argentina, 1778–1810." In *Sexuality and Marriage in Colonial Latin America,* edited by Asunción Lavrin, 209–46. Lincoln: University of Nebraska Press, 1992.

Stephens, Walter. "Witches Who Steal Penises: Impotence and Illusion in *Malleus Maleficarum.*" *Journal of Medieval and Early Modern Studies* 28 (1998): 495–529.

Stolberg, Michael. "A Woman Down to Her Bones: The Anatomy of Sexual Difference in the Sixteenth and Early Seventeenth Centuries." *ISIS* 94, no. 2 (June 2003): 274–313.

Stone, Lawrence. *Broken Lives: Separation and Divorce in England 1660–1857.* Oxford: Oxford University Press, 1993.

———. *Road to Divorce: England, 1530–1987.* New York: Oxford University Press, 1990.

———. *Uncertain Unions: Marriage in England, 1660–1753.* New York: Oxford University Press, 1992.

Stone, Marilyn. *Marriage and Friendship in Medieval Spain: Social Relations According to the Fourth Partida of Alfonso x.* New York: P. Lang, 1990.

Testón Nuñez, Isabel. *Amor, Sexo y Matrimonio en Extremadura.* Badajoz: Universitas Editorial, 1985.

Thomas, Keith. *Religion and the Decline of Magic.* New York: Scribner's, 1971.

Tomás y Valiente, F. "El crimen y pecado contra natura." In *Sexo barroco y otras transgresiones premodernos,* edited by Francisco Tomás y Valiente. Madrid: Alianza Editorial, S.A., 1990.

Torremocha, Margarita. *La vida estudantil en el Antiguo Régimen.* Madrid: Alianza Editorial, 1998.

Turner, Bryan S. *The Body and Society: Explorations in Social Theory.* Oxford: Basil Blackwell, 1984.

Twinam, Ann. "Honor, Sexuality, and Illegitimacy in Colonial Spanish America." In *Sexuality and Marriage in Colonial Latin America,* edited by Asunción Lavrin, 118–55. Lincoln: University of Nebraska Press, 1992.

Vasoli, Robert. H. *What God Has Joined Together: The Annulment Crisis in American Catholicism.* New York: Oxford University Press, 1998.

Vasvári, Louise. "Intimate Violence: Shrew Taming as Wedding Ritual in the *Conde Lucanor.*" In *Marriage and Sexuality in Medieval and Early Modern Iberia,* edited by Eukene Lacarra Lanz, 21–38. New York and London: Routledge, 2002.

Waldron, Kathy. "The Sinners and the Bishop in Colonial Venezuela: The *Visita* of Bishop Maríano Martí 1771–1784." In *Sexuality and Marriage in Colonial Latin America,* edited by Asunción Lavrin, 156–77. Lincoln: University of Nebraska Press, 1992.

Watt, Jeffery. *The Making of Modern Marriage: Matrimonial Control and the Rise of Sentiment in Neuchâtel, 1550–1800.* Ithaca, NY: Cornell University Press, 1992.

Weissberger, Barbara. "'A tierra, puto!': Alfonso de Plaencia's Discourse of Effeminacy." In *Queer Iberia: Sexualities, Cultures, and Crossings from the Middle Ages to the Renaissance,* edited by Josiah Blackmore and Gregory S. Hutcheson, 291–324. Durham, NC: Duke University Press, 1999.

Wiesner-Hanks, Merry E. *Christianity and Sexuality in the Early Modern World: Regulating Desire, Reforming Practice.* London: Routledge, 2000.

———. "Lustful Luther: Male Libido in Luther's Lectures on Genesis." In *Sexuality and Culture in Medieval and Renaissance Europe,* edited by Philip M. Soergel, 123–48. New York: AMS Press, 2005.

———. *Women and Gender in Early Modern Europe.* 2nd ed. Cambridge: Cambridge University Press, 2000.

Whiteway, A. R. "Customs of the Western Pyrenees." *English Historical Review* 15, no. 60 (October 1900): 625–40.

Young-Bruehl, Elisabeth, ed. *Freud on Women: A Reader.* New York: W. W. Norton, 1990.

INDEX